Statistical Modelling for Social Researchers

This book explains the principles and theory of statistical modelling in an intelligible way for the non-mathematical social scientist looking to apply statistical modelling techniques in research. The book also serves as an introduction for those wishing to develop more detailed knowledge and skills in statistical modelling. Rather than present a limited number of statistical models in great depth, the aim is to provide an overview of the statistical models currently used in social research, in order that the researcher can make appropriate choices and select the most suitable model for the research question to be addressed. To facilitate application, the book also offers practical guidance and instruction in fitting models using SPSS and Stata, the most popular statistical computer software available to most social researchers. Instruction in using MLwiN is also given.

Models covered in the book include; multiple regression, binary, multinomial and ordered logistic regression, log-linear models, multilevel models, latent variable models (factor analysis), path analysis and simultaneous equation models and models for longitudinal data and event histories. An accompanying website hosts the datasets and further exercises in order that the reader may practice developing statistical models. The website address is: www.routledge.com/textbooks/9780415448406

An ideal tool for postgraduate social science students, research students and practicing social researchers in universities, market research, government social research and the voluntary sector.

Roger Tarling is Professor of Social Research at the University of Surrey, a post he has occupied since 1996. Before that he was for 23 years a member of the Home Office Research and Planning Unit, for the last six as Head of RPU. Throughout his career he has used statistical modelling in research and has had to explain statistical models and the inferences from them to research assistants, policy makers and to the students he has taught. He is a Certified Statistician of the Royal Statistical Society.

Social Research Today
Edited by Martin Bulmer

The *Social Research Today* series provides concise and contemporary introductions to significant methodological topics in the social sciences. Covering both quantitative and qualitative methods, this new series features readable and accessible books from some of the leading names in the field and is aimed at students and professional researchers alike. This series also brings together for the first time the best titles from the old *Social Research Today* and *Contemporary Social Research* series edited by Martin Bulmer for UCL Press and Routledge.

Other series titles include:

Principles of Research Design in the Social Sciences
Frank Bechhofer and Lindsay Paterson

Social Impact Assessment
Henk Becker

The Turn to Biographical Methods in Social Science
edited by Prue Chamberlayne, Joanna Bornat and Tom Wengraf

Quantity and Quality in Social Research
Alan Bryman

Field Research
A Sourcebook and Field Manual
Robert G. Burgess

In the Field
An Introduction to Field Research
Robert G. Burgess

Qualitative Analysis
Thinking, Doing, Writing
Douglas Ezzy

Research Design (second edition)
Catherine Hakim

Measuring Health and Medical Outcomes
edited by Crispin Jenkinson

Methods of Criminological Research
Victor Jupp

Information Technology for the Social Scientist
edited by Raymond M. Lee

An Introduction to the Philosophy of Social Research
Tim May and Malcolm Williams

Research Social and Economic Change
The Uses of Household Panel Studies
edited by David Rose

Introduction to Longitudinal Research
Elisabetta Ruspini

Surveys in Social Research (fifth edition)
David de Vaus

Researching the Powerful in Education
edited by Geoffrey Walford

Researching Race and Racism
edited by Martin Bulmer and John Solomos

Managing Social Research
A Practical Guide
Roger Tarling

Martin Bulmer is Professor of Sociology at the University of Surrey. He is Director of the Question Bank (a WWW resource based at Surrey) in the ESRC Centre for Applied Social Surveys (CASS), a collaboration between the National Centre for Social Research (NatCen), the University of Southampton and the University of Surrey. He is also a Director of the department's Institute of Social Research, and an Academician of the Academy of Learned Societies for the Social Sciences.

Statistical Modelling for Social Researchers

Principles and practice

Roger Tarling

Routledge
Taylor & Francis Group

LONDON AND NEW YORK

First published 2009
by Routledge
2 Park Square, Milton Park, Abingdon, Oxon, OX14 4RN

Simultaneously published in the USA and Canada
by Routledge
270 Madison Avenue, New York, NY 10016

Routledge is an imprint of the Taylor and Francis Group, an informa business

Typeset in Times New Roman by
RefineCatch Limited, Bungay, Suffolk
Printed and bound in Great Britain
by The Cromwell Press, Trowbridge, Wiltshire

British Library Cataloguing-in-Publication Data
A catalogue record for this book is available from the British Library

Library of Congress Cataloging in Publication Data
Tarling, Roger
Statistical modelling for social researchers / Roger Tarling
p. cm.
1. Social sciences—Research—Statistical methods.   2. Social sciences—
Statistical methods.   I. Title.
HA29.T28 2008
519.5—dc22   2008008888

ISBN10: 0–415–44840–9 (pbk)
ISBN10: 0–415–44837–9 (hbk)
ISBN10: 0–203–92948–9 (ebk)

ISBN13: 978–0–415–44840–6 (pbk)
ISBN13: 978–0–415–44837–6 (hbk)
ISBN13: 978–0–203–92948–3 (ebk)

Contents

Preface

My motivation for writing this book stems from my experience of teaching social science graduates undertaking a Master's Programme in Research Methods and from a long association of working with social researchers in higher education, in government, in the voluntary and commercial sectors. While many excellent introductory statistics texts are available and written with social scientists in mind, there is a dearth of accessible texts on statistical modelling for this audience. There is, of course, a vast array of excellent texts on statistical modelling but they adopt a mathematical and theoretical approach to the subject (for example, Dobson, 2002). Obviously I do not wish to deride mathematics and theory nor minimise their importance, but for many social scientists without a background in mathematics, an undue emphasis on notation and formulae too early in their exposure to statistical modelling can be off-putting, if not fatal.

A second limitation of existing texts on statistical modelling, even the few that are not overly mathematical (such as the exemplary text by Allison, 1999), is that they invariably concentrate on one or two aspects of the subject, which they treat in some depth. As a result, they do not provide an overview, which enables the new recruit to understand how the various elements of statistical modelling relate to each other. A minor issue, but often a disconcerting one, is the myriad of alternative terms used by different writers, which leads to unnecessary confusion amongst students when they switch between different texts, computer software and manuals.

The purpose of this book is thus to provide students who have completed a basic statistics course with a first and readily accessible entry point into statistical modelling. As such the book is intended to be a guide or a map of the entire terrain. It aims to explain the issues in everyday language rather than in mathematical notation, which is kept to the barest minimum. It is not a cookbook and will not provide the recipe for a particular research problem. Instead it is hoped that readers will gain a 'feel' for the subject and will be encouraged to acquire further insight by reading more advanced accounts.

Before embarking on the material covered in this book, students should be familiar with some basic statistical concepts, including descriptive statistics (measures of central tendency and dispersion), frequencies and tables. It is also necessary to have prior knowledge of the principles of significance testing, the z, t and chi-square tests in particular, as well as measures of association and correlation (although some of these concepts are reviewed in Chapter 3). It is not essential, however, to have studied regression beforehand as it is covered in this book.

Having received instruction in basic statistical methods it is assumed that readers will also have gained some proficiency in statistical computing. The audience I have in mind is unlikely to be developing new statistical methods (but perhaps they will do so at a future stage in their career). Instead they will be wishing to use software with statistical modelling techniques pre-programmed and operated through drop down menus and dialogue boxes or by issuing straightforward commands. In my experience, the software most readily accessible to social scientists is SPSS, but Stata has superior modelling capabilities and is rapidly gaining in popularity amongst this group. Both are employed to fit models in this book. MLwiN is also chosen in order to fit multilevel models and, although not discussed, I find Excel useful to structure data in a form suitable for inputting into more specialist statistical software. Furthermore, much administrative data is stored and supplied as Excel files.

It is beyond the remit of this book to be a manual for any software. However, as the models presented in this book have been fitted by SPSS, Stata or MLwiN, I comment on what I regard as the strengths and weaknesses of each product at appropriate points in the text. Insights into using SPSS, Stata and MLwiN can be thought of as a feature of the book but not its main focus. Throughout the text I have reproduced output from the software but I would not endorse this practice when presenting results of analyses in journals articles, reports and official documents. It is only followed here in order that readers can relate models to the software. For the same reason I have often reported numbers to more decimal places than would be good practice in published accounts.

Many of the datasets analysed in this book can be found at the accompanying website together with suggestions for further analysis. The website address is:

www.routledge.com/textbooks/9780415448406

I am indebted to the help and assistance of many people and organisations in preparing this text. First and foremost I would like to thank Clive Payne who has given me invaluable advice and support on statistical modelling and computing over a period of more than thirty years. More specifically here, Clive made available his data on Training for Work, which is used to illustrate event history models in Chapter 13. Clive also assisted in preparing the SPSS and Stata code to convert data files from one format to another. In addition, Clive provided invaluable comments on an earlier draft of this book.

Ian Brunton Smith, my colleague at the University of Surrey, greatly helped me with multilevel modelling, which is featured in Chapter 9. Ian also read and commented on earlier drafts of many other chapters.

I am particularly grateful to two former Master's students who generously allowed me to draw on some of the data that they had assembled for their dissertations. Veronica Hollis made available the data on sentencing offenders convicted of shop theft and Elizabeth Whiting the multilevel data combining the Labour Force Survey with area level data on social deprivation.

I am also extremely grateful to the Home Office, the Office for National Statistics and the UK Data Archive for supplying me with the data sets analysed in this book. Further details are given in the text, at the point where the data are analysed. Citations appear in the Bibliography. These organisations have asked me to record that although all efforts are made to ensure the quality of the materials, neither the original data creators, depositors or copyright holders, the funders of the Data Collections, nor the UK Data Archive bear any responsibility for the accuracy or comprehensiveness of these materials nor for their further analysis or interpretation.

Roger Tarling
July 2008

1 Statistical modelling: An overview

1.1 Introduction

In defining a model, the dictionary talks of making a representation, an imitation, an image, a copy or a paradigm.

We talk of models and use them in many different contexts. Perhaps the term is used too readily or too loosely, devaluing its meaning and power. Nevertheless, in the built environment it is common to physically build a mock-up (models) of how the construction will look. Engineers will build prototypes (models) of a new machine, for example a car. Planners build simulation models to represent traffic flows as a way of assessing new road layouts.

In their objective, models in the social sciences are no different. What the theoretician or researcher is attempting to produce is a representation of how phenomena or concepts (as measured by their variables) relate to each other. In other words, the social scientist is attempting to understand the complex social world and represent the essential inter-relationships in a simplified but meaningful way.

What distinguishes a statistical model is that it is constructed from empirical quantitative data and uses statistical theory to guide its development. The details of this will be given later but at this stage it is important to note that the theory or the research question guides the construction of the model. Statistical modelling is a technique to aid understanding, it is not an end in itself.

1.2 Why model?

Statistical modelling is an important analytical tool as it enables social researchers to consider in a coherent and unified procedure complex inter-relationships between social phenomena and to isolate and make judgements about the separate effects of each. More specifically, in social science statistical modelling is undertaken for one of four main reasons: (1) to improve understanding of causality and the development of theory, (2) to make predictions, (3) to assess the effect of different characteristics, (4) to reduce the dimensionality of data.

To aid the development of theory

Constructing models can help develop theoretical perspectives or test the claims of competing perspectives. Relatively recently attention has been given to the part lifestyle plays in crime victimisation and routine activity theories have been promulgated.

These theoretical perspectives can be informed by developing models examining how aspects of people's lives, such as where they work, what recreational activities they take part in, how they travel, what time they travel and who with, relate to their experience of being a victim of crime.

To make predictions

Many models, particularly in the economic sphere, are constructed with the purpose of making forecasts or predictions about the future. The ability to anticipate any changes in unemployment or interest rates or the cost of living offers decision makers the opportunity to take any necessary remedial action. Similarly, statistical models can be used to estimate the relative risks of certain outcomes, for example, the risk that an offender will reoffend within a particular time period. Knowledge of the risk can be an aid to decision making; in this example it may inform decisions about when the offender is to be released from prison or whether or not the offender should be placed on a particular programme.

To assess the effect of different characteristics

Often the aim of a social research project is to evaluate the effect of a particular characteristic on an outcome, for example are women offenders treated differently from male offenders in terms of the sentence they are awarded at court? Are women dis-criminated against in the workplace and paid less than men? In answer to the first question, women are generally awarded lesser sentences than men but can it be inferred that women are treated differently? Other attributes contribute to the sentence imposed – the seriousness of the offence, the age of the offender and the previous criminal history of the offender. Compared with men, women offenders generally commit less serious offences and have less extensive criminal careers so it is not surprising that on average they receive lesser sentences. To answer the important question of whether women are treated differently from men, account has to be taken of the offence committed, age and criminal record, in order that we may treat 'like with like'. A statistical model enables us to assess the effect of gender on sentencing after adjusting for the other important characteristics known to influence sentencing decisions.

To reduce the dimensionality of data and to uncover latent variables

A situation may exist where many variables are highly inter-correlated, for example a child's marks on various school tests, or a person's answers to a large number of similar attitudinal questions. Leaving until later the technical problems encountered by includ-ing all these similar variables in a model, one might, in any case, prefer a summary measure of them. An average (which is itself a linear model) could be calculated and used to represent the set of variables or a more sophisticated model, which weighted each of the variables differently, could be constructed.

In other applications the purpose may be to uncover *latent variables*, which are underlying social constructs (such as social deprivation, quality of life or fear of crime) but for which no direct measurement scale exists. In order to undertake research and perform analysis on these concepts, a measurement scale has to be constructed from *manifest variables*, that is, from variables that can be measured. Latent variables are discussed further in Chapter 10.

Before concluding this section it should be emphasised that the four purposes outlined above are not themselves mutually exclusive. Models that are firmly grounded in theory are likely to achieve better predictions and will be better placed to isolate the relative effects of different characteristics. That is, the better the model represents true relationships between the underlying phenomena the better able it is to achieve any of the objectives set out above.

1.3 The general linear statistical model

A statistical model takes the form of a mathematical equation in which the concepts of interest (as measured by their variables) are hypothesised to be related to each other in some way. The statistical model of interest in this book is known as the general linear statistical model and is defined in Equation (1.1).

$$y_i = b_0 + b_1 x_{1i} + b_2 x_{2i} + \ldots + b_p x_{pi} + e_i \tag{1.1}$$

where:

> y is the dependent variable, y_i is the value of the dependent variable for the ith subject
>
> $x_{1i}, x_{2i} \ldots x_{pi}$ are any number (from 1 to p) of explanatory/independent variables. The value of x_p will vary between the i subjects.
>
> $b_1, b_2 \ldots b_p$ are the coefficients, or parameters, of the corresponding explanatory variables, $x_1, x_2 \ldots x_p$.
>
> e is the error term or residual, e_i is the residual for the ith subject.

Each variable is explained in turn.

Dependent variable, also known as response variable or outcome variable

The dependent variable is the variable of prime interest in our research, that is, the variable which we wish to explain or predict. The dependent variable is regarded as a random variable, which is free to vary in response (hence response variable or outcome variable) to the explanatory variables. Note that in Equation (1.1) there is only one dependent variable although we may have alternative definitions and measures of it. (For example, if the focus of the study was the remuneration people received, the dependent variable could be annual salary or hourly rate of pay. Remuneration could also include pensions and/or interest on savings and investments, etc.) Although there is only one dependent variable per equation, we will also consider in Chapter 11 the situation where there is more than one equation (each with its own y) which are related or need to be analysed simultaneously.

SPSS and Stata consistently use the term dependent variable in all their models and it is the convention in texts and computer program manuals to denote the dependent variable by the letter y.

Explanatory variables, also known as predictor variables, covariates, factors or independent variables

In most real-life applications there is more than one, and potentially many, explanatory variables. As the name implies, these variables are associated with the dependent variable and explain or predict values of the dependent variable.

Although in common usage, the term independent variable is not favoured by statisticians as it does not accurately convey the nature of the relationship between such a variable and the dependent variable. As will be seen later, these variables are far from independent in statistical models but are often highly correlated with the dependent variable and each other. I prefer the term explanatory variable as it better describes the nature of the relationship between it and the dependent variable. However, I concede that the use of independent variable is pervasive and I will continue to use it interchangeably with explanatory variable.

Explanatory (independent) variables can obviously be continuous or categorical (these terms are defined in section 2.4). Continuous explanatory (independent) variables are often called covariates – to signify that they vary in some relationship with the dependent variable. Categorical explanatory (independent) variables are also called factors or indicators and the individual categories of the factor are sometimes called levels.

Stata consistently uses the term independent variable throughout. However, SPSS is not so consistent. Rather confusingly it uses independent variable in the regression component, but covariate in the logistic regression component, regardless of whether the variable is continuous or categorical. The terminology changes again for the multinomial where covariates and factors are separately identified.

In most texts and computer program manuals it is the convention to denote explanatory variables by the letter x, and if there is more than one to number them sequentially with a subscript: x_1, x_2, x_3 and so on.

Whether a variable is considered to be a dependent variable or an independent variable depends wholly on the context, that is, the nature of the research being undertaken. In one study a variable may be considered as the dependent variable but in another as an explanatory variable. For example in a study of school pupils' achievements, some measure of educational attainment might be taken as the dependent variable. However, in a study of adults' occupations or salary, school attainment might well be considered as an explanatory variable. Furthermore, in any one study, a variable may be considered as both a dependent variable and an explanatory variable at different stages of the analysis, especially when developing causal models (which are the subject of Chapter 11).

Coefficients or parameters

Associated with each explanatory (independent) variable x_p is a coefficient or parameter b_p. b_p indicates the magnitude by which y changes as x_p changes after taking into account (or adjusting for) the other explanatory variables included in the model. To be more precise, for a one-unit change in x_p, y will change by an amount b_p after adjusting for the contribution of the other explanatory variables. Thus b_p is the *partial* effect of x_p given the other xs in the model. It is important to understand that the value of b_p may well change from model to model depending on which other variables are included. In addition, b_p will also depend on the units of measurement chosen. For example, if y represented a person's weight and x his or her height, b would take a different value if weight was measured in pounds or kilograms and height was measured in feet or centimetres. However, whatever units of measurement were chosen, b would represent the same change in the quantum of weight due to a one-unit change in the quantum of height.

b_0 is a constant term and represents the value of y when all the explanatory variables equal zero, that is, when no explanatory variables are included in the model. It will be seen that the constant value, b_0, is itself often meaningless; its only importance is to help determine the values of b_p. (The exception is where the explanatory variables are categorical when b_0 represents the effect on y of being in the reference category; discussed in section 3.5) It is also possible to fit the models to eliminate the constant term altogether (in effect to set it to zero).

The element of the model containing the explanatory variables and the coefficients, that is:

$$b_0 + b_1 x_{1i} + b_2 x_{2i} + \ldots + b_p x_{pi}$$

is known as the fixed component (or systematic component) of the model.

Error term

The final term in the model is e, which represents the random component of the model, and is the error term or the residual (sometimes called the disturbance term). The fixed component of the model does not predict y exactly as in reality there are always other influences not represented by the explanatory variables, however exhaustive they may appear to be, which help determine the value of y. In addition, some of the variation in y may just be unexplainable random variation (which is often referred to as noise). The term e is called the error term or residual as it represents what is not explained by the fixed component of the model and thus represents unmeasured effects and noise. In numerical terms it is the difference between the observed or actual value of y and the value of y predicted by the explanatory variables in the model. Assumptions about the nature of the error term are important in defining the particular model and examining residuals can provide insights into whether the assumptions are correct.

Linearity

The model above was labelled the general *linear* model and this review is limited to linear models. What then does linear mean in this context? The model is defined to be linear in the *coefficients*. This means that the coefficients, the bs, are added together. Of course each b is multiplied by its corresponding x before being added to another term, but it does not matter what that x is. It is the fact that the terms are added together that makes the model linear.

Because the only requirement is that the terms are added together, the framework of the general linear model is very flexible. The xs need not be linear to conform, a point we shall develop in section 3.8.

Many of the models discussed in this book have been found to be related under the unifying concept of the generalised linear model. But to avoid introducing too many concepts at the outset, a description of the generalised linear model is given in Appendix 1.

1.4 Model development

There are essentially six stages in developing a statistical model. A brief overview is given here and further details will be provided in later chapters.

Clarifying the research question/designing the study

The first stage involves being clear about the purpose and nature of the research and in defining the specific research questions or hypotheses to be explored and evaluated. The need for the study will have emerged as a result of theoretical development and/or in response to a policy issue. Either way, there will be a context and often previous research which will shape the design of the study to generate appropriate data.

Data collection

New data could be gathered from primary sources (for example, by conducting a survey) or data from secondary sources could be used (either data generated from a previous survey or from existing, often administrative, records). Regardless of the source, the data will need to be coded (or recoded) and new variables derived. Finally the data will need to be assembled in an appropriate form in readiness for analysis. This stage will also entail a good deal of initial preliminary statistical analysis to clean up the data and identify potentially important relationships which need to be examined further.

Specifying the model

In statistical modelling, statisticians talk of specifying a model, that is, making an initial assumption about how variables might be related and hence included in the model. Theory, previous research and the hypotheses to be tested will identify which explanatory variables need to be considered. Of course, if important variables are not included in the model the model will be mis-specified. The problems arising from mis-specified models are discussed in section 3.10.

A further aspect of specifying the model involves choosing the form of the model to be adopted (multiple regression, logistic regression and so on) which is governed by the *type* of response variable.

Fitting and estimating the model

Having specified a model, the next stage is to map it onto the data. Statisticians call this process model fitting or estimation. This stage estimates the values of the coefficients or parameters of the model.

There are two main procedures for estimating models, known as least squares and maximum likelihood. Ordinary least squares (often referred to as OLS) will be described in Chapter 4 as it is the procedure used for estimating regression models. As will be seen, it is a procedure for minimising the distance of the regression equation from the data points, and in that sense provides the best possible fit to the data. In addition to ordinary least squares, there are variants including weighted least squares, generalised least squares, two-stage and three-stage least squares.

Maximum likelihood is mathematically more technical and no attempt will be made here to provide a detailed explanation. In essence a maximum likelihood estimate of our parameters, b_p, is the one that makes the observed data most likely. The estimates forthcoming from maximum likelihood procedures can be shown to have very desirable properties and thus maximum likelihood is considered a good method of estimating the parameters of a model.

Interestingly, ordinary least squares is, in fact, a maximum likelihood method under certain conditions (technically that the error term is normally distributed). This may explain why OLS is still used to estimate regression models but maximum likelihood is used to estimate other models.

Statisticians developing new types of models, or wishing to modify existing standard models, will 'go back to basics' and formulate the appropriate likelihood function to estimate the parameters of their models. However, in reality, most social scientists will not be developing new models but simply applying those already available within existing statistical software. We mortals will have to take on trust the estimation procedures incorporated within the software, satisfying ourselves that the creators of reputable computer software such as SPSS and Stata have adopted the best possible procedures. The reason why OLS is described in any detail (in the Chapter 4) is that some appreciation of how models are fitted helps clarify the essential features of a statistical model and illustrates why certain procedures are followed in developing models.

Assessing the adequacy of the fitted model

How good is the model? Intuitively this question can be answered in three ways. First, how good is the model as a whole in explaining the variation in the dependent variable, y? And how much of the variation in the response variable does the model explain? How does one model compare with other, alternative models? For this we require global measures of the model (often referred to as goodness of fit statistics) and significance tests in order to indicate whether the model in its entirety shows evidence of an underlying relationship or whether it falls within the boundaries of a chance occurrence. Tests are also needed to assess whether one model is better than another model.

Second, how do the elements (variables) in the model compare? Which ones are important and which ones are not? We need a significance test for each component of the model, the explanatory variables x_p, to see whether each individually is making an important contribution to the model in explaining y over and above other variables included in the model. In practice, it is not the x_p that is tested but the coefficient, b_p, to see if its value is significant. If not, this is tantamount to inferring that the corresponding x_p makes no significant contribution to the model.

Third, if the purpose is to construct a model which best represents the data then intuitively a model that 'comes close' to all the data points is preferred. Does the model adequately represent (or fit) all the data points? This question can be answered by following certain diagnostic procedures. A well-respected method here is to examine residuals. The model can be used to predict the value of each data point and the predicted value can be compared with the actual data point. As previously stated, the difference between the two is the residual. Residuals thus provide important information on how well the model fits the dataset generally and each data point individually. We may well find that the model fits the data well within a range of values of y but not all values of y. Furthermore, exceptional values of y or combinations of x values (often referred to as outliers) may have undue or disproportionate influence when estimating the model and on the values of the coefficients, b_p. An example here might be income where a relatively small proportion of people have exceptionally high incomes, way above the income of the majority. Residuals are discussed further in section 3.9.

Drawing conclusions

The final stage is to draw out the conclusions from the model and to assess how much light it sheds in answer to the original research question. A model might have passed statistical tests which indicate that it is good or best, but how does it help shape our understanding of the real-world problem? Is it good or useful in a substantive sense?

Determining the final or 'best' model

The previous section sets out the distinct stages, however, it is extremely unlikely that the final or best model will be developed in the first instance. The modelling process invariably involves repeating or iterating through certain stages of the cycle. Stage 1 may not be revisited but it may be necessary to re-examine the data at Stage 2, perhaps to derive new variables. Stages 3, 4 and 5 will be repeated, often many times. Information obtained from testing one model will feed back to re-specifying the model (dropping some variables, including others, considering interactions, etc.), trying alternative models and comparing them with previous models.

Perhaps because of the complexity of many of the relationships within social science or because of the imperfections in measuring some of the information, it is invariably the case that models developed provide some, but only limited, explanation of the phenomenon under consideration. It is also a common experience in social research to have explanatory variables which are highly related to each other because they reflect the same underlying condition. For example, poor housing, low pay, high unemployment may all be manifestations of social deprivation. The problem caused by highly inter-related variables is known as multicollinearity (discussed in section 3.6).

Throughout this process the social researcher will be balancing the explanatory power of the model with simplicity or parsimony. As result of either the complexity of the relationships and/or multicollinearity, many different models may be found to be nearly as good as each other. Leaving to one side theoretical or substantive considerations, when choosing between equally good competing models the simpler or less complicated model is to be preferred. However, it may take several iterations to arrive at the best model (or a small set of alternative models) and to clarify what messages are forthcoming from the entire modelling exercise.

1.5 Model selection by the computer

In the above description of the process the social researcher has been taking the decisions regarding which variables to enter into each of the alternative models. The researcher could, however, take the 'easy way out' and delegate this task to the computer package and let it find the best fitting model which is an option in SPSS.

The default procedure in SPSS is Enter – under which the researcher specifies all the variables to be included in the model. However, SPSS offers the researcher alternative procedures, including Stepwise and Backward. Choosing either method will lead SPSS to find what it considers to be the best model according to the criteria it has been set to follow. All the researcher has to do is to ensure that the explanatory variables that he or she would like to be considered are included in the appropriate box. In Stepwise SPSS will, at Step 1, find the best model with one variable (that is, the variable that is most significantly related to the dependent variable). At Step 2, SPSS will search for the best fitting model with two variables, at Step 3, three variables, and so on. The procedure terminates at the point where any further variables would not make a significant additional contribution to those already included. A point to bear in mind is that a particular variable might be included in an earlier step but excluded at a later step because a different set of variables might make a greater contribution. Backward undertakes the process in reverse. All the variables are included at the outset and SPSS eliminates them one by one, starting with the least significant, until it arrives at the subset where all remaining variables are significantly related to y.

Automated procedures used sparingly can be helpful in model development but they should not be used slavishly and they are certainly not a panacea. Theory, prior research and substantive knowledge should always play a major part in guiding model development. Insights and understanding are gained from thoughtfully specifying and testing alternative models. Simply throwing the data at SPSS and leaving it to arrive at a solution can also lead to misleading results and unintelligible models. The computer software can only apply statistical algorithms, it cannot make thoughtful decisions. In some software further restrictions can be placed on how the computer implements selection criteria, but imposing restrictions is tantamount to specifying the model. Furthermore, in a study where a large number of variables have been collected, it is impractical to offer them all for selection.

Some commentators take a purest line and will not allow the computer to select the model, whereas I am more pragmatic. It may be helpful during a session of model development just to see what the 'computer would have made of the problem' and whether the computer-generated solution suggests developments that might otherwise have been overlooked. However, I am not keen on backward procedures, especially in situations where there are a large number of explanatory variables and even more so if the sample size is relatively small in relation to the number of explanatory variables.

1.6 Statistical software

Many statistical packages are available to fit statistical models. Statisticians would probably favour S-Plus, a freeware version R, or perhaps SAS. However, in reality (and it is certainly my experience) most social researchers will choose to use, or more likely will simply have available to them, SPSS or increasingly now Stata. Furthermore, datasets obtainable from the UK Data Archive (www.data-archive.ac.uk) are available as SPSS files or, alternatively in the case of more recent data files, Stata files. It is for these reasons that SPSS and Stata are used to fit the models discussed in this book.

Although SPSS is easy to use and has many strengths, it is somewhat frustrating for statistical modelling. It will be seen that each component is different in the terminology it adopts, its facilities for handling categorical data, creating interaction terms and in other ways. It seems that different components have been produced at different times by different teams without reference to previous components. Furthermore, earlier modules have not been updated to conform to later developments. There appears to be no one unifying architecture, structure or language, leaving users to learn each module as a separate entity. I find students can be confused when moving between the modules simply because they do not appreciate that a different terminology has been adopted. (It is for this reason that alternative terminology is presented in this book.)

Stata may be a little more difficult to learn initially but does have a unifying framework with commands following a consistent pattern. Stata fits a wider range of models and also benefits from having a large user base, members of which create additional routines that are available and can be incorporated within Stata. It is possible to access the web-based user group while in Stata, via the Help facility.

Both software have a Windows interface with drop-down menus and dialogue boxes and models can be specified by point and click. But both software can be command driven. Whichever approach is taken it is good practice to keep a record of commands issued, especially records of any changes to variables, such as recoding existing variables or deriving new variables. This can be accomplished in SPSS by opening a syntax file and in Stata by opening a log file. Apart from keeping a record for future reference, the commands contained in the files can be adapted to run subsequent analysis. In addition to preserving a permanent record, Stata also has the facility of storing a list of commands initiated during the current session in a Review window. This is valuable as the researcher can click on a previous command specifying a model and simply add or delete further variables.

From Version 14 onwards, SPSS has the facility to save SPSS files as Stata files and also to read Stata files. This is a welcome development as it enables the researcher to undertake initial analysis in SPSS and to convert to Stata to take advantage of its additional capabilities or to switch files between packages for any other reason. Stata have also produced a separate program called Stat Transfer which can be used to convert data files from any one of many computer software formats into any other.

To fit multilevel models, a separate package, MLwiN, is preferred even though Stata does have an 'add on routine' gllamm which will fit a broad range of multilevel models. (SPSS can only fit a limited range of multilevel models.) (MLwiN can, of course, also fit the more common single level linear models but we shall not adopt it in those situations as a principal purpose is to demonstrate SPSS and Stata.) Further details of MLwiN are left until Chapter 9 which describes multilevel models.

Although they are not discussed in any detail in this book, I sometimes find myself using Microsoft Excel and Access to prepare data files for statistical modelling. In addition, much administrative data is made available from organisations in either format so some knowledge of Excel and Access is useful.

Further reading

References to texts on statistical modelling will be given at the end of the chapters describing particular models.

A large number of introductory texts on SPSS are available and a growing number on Stata. (For details of books on Stata, see the Stata website www.stata.com: click Purchase → Bookstore → Books on Stata.)

Free guides to SPSS and Stata are available at the Economic and Social Data Service (ESDS) website (www.esds.ac.uk). They are: Norman, P. and Wathan, J. (2006) and Rafferty, A. (2006).

Both guides contain appendices detailing further resources and references.

2 Research designs and data

As noted in the previous chapter, stage one of any study is to clarify the research question and the focus of the research. This in turn will identify the type of data required to answer the question and the method by which the data is collected. Both will have a bearing on the approach to statistical modelling and the type of model fitted. Thus before discussing statistical modelling, it is necessary to review research designs, how variables are defined and measured and the problems posed by missing data. These topics are the subject of this chapter.

2.1 Units of analysis

At an early stage a decision must be taken on the units of analysis, that is, the subjects on which we are going to collect information. (Once assembled in a data file, subjects are often referred to as cases.) In many studies the unit of analysis or subjects will be people (voters, employees, children, offenders, for example). Data on people is often referred to as data at the individual level. Alternatively, the unit of analysis could be an organisation, institution or region such as schools, hospitals, police forces or counties and countries. For these units of analysis, data might be collected on the characteristics of the organisation or institution, such as the type of school or hospital, whether the police force covers a rural or urban area and so on. In addition, aggregate data might be assembled for the organisation based on the individual data for that institution, such as the number or proportion of pupils passing examinations (in the case of schools) or the number of crimes per number of people living in the police force area (in the case of police forces). Such measures are thus in the form of proportions (or percentages) or rates – the latter being common when comparing countries where measures often include population density, Gross Domestic Product per capita, literacy rate and so on.

Of course, in any study, and depending on the topic of interest, data may be collected both at the individual and at the organisation or institutional level. If the research interest were to identify the factors contributing to educational attainment, we would collect information on the pupils and on the schools. Such research would result in hierarchical data, now more commonly called multilevel data where data is collected on units at two levels, pupils and schools. Multilevel data arises in many research applications and need not be confined to two levels, but conceptually can extend to any number of levels. For example, a study may be interested in examining individuals within households which are situated within neighbourhoods which in turn are located within geographic regions. (Models for multilevel data are presented in Chapter 9.)

2.2 Research designs

Research can be classified into two broad categories, cross-sectional studies and longitudinal studies.

Cross-sectional designs

In many research studies data is collected with reference to one point or period in time, usually on a representative sample or 'cross-section' of subjects (individuals, organisations, whatever) from the relevant population. The National Travel Survey asks those interviewed (interviewees, respondents) what journeys they made in a previous fixed time period, why they undertook those journeys and what mode of transport they used. Individuals need not be interviewed as data about them may be gathered from official, administrative records; for example from registers of unemployed people, or from prison records. If the subjects are institutions or organisations, such as schools, data may be gathered from administrative records or by interviewing a representative of the institution or by requesting that representative to complete a questionnaire on behalf of the institution.

Most of the models described in this book can be readily applied to cross-sectional data.

Longitudinal designs

Longitudinal studies essentially collect data over a period of time on the same subjects (individuals, organisations etc.) and by so doing monitor and record social change or changes in life events. By recording events over time, longitudinal studies are better placed to disentangle the temporal and sequential occurrence of different social processes and thus, potentially at least, facilitate greater understanding of causal mechanisms and relationships.

However, the broad category of longitudinal research design can be further subdivided into several sub-types: time series, repeated cross-sections and panel studies. Each sub-type poses particular issues for statistical modelling. Further details of longitudinal designs and models are left until Chapters 11, 12 and 13.

2.3 Sampling, surveys and weighting

Much of statistical theory, including the theory underpinning statistical modelling, is based on the assumption of a simple random sample, that is, a situation where every member of the given population of interest has the same probability of being selected for inclusion in the sample. However, in reality many research studies and surveys that are conducted do not yield simple random samples but complex sample surveys. They are probability samples, where the method of selection enables every member of the population the opportunity to be selected, but the probability of selection is different for different subjects.

Consider the British Election Survey, which is typical of many large-scale surveys undertaken by government or other public bodies. At the time of each general election, a survey is carried out to ascertain whether people voted, which party they voted for and their reasons for choosing one party over another. Individual characteristics are also obtained. The survey is not a simple random sample as this would entail selecting for interview individuals from all parts of the country and the costs and effort of contacting and visiting them (possibly more than once) would be considerable as well as impractical. The British Election Survey (BES) that followed the 1997 general election is typical. To keep costs to an acceptable level, a multistage or clustered random probability design was adopted. The first stage entailed selecting 218 postal sectors (small areas of the country), thus postal sector is the primary sampling unit (or psu). The second stage entailed sampling 30 'delivery points' within each sector (a delivery point is an address where mail is delivered which may have more than one household at the address). The third stage then randomly selected households at the address and the fourth randomly selected an individual over the age of 18 (that is of voting age) living in the household for interview.

The multistage procedure reduces costs because fieldwork is concentrated or clustered in fewer areas of the country. The selected households are not evenly scattered across the country as they would be if a simple random sample had been drawn. Unfortunately there is no such thing as a free lunch. The price to be paid is that clustering can, and generally does result in larger standard errors (if correctly estimated). This is because households and individuals in a small area (postal sector) are likely to be more similar in their composition, background and voting behaviour than the same number of households or individuals evenly spread around the country (that would be selected in a simple random sample). Choosing many different postal sectors throughout the country will minimise the 'clustering effect', but it is unlikely to eliminate it entirely. The upshot will be that standard errors of estimates from a multistage clustered sample will be greater than the standard errors resulting from a simple random sample of the same size. Intuitively this can be conceived in one of two ways. First, a multistage clustered sample does not capture all the variation that would be captured by a simple random sample. Or, second, because many households are more similar within clusters than would be the case in a simple random sample it is as if the sample size of the multistage clustered sample is not as large as a simple random sample.

The clustering effect is known in other statistical contexts as the intra-class correlation, ρ (the Greek letter rho) and is a measure of within group or cluster homogeneity. For example, a ρ of .15 indicates that individuals within the same cluster or group are 15% more likely to have the same value on a variable of interest than individuals in the population as a whole. (The intra-class correlation is also important in the context of multilevel models and is discussed again in Chapter 9.)

Greater precision in surveys can be achieved by stratification. This can be explained by way of an example. Suppose we wish to obtain a sample of different ethnic groups. For simplicity we will assume that there are only two groups, white and non-white, and it is known from the Census that x% of the population are white, y% non-white. An approach could be to stratify our sample into the two groups (or strata) and select a subsample from within each strata. If the total sample was to be of size 1000 we would select x% of 1000 from the white subsample and y% of 1000 from the subsample of non-whites. The stratified sample of 1000 would provide more precise estimates of the population, as it would be more representative of ethnic groups, than a simple random sample of 1000, which runs the risk of selecting, by chance, slightly more of one ethnic group and slightly less of the other group. By better reflecting the population, stratification will improve precision of the estimates but only if the strata have been constructed on variables that are related to the research question of interest.

In the example above, ethnic groups were chosen for the sample in proportion to their occurrence in the population. However, if it is intended to undertake detailed analysis within each group separately we may wish to select a greater proportion, or over sample, a particular group in order to have a larger number from that group. It is common practice in many UK surveys to include such 'booster' samples for Wales, Scotland and Northern Ireland.

Stratification was adopted for the 1997 BES. The postal sectors were stratified on the basis of sub-region of the country, population density and SEG profile (percentage of household heads who are employer/managers). These three stratification variables are related to voting patterns and thus the strata created helped achieve a more representative sample of voting patterns.

A further bias arises in the BES and similar surveys due to differential selection probabilities in that only one household at an address is selected and only one person within the household is selected for interview. Thus, for example, individuals living in single-person households are more likely to be selected than individuals living in large households. Non-response can also cause bias as some individuals may be less easily contactable than others. To correct for these biases, and produce a sample representative of the population, the sample needs to be weighted to give less weight to those over-represented in the sample and more weight to those under-represented in the sample.

Calculating weights is a complicated subject outside the scope of this book. However, it need not concern us unduly because the calculation is undertaken by specialist survey methodologists employed by the survey company carrying out the survey and the weights are included as variables in the data file. There may be (and often are) more than one weight variable and of concern to the researcher is to know which weight to use in what circumstances. Guidance should be available in the documentation accompanying the data file.

So far the discussion has centred on complex sample surveys, but many research studies are multistage designs and thus give rise to the issues presented in this section. In studies of school pupils it is common to first randomly select schools and then select pupils within schools. Similarly, when sampling prisoners for interview, it is common to first randomly select prisons and then select prisoners within those prisons. Furthermore, it should be noted that random selection is often compromised in such studies when one (or more) randomly selected schools or prisons request not to participate for logistical reasons and another school or prison is substituted.

When analysing data arising from complex samples it is important to be aware of the design factors and to take account of them in the analysis as far as possible. While weight variables are invariably provided, unfortunately many major surveys do not include variables indicating clustering (the psus) and stratification. The BES is one exception to the general rule and does include all the relevant information needed. For that reason, analysis of the survey, incorporating complex design factors, is presented in Chapter 6.

As to choice of software, Stata is better suited to model data from complex surveys as it can incorporate the full range of design features. SPSS cannot. How Stata handles design features is also explained in Chapter 6.

2.4 Variables and their measurement

In the previous section consideration was given to how the data might be generated. Here we outline what form that data might take.

A variable is simply a trait of a subject (our chosen unit of analysis) which can take different values for different subjects. Familiar variables would include age, height and weight, or in the case of an organisation, type of school or prison. Each person or organisation in the population will have a value for each variable but different subjects may have different values. A distinction can be made between time-varying variables and time-invariant variables. Some variables remain fixed throughout a subject's life, such as their sex or ethnicity. These variables are invariant over time. However, many variables can change over time, such as marital status – where a person will start out as single but then may marry, and later may get divorced or become widowed.

It is important to understand the different levels or scales on which variables can be measured as different statistical models are applicable for the different types of response variable.

Continuous data

Variables measured on a continuous scale can, in theory, take any value on that continuum. Age, height and weight are examples of continuous variables. In theory age could be measured to the gradation of minutes, hours, days, weeks, months or years. In practice however, how age is defined in any study will be determined by two considerations. First it is dependent on what is recorded in the original source data – in many cases the source may record date of birth, which permits a level of measurement to the nearest day. Second, the researcher needs to reflect on what degree of detail is required and in many cases a person's age in years is sufficient (although if the research study was of newly born children age might need to be measured in finer detail such as days or weeks).

Continuous data is measured on an interval or ratio scale. In both cases the distance between successive measures are the same. For example, a 21-year-old is one year older than a 20-year-old and a 41-year-old is one year older than a 40-year-old. An important feature of continuous data is that one can perform arithmetic operations so that it can be said that a 40-year-old is twice the age of a 20-year-old and their combined age is 60.

Because of the ability to carry out arithmetic, continuous data is considered to be measured at the highest level.

A distinction can be made between an interval and a ratio scale. A ratio scale (such as income or age) has a natural zero value whereas many constructed scales (such as intelligence, deprivation or attitudinal scores) do not.

Categorical data

Categorical data is a term which includes data measured on a nominal scale or on an ordinal scale. To confuse matters further, in some of its models SPSS calls categorical variables factors and Stata calls them indicators. Qualitative data has also been used as a term for categorical data (e.g. Agresti and Finlay, 1997) as opposed to quantitative data, which refers to continuous data. I shall avoid both terms, qualitative and quantitative, as qualitative data can take on a different meaning in social science.

The nominal scale is the lowest level of measurement. A variable measured on a nominal scale consists merely of separate categories (called levels in some statistical software). An example is the variable religion, which could have the categories, Christian,

Hindu, Jew, and Muslim. Here the categories are simply logically different and distinct from one another. The categories must be mutually exclusive and each person can fit only one category. Categories must be exhaustive so that any subject can be placed in one of the categories. To accommodate this it is usual to include a category 'other' for the small number of cases that fall outside the schema (as well as a category 'not known' for cases where information is missing or has not been recorded).

It is not possible to perform arithmetic on categorical data in the way one can on continuous data. For example, it makes no sense to say a Christian is twice a Hindu or that Christian plus Hindu equals a Jew. All that we have for categorical variables is count or frequency data, that is, the number of people who are in each of the categories Christians, Hindus etc. in the sample or population.

In many cases there may be only two categories, for example gender, male or female. Similarly many outcome measures may have two categories, passed or failed (a test), survived or died, reoffended or not reoffended, and so on. In situations where there are only two categories (or levels) the variables are most commonly known as binary variables but also as dichotomous variables. If the categorical variable has more than two categories (such as religion above) it is called polychotomous or (as is becoming increasingly common) multinomial – the term favoured here. Categorical variables can be converted readily into proportions. For example we can present, or analyse, the data in terms of the proportion that passed, survived, reoffended or were of a particular religious faith, etc.

Categorical variables may also be measured on an ordinal scale, that is, the categories may fall into a natural order. An example of an ordered variable is educational attainment which could be defined to have the four ordered categories (starting with the lowest), 'no qualifications', 'GCSE', 'A-levels', 'university degree'. Compared with religion above we have additional information on educational attainment in that we can rank the various categories. However, unlike a continuous variable, such as age, we do not know the intervals between the categories (what is the difference between GCSE and A-level in terms of educational attainment?) so it is not possible to perform arithmetic operations.

Ordered variables are especially common in studies of attitudes, beliefs or preferences where people are asked whether they:

Strongly agree / Agree / Neither agree nor disagree / Disagree / Strongly disagree

on a particular issue. Variables measured in this way are said to be measured on a Likert scale.

Relationship between continuous and categorical variables

Continuous variables can always be collapsed into ordinal and nominal categorical variables. Age measured in years as a continuous variable can be recoded into ordered categories such as children, juveniles, young adults, middle-aged, older persons. The ordering can be ignored and the categories can be treated as if they were measured on a nominal scale, that is, as separate entities. Any ordinal variables can be regarded as nominal. However, it is not possible to reverse this process. Variables such as religion cannot be considered as ordinal or continuous.

It will be seen later that the level of measurement of the response variable determines the form of the statistical model to be adopted. Furthermore, the level of measurement of the explanatory variables determines how they are to be included in the model.

2.5 Missing data

It is rare (but fortunate when it happens) not to be confronted with problems posed by missing data. If data is missing statistical models and the inferences that can be drawn are weakened. The extent to which missing data is a problem and how its impact might be minimised depends on the circumstances which gave rise to its being missing.

In the first instance subjects may be missing. This can arise in survey research where individuals or organisations cannot be contacted or where they refuse to participate. In longitudinal studies members may have died or moved during the course of the study and not be contactable at later dates. Omission of subjects can also arise in studies based on administrative data. Records of hospital patients, school children, prisoners, etc. can be unavailable, mislaid or lost at the time of data collection – as anyone who has extracted such data can testify.

In survey research the number interviewed is called the achieved sample and the achieved sample expressed as a percentage of the intended sample (those initially selected for interview) is the response rate for the survey. Most government-sponsored surveys aim for a response rate of around 80%, which is considered to be a high and acceptable level. Unfortunately response rates tend to be falling as individuals become less inclined to be interviewed – perhaps through over-exposure to this form of data collection (not to mention a proliferation of more dubious and off-putting attempts to dress up product selling under the disguise of a research survey).

Nevertheless, even with a response rate of 80% one in five individuals (organisations or institutions depending on the subject of the survey) who were intended to be in the sample are not. If the one in five are no different from the 80% who did respond (the reason or process causing them to be missing was just random – known as missing completely at random or MCAR) then all is well and good. The achieved sample can be assumed to be an unbiased sample – the only disadvantage being that it is smaller than intended. (Often even this is not a problem as sponsors or survey contractors invariably work towards achieving a particular size sample and then select more for interview on the expectation of a certain level of non-response.)

Unfortunately however, in most cases it is unlikely that non-respondents are merely a random subset of the initial sample. Non-respondents are likely to be a biased group in some way. How biased and the extent to which one needs to be concerned is not always known. (Missing data is, by definition, missing.) From cumulative experience of conducting surveys and from undertaking detailed analysis of those who were contacted but after a good deal of effort, it is possible to gain some insights. Young people living alone, for example, may be most difficult to reach for face-to-face interview. This knowledge can be used to reweight the sample to minimise bias (as described in section 2.3). However, while it might be possible to compensate for obvious deficiencies in the basic composition of the survey, if the purpose of the survey is to enquire into very personal experiences or illegal or deviant behaviour some subjects may not participate because they do not wish to divulge their sensitive information.

So far we have considered non-response, where *no* information is available for a selected subject. In addition, it is often the situation that even if the subject is included only certain items of information are available. A person may participate but refuse to answer certain questions or partial information may only be available from administrative records. Whatever the reason, the case will be present but data is missing on particular variables. Three types of missing data can be distinguished. First, respondents refuse to answer the question or may have simply overlooked it. Second, respondents may genuinely not know the answer to the question or do not have a view or opinion to express. Thirdly, a question may not be applicable to that respondent, such as asking a person who did not go to university about their experience of university.

SPSS has three missing-value codes allowing the researcher to take account of the three different kinds of missing data: non-response, not known and not applicable. Stata, on the other hand, does not make this allowance, permitting only one missing-value code. It is important to be aware that Stata assigns a very large number as the missing value which can lead to problems for the unsuspecting. For example, if one recodes a continuous variable, like income, in such a way that a new recoded value is given to all values greater than a certain value, it will assign the new value to cases with the missing value as well. To avoid this error it is necessary to define the recode as 'greater than x, except missing value' or to adopt an increasingly common convention of coding missing data as a negative number for those variables where true values can only be positive.

Faced with missing data for a fraction of cases on a particular variable, the researcher should consider the mechanism for generating the missing values. Is the mechanism MCAR, in which case the missing data is not related to the observed data or to the unobserved data – it is simply random? A weaker assumption is that the data are missing at random (MAR). Under MAR, data missing on a variable may be explained by other variables collected in the study. Allison (2002) gives the example of the probability of missing data on income being related to a person's marital status, but within each marital status category, the probability of missing data on income was unrelated to a person's income. The final situation is missing not at random (MNAR). Here the reason for the missing data is not related to the other data collected but to unobserved data or some external reason.

Considering the missing mechanisms and exploring the data helps the researcher to identify solutions. Basically the researcher is faced with four options. First the variable with a high amount of missing data can be omitted from the analysis. This is a satisfactory course of action if the variable was not particularly crucial to the analysis or a substitute is available.

If the option of using an alternative is not available and the variable is pertinent to the analysis, the researcher has to choose between one of the three remaining options: casewise (or listwise) deletion, pairwise deletion and imputation.

Casewise (or listwise) deletion simply removes from the dataset all cases that have data missing on any of the variables to be included in the model. The modelling is then undertaken on the subset of cases for which data is complete on all variables. This is a simple and straightforward method but is only strictly valid if the missing mechanism is MCAR. However, if many variables are to be included in the model and each has only a small proportion of cases without data, but the missing data on all variables is spread evenly and thinly across the dataset, the result can be a large number of cases being discarded resulting in a considerably reduced sample. Losing many cases may also weaken the underpinning MCAR assumption.

Pairwise deletion (sometimes known as available case analysis) is more complex.

Some statistical models, for example multiple regression, can be developed from summary statistics (means, standard deviations, correlations etc.). The summary statistics can be calculated for a variable or pair of variables from the cases that have complete information on that variable or variables. The advantage is that more of the data is used compared with casewise deletion as fewer cases are deleted (or more are retained) at each stage of the analysis. The disadvantages are that the sample size differs for different parts of the analysis, making the calculation of the standard errors difficult. Perhaps more importantly from a practical point of view, the model still has to be derived from the summary statistics – a task that is not possible within SPSS. It can be done within Stata but it is not straightforward as it requires knowledge of a model's underlying mathematical structure and knowledge of matrix algebra.

The final option is to impute (infer then substitute) a value for the missing value. One could simply replace the missing value by the mean or mode estimated from the cases that have the information. Under MAR the missing data is related to the other observed data, thus the observed data can be used to impute the missing values. Various methods have been suggested and there are ever more sophisticated methods that fit models to provide the best estimate of the missing value, ranging from regression (to provide the predicted value for the missing data) to multiple imputation.

Allison (2002) has recently surveyed the three options outlined above and concludes that casewise deletion is attractive, satisfactory and robust, even if the underlying process leading to the data being missing is not entirely random. He dismisses pairwise deletion for the disadvantages and impracticalities stated above. Of the many imputation methods he advocates two recently developed procedures: (1) maximum likelihood and (2) multiple imputation.

As part of a recent methodology initiative, the Economic and Social Research Council (ESRC) has supported further work on missing data by a team at the Medical Statistics Unit at the London School of Hygiene and Tropical Medicine. The work of the Unit can be found at www.missingdata.org.uk. Members of the Unit are less sanguine than Allison regarding casewise deletion, feeling it can lead to substantial bias in models. However, in their *Guidelines for Handling Missing Data in Social Research*, they emphasise the need at the outset, when designing the research, to think through issues that may lead to missing data and to take all possible steps to reduce the potential problem. Furthermore, they suggest that if certain information is thought to be difficult to collect, researchers should carefully consider what other information could be collected that might shed light on the missing data. Once the data has been collected they suggest ways that initial data analysis might explore the reasons for the missing data. Of the imputation methods they discount simple methods and opt for multiple imputation, the procedure now favoured by many statisticians. Multiple imputation, as the name implies, produces several estimates, typically five, of the missing data which leads to five completed datasets. Each dataset is then analysed and the results combined.

Missing data is thus receiving a good deal of attention and in the near future it is likely that more advanced methods for handling missing data will be more readily accessible. Social researchers can track developments at the missing data website. In the meantime it makes good sense to think carefully about missing data (and avoid its occurrence as best one can). However, the reality is that only limited options are readily available at present within SPSS or Stata. Stata has an impute command which estimates missing values using a regression model. SPSS has the command Transform → Replace Missing Values, which gives a range of options. However, MLwiN, the only other statistical software package considered in this book, has available other, more advanced, options.

2.6 Data structures

Most data collected for a research study or made available for secondary analysis will be set out in a standard form with information for each subject or case recorded on a separate row of the data file. As already emphasised, the subject or case may be an individual, a household, a school, a police force, a country (or whatever the unit of analysis is for the study). The statistical software assigns a line number to each row of the data file. There may be any number of columns but they will fall into one of three categories:

1   Each subject or case needs to be given at least one (but usually more) unique identifier to distinguish it from all other subjects. It is not essential to have the identifier(s) in the first column(s) but it is common practice (because it is most convenient) to do so.
2   Most columns will be assigned to the variables.
3   The third item of information (which may or may not be included) is a weight or some other item which defines the sample design, such as the primary sampling unit (psu).

The standard data file described above is also referred to as a flat file or a rectangular file.

There are many variations and adaptations of the standard file, especially when recording multilevel (hierarchical) or longitudinal data. However, details of additional data structures are not given here but are presented alongside the relevant statistical models. Thus more is said about multilevel data files in section 9.1 and longitudinal data files in sections 12.6, 12.7 and 13.6.

On occasion data is not available for each individual subject and set out in the standard format, but aggregated and set out in the form of a multiway table. However, tabular data can be entered into an SPSS or Stata file and analysed as if it were a standard file of individual cases. The procedure is to weight the data by the number in the cell of the table. Instructions on how to handle tabular data are given in Appendix 2.

Further reading

For more information on research designs a good starting point is De Vaus (2001). Another book by the same author, De Vaus (2002), is a basic introduction to data preparation.

Theoretical and practical advice on surveys can be found in Groves *et al.* (2004).

A more detail account of weighting data is available at the Economic and Social Data Service (ESDS) website (www.esds.ac.uk): Crockett (2006).

For more information and practical advice and guidance on handling missing data, see Allison (2002). Also visit the website www.missingdata.org.uk.

3 Statistical preliminaries

In preparing this book it has been assumed that the reader has some understanding of basic statistics. Nevertheless, some concepts which are essential when fitting and interpreting statistical models are reviewed here.

3.1 Odds and odds ratios

Odds and odds ratios are a very informative way of expressing the relationship between categorical variables, and, as we shall see later, form the basis of models for binary, multinomial and ordinal response variables.

Odds is defined as the probability of an event occurring divided by the probability of the event not occurring.

If p is the probability of the event occurring then $1 - p$ is the probability of the event not occurring.

Thus:

$$\text{odds} = \frac{p}{(1 - p)}$$

An odds ratio is simply the ratio of two odds.

We illustrate odds and odds ratios by considering the relationship between the sentence awarded by the court and sex of the offender. The data has been extracted from the Offenders Index which is a database of all persons convicted at a court in England and Wales between 1963 to the present date. The sample here is of all offenders convicted of shop theft in the six-week period prior to July 2001.

The relationship between sentencing and sex is displayed as a two-way table (Table 3.1).

Most of the sentences displayed in Table 3.1 are self-explanatory. Custody is obviously imprisonment or some other form of incarceration. A community penalty is most often probation or a community service order – where the offender is required to undertake work in the community for a prescribed number of hours. Fine is a monetary penalty but could also include a payment of compensation to the victim. Discharge should not be confused with a finding of not guilty. The offender has been found guilty (or has admitted guilt) but the court chooses not to impose a punishment. Discharges are usually conditional for one or two years, meaning that if the person reoffends within that period an additional sentence might be imposed to take account of the

Table 3.1 Type of sentence awarded by sex: adults aged 21 and over convicted of shop theft

Sentence	Males		Females		Total	
	Number	%	Number	%	Number	%
Custody	650	29.4	90	13.9	740	25.9
Community penalty	537	24.3	181	27.9	718	25.1
Fine	595	26.9	151	23.3	746	26.1
Discharge	429	19.4	227	35.0	656	22.9
Total	2211	100	649	100	2860	100

Pearson chi-squared: 104.975; df, 3; $p < .001$
Likelihood ratio: 106.887; df, 3; $p < .001$

Note: It is not necessary to quote these statistics to three decimal places. They are only reported here in order to make comparisons with subsequent computer output.

breach of the conditional discharge. The implication of a discharge is that the offence is added to the offender's criminal record.

From Table 3.1 it can be seen that there is an association between the sentence awarded and the sex of the offender. Females are much less likely to be given a custodial sentence and much more likely to be discharged; only 13.9% are sentenced to custody but 35.0% are discharged. They are also slightly more likely to be given a community penalty (27.9%) than fined (23.3%). In contrast, males are more likely to be sentenced to custody (29.4%) and less likely to be discharged (19.4%). A similar proportion (about one quarter) is given each of the other two sentences.

As an alternative to percentages, we can express the relationship between sentence and sex as odds and odds ratios.

Consider the odds of males being sentenced to custody.

The probability, p, of a male being given a custodial sentence is

$$\frac{650}{2211} = .294$$

The probability of a male not being given a custodial sentence is $(1 - p) = 1 - .294 = .706$

Thus the odds of a male being sentenced to custody is

$$\frac{p}{(1 - p)} = \frac{.294}{.706} = .416$$

We have chosen to express the odds of a male being sentenced to custody (.416), but we could equally have expressed the odds of a male not being sentenced to custody. This is simply the inverse of the odds of being sentenced to custody, or

$$\frac{1}{.416} = 2.403$$

Thus males are nearly two and a half times as likely to be given a sentence other than custody as they are to be sentenced to custody.

The same steps can be applied to calculate the odds of a female being given a custodial sentence.

The probability, p, of a female being given a custodial sentence is

$$\frac{90}{649} = .139$$

The probability of a female not being given a custodial sentence is $(1 - p) = 1 - .139 = .861$

Thus the odds of a female being sentenced to custody is

$$\frac{p}{(1 - p)} = \frac{.139}{.861} = .161$$

As in the case of males, we could equally have chosen to express the odds of females not being sentenced to custody. For females it is

$$\frac{1}{.161} = 6.211$$

The odds ratio compares the odds for males with those of females (or the odds for females with those of males – it does not matter which).

The odds ratio of males to females of being sentenced to custody is

$$\frac{.416}{.161} = 2.58$$

thus males are about two and a half times more likely to be sentenced to custody than females.

Alternatively, the odds ratio of females to males is

$$\frac{.161}{.416} = .387$$

thus females are only 40% as likely to be sentenced to custody as males.

So far we have considered the odds of males and females receiving a custodial sentence, but we could easily extend our analysis to consider the odds of males and females receiving alternative sentences. Consider the odds of males and females receiving a discharge as opposed to a custodial sentence.

From Table 3.1 it can be seen that 650 males were sentenced to custody and 429 males were awarded a discharge. Thus 1079 males were sentenced to either custody or discharge. Similarly from Table 3.1 it can be seen that 90 females were sentenced to custody and 227 received a discharge.

The odds of custody rather than discharge for males is

$$\frac{p}{(1-p)} = \frac{\left(\dfrac{650}{1079}\right)}{\left(1 - \dfrac{650}{1079}\right)} = 1.51$$

The odds of custody rather than discharge for females is

$$\frac{p}{(1-p)} = \frac{\left(\dfrac{90}{227}\right)}{\left(1 - \dfrac{90}{227}\right)} = .396$$

Thus the odds ratio is

$$\frac{1.51}{.396} = 3.813$$

which can be interpreted that males are nearly four times as likely to be given a custodial sentence rather than receive a discharge than are females.

Following identical steps we can calculate that the odds ratio of community penalties to discharge, males to females, is 1.570 and the odds ratio of fine to discharge, males to females, is 2.085.

In a research study our particular interest may be in the imposition of custody and community penalties for males and females. We could calculate the odds ratio custody to community penalties in the same way as we did above. But we have already calculated the odds ratio custody to discharge and community penalties to discharge (both males to females). As both custody and community penalties are referenced to discharge the odds ratio custody to community penalties can be derived directly from them.

Odds ratio custody/community penalties males to females =

$$\frac{3.813}{1.570} = 2.428$$

Thus males are two and a half times as likely to receive a custodial sentence rather than a community penalty than are females.

While proportions range from 0 to 1, and percentages from 0 to 100, odds range from 0 to ∞ (infinity).

3.2 Logarithms

Mathematicians invent different numbering scales but whether they are adopted, and in what circumstances, depends on whether they or others find a use or application for them. One example is the binary numbering system in which any number can be expressed as a combination of 0s and 1s. This system has found an application in computing as it can be represented as the absence or presence of an electrical current. Computers utilise this representation to store and manipulate numbers.

Logarithms are yet another numbering system. The natural logarithm of a number is the power that raises the natural number, e (= 2.718), to equal the number in question. That is, if $y = e^x$, $x = \log_e y$ (or alternatively expressed as $x = \ln y$). Hence x is said to be the natural logarithm of y.

Thus the natural logarithm of 100 (ln 100) = 4.605 (because $100 = 2.718^{4.605}$).

The process can be reversed and the natural log can be transformed back to the number (known as the antilog) by $2.718^{4.605} = 100$.

So what, why bother with logarithms? Well it just so happens that logarithms have certain advantages and benefits in statistical modelling. There are three that concern us.

First, taking the natural logarithms of the odds (also known as the logit) changes the scale from 0 to ∞ (for odds), to $-\infty$ to $+\infty$ for log odds, centred on 0. Odds less than 1 have negative values of log odds whereas odds greater than 1 have positive log odds.

The logit is defined as:

$$\log_e \left(\frac{p}{1 - p} \right)$$

Second, logarithms have another useful property in that any two numbers multiplied together is equivalent to adding their logs. Thus multiplicative models can be converted to additive models, thereby conforming to Equation (1.1). We will come back to this when we consider loglinear models in Chapter 7.

Third, a statistic that we will come across later, −2loglikelihood (pronounced minus two log likelihood), which measures the fit of our model has a chi-squared distribution. This, and other properties of chi-squared (presented in section 3.3) provide a means of testing the fit of our models and a means of comparing one model with another.

We need not be unduly concerned with the details of logarithms as the statistical software constructs log odds, performs the analysis on the log odds and converts log odds back to odds for us. (Having said that, frustratingly SPSS does not undertake this conversion – or provide the option to convert – in some of its models.) Similarly, we do not need to be concerned with −2loglikelihood, but with the difference between the −2loglikelihoods for different models (also known as deviance) which results in chi-squared goodness-of-fit test statistics for our model(s).

3.3 z, t and chi-squared (χ^2)

z, t and chi-squared statistics are calculated by SPSS and Stata and given as tests of various elements of a statistical model. They are thus crucial in drawing inferences about a model.

Recall from basic statistics that z is:

$$\frac{\text{(the statistic of interest − the expected value of the statistic under the null hypothesis)}}{\text{the standard error of the statistic (s.e.)}}$$

In most introductory texts the statistic of interest is usually the mean and students often think z applies only to the mean (or the difference between two means). But z can be applied to all statistics of interest so long as we can estimate the standard error. Mathematical statisticians work out the formula for the standard error and the software incorporates and applies those formulae.

In statistical modelling, a statistic of primary interest is the coefficient b. It was pointed out in section 1.4 that the second of our three tests was to examine whether a particular variable, x_p, made a significant contribution to the model. To test the contribution of an explanatory variable we test whether its coefficient, b, is equal to 0. Under the null hypothesis $b = 0$. If $b = 0$ then $bx = 0$, thus testing for $b = 0$ is tantamount to testing that x is not related to y or has no effect on y.

Thus

$$z = \frac{b - 0}{\text{s.e. } b}$$

which simplifies to

$$\frac{b}{\text{s.e. } b}$$

Having calculated z how do we interpret it? If we can invoke the Central Limit Theorem, z conforms to a normal distribution with mean 0 and variance 1. Furthermore, 95% of the distribution lies within a z of ± 1.96 or 5% lies outside the range ± 1.96. This offers us a test statistic because if the absolute value of z (that is, ignoring whether it is positive or negative) is greater than 1.96 the probability that the value of b is equal to 0 is less than 5%. If our criterion for rejecting the null hypothesis is 5%, a value greater than 1.96 provides grounds for rejecting the null hypothesis and accepting the alternative hypothesis that b is not equal to 0. (We will make the point later that the criterion of a 5% significance test should not be slavishly applied.)

Student's t

The theory for z outlined above holds if the sample size is relatively large, usually taken to be 100 or more. However, Gossett, publishing under the pseudonym Student, identified the t distribution which is applicable for small samples. When the sample size is 120 or more, the normal distribution and the t distribution are indistinguishable and $z = t$. Because t is suitable for both large and small samples (and is z for large samples) t is the statistic produced by SPSS and Stata and appears in the output.

Robust standard errors

From the above it can be seen that the denominator of z and t is the standard error of the coefficient. One condition of estimating the correct value of z or t (and hence a correct estimate of the p-value) is thus to have an accurate estimate of the standard error. Like all statistics, the estimate of the standard error rests on certain assumptions and statistical theory. Violations of those assumptions and theory can lead to biased estimates but statisticians have developed what are known as *robust* statistics which are less prone to bias if the assumptions are not fully met. Stata has an advantage in that it can calculate robust standard errors if requested and this option is chosen when multiple regression models are fitted in section 4.9 and section 11.2. (As pointed out in section 2.3, Stata can also take into account complex designs when calculating standard errors, which is demonstrated in section 6.6.)

Confidence intervals

From the data the model estimates the coefficients b_p. But the estimates are based upon one sample of data that was obtained for the study. Had another sample been drawn, a slightly different estimate would have been obtained. So what confidence can be placed on the estimates we have from the study? The theory of the normal distribution outlined above can help. If the sampling distribution of b is normal then we can be 95% confident that the true value of b lies within the range ± 1.96(standard error of b). This range is called the 95% confidence interval. Obviously, if we wish to be more confident of our estimate, say 99%, then z changes from 1.96 to 2.58 and the range increases accordingly.

Confidence intervals are related to significant tests. The purpose of the significance test was to find evidence to reject the null hypothesis, $b = 0$. If the z or t value emanating from the test was greater than 1.96 (or less than -1.96) we would reject the null hypothesis and conclude that b was not equal to 0. We can then estimate a 95% confidence interval around b. In this situation the 95% confidence interval would *not* contain the value 0; because if the probability is less than 5% that b is 0 then we can be 95% sure that whatever range b lies within, 0 will not be in that range. Conversely, if our test had resulted in a z or t value less than 1.96 we would conclude that there was more than a 5% probability that b is 0. If we then calculated a 95% confidence interval for b it *would* contain the value 0.

Chi-squared

The chi-squared distribution is extremely important in statistical modelling as it is the basis of many tests which enable the researcher to compare models and to judge the importance of individual variables.

From first course statistics, it will be remembered that chi-squared tests the association between two categorical variables set out as a two-way table by comparing the observed numbers in each cell with the number that would be expected under the null hypothesis of no association (or independence). Consider Table 3.1 in which the two categorical variables are sentence and sex. Are they independent or is there an association between them? If sentence is independent of sex then both males and females would receive broadly the same sentences. 'Broadly' because there will always be some small difference between the observed and expected values due to sampling variability.

Consider the first cell: males sentenced to custody. Under the assumption of no association we would expect the probability of males sentenced to custody to be the same as the probability for females. Both would be equal to the probability of the entire sample being sentenced to custody, that is:

$$\frac{\text{Total number sentenced to custody}}{\text{Total sample}} = \frac{740}{2860} = .26$$

This is known as the marginal probability of custody: *prob(custody)*

However, to be in the first cell the offender also has to be a male. The probability of being a male in this sample is:

$$\frac{\text{Total number of males}}{\text{Total sample}} = \frac{2211}{2860} = .77$$

This is known as the marginal probability of being a male: *prob(male)*

The joint probability of being both a male and of being sentenced to custody (that is the probability of being in the first cell) is the product of the two marginal probabilities. Thus the expected number in the first cell is simply the probability of being in the first cell multiplied by the sample size. That is:

$$N \times \text{Row marginal prob (custody)} \times \text{Column marginal prob (male)} \qquad (3.1a)$$

Or, alternatively:

$$\text{Total sample} \times \frac{\text{Total number sentenced to custody}}{\text{Total sample}} \times \frac{\text{Total number of males}}{\text{Total sample}} \qquad (3.1b)$$

Note that by cancelling Total sample from the top and bottom, Equation (3.1b) reduces to:

$$\frac{\text{Row total} \times \text{Column total}}{\text{Total sample}}$$

which is the formula given in introductory statistics texts for calculating the expected values when calculating the chi-squared test of association for two-way tables. However, the conceptualisation of Equation (3.1a) has advantages which we will come to appreciate when loglinear models are described in Chapter 7.

Substituting values in Equation (3.1a) gives:

$$2860 \times .26 \times .77 = 573$$

This formula can be applied to each cell of the table by suitably adapting the row and column marginal probabilities depending on which row and column the cell falls.

Having calculated the expected value for each cell of the table, the chi-squared statistic is calculated as:

$$\chi^2 = \Sigma \frac{(O-E)^2}{E} \qquad (3.2)$$

where Σ means the sum of $\dfrac{(O-E)^2}{E}$

Equation (3.2) results in the Pearson chi-squared statistic. This was calculated by SPSS and found to be 105.0. However, to interpret chi-squared we need to know its associated degrees of freedom (df). A given value of chi-squared will lead to a different probability value (hence a different interpretation) depending on its degrees of freedom.

Degrees of freedom indicate the extent to which the data is 'free' to vary across the table. Given the sample size, which in Table 3.1 is 2860, three of the row marginal totals can vary, but not the fourth – its value must equal 2860 minus the sum of the other three row totals. (It does not matter which three rows vary.) Similarly, considering the columns, the number of males in our sample could vary but the number of females is fixed as (2860 – number of males) (or the number of females could vary and then the number of males would be fixed). Thus the data can vary across three rows and one column or $3 \times 1 = 3$. (In introductory texts the formula for the degrees of freedom is given as $(r-1)$ $(c-1)$ where r is the number of rows and c the number of columns.)

In practice the computer software will calculate chi-squared, the number of degrees of freedom and record the probability of obtaining that chi-squared value with its associated degrees of freedom. In Table 3.1 the chi-squared of 105 with 3 degrees of freedom results in a *p*-value of less than .001. By any account the probability of obtaining that result by chance is very small and we would conclude that sentencing outcomes are associated with sex of the offender.

Likelihood-ratio chi-squared statistic

At the foot of Table 3.1 another statistic is reported, named 'likelihood ratio'. (In fact SPSS produces three statistics but the third 'linear-by-linear' is of no interest to this book.) The likelihood-ratio chi-squared statistic (to give it its full name; often referred to as G^2) is complicated and details are not given. However, for two-way tables it simplifies to:

$$G^2 = 2 \Sigma \, O \log \left(\frac{O}{E} \right) \tag{3.3}$$

The likelihood-ratio statistic also has a chi-squared distribution and in most cases is similar in value to the Pearson chi-squared and will lead to the same inference. From Table 3.1 it can be seen that the likelihood-ratio statistic is 106.9, little different from the value of the Pearson chi-squared. However, as we shall see, it is the likelihood-ratio statistic that is reported in statistical modelling output (although it is often simply referred to as 'chi-squared') rather than the Pearson chi-squared. The reason for preferring the likelihood-ratio statistic is that it can be exactly partitioned whereas the Pearson chi-squared cannot. We explain what is meant by partitioning below.

Properties of chi-squared

One of the most important properties of chi-squared is that it is additive, by which we mean that the sum of two chi-squareds is also a chi-squared (with degrees of freedom the sum of the two degrees of freedom). This additive property extends to any number of chi-squared statistics. Of course, if chi-squareds can be added together they can also be disaggregated (or partitioned, to use the statistical parlance). This property is very useful because it means that we can compare chi-squareds (or more precisely the likelihood ratios) emanating from different models. In practice we can fit a model and obtain a chi-squared which will indicate the contribution of the model. We can then add more explanatory variables and obtain another chi-squared statistic which will indicate the importance of the second fitted model. However, the difference between the two chi-squareds will also be a chi-squared and will indicate the contribution of the added explanatory variables.

Another interesting property of chi-squared is that it is related to the normal distribution and the z score referred to above. In fact z^2 has a chi-squared distribution with 1 df. (This can be verified in statistical tables as the 5% value for z is 1.96 and $1.96^2 =$ 3.84, the 5% value of chi-squared with df = 1.) In statistical models z (or t) is simply (b/s.e.b), and squaring this is known as the Wald statistic. As the coefficients of the statistical model have one degree of freedom we will see that the Wald statistic is often given instead of the t statistic. By giving the Wald statistic all tests are then based on chi-squared.

3.4 Tests of significance

I have found that many students (often psychologists) have been led to believe that a p value of less than 5% is taken as significant whereas a p value greater than 5% is interpreted to be not significant and that this rule is immutable and never to be transgressed regardless of any other considerations. Thus a p value of .049 indicates significance whereas a p value of .051 is not significant even though there is little difference between them. Also immutable, it seems, is adherence to a two-tailed test. But if the direction of the effect is part of the research hypothesis, for example that women are paid less than men, it is appropriate to use a one-tailed test. (I was once told by a criminologist that using a one-tailed test was cheating as it doubled my chances of obtaining a significant result.)

The 5% level is an appropriate yardstick or starting point but should not be taken as immutable. The fact that it has become enshrined in folklore is perhaps a throwback to the days before computers. Then one had to calculate z, t or χ^2 by hand (or with the aid of an elementary calculator) and to estimate the corresponding p value entailed further time-consuming calculations. To make life easier, lookup tables were produced giving z, t and χ^2 values at key p values, usually 5%, 1% and .1%. (Such tables can still be found as appendices to most introductory texts.) By consulting these tables one could see whether the z, t or χ^2 obtained reached one of the three p threshold values. However, this way of proceeding is a thing of the past. It is trivial for a computer to calculate the exact p value associated with any z, t or χ^2 value and all the computer software used in this book reports exact p values.

Nowadays (if it wasn't before) it is more important to form a judgement about how much weight should be placed on the p value, and in reaching a judgement there are various points to consider. All statistical theory is based on the notion of a random sample but it has already been mentioned that we rarely have the luxury of a pure random sample as compromises may have been necessary when selecting a sample. Even if a random sample was drawn initially, non-participation, non-response or data missing for other reasons will affect the extent to which it can still be considered to be a random sample.

Significance tests will also be affected by the size of the sample. Results will assume greater significance (smaller p values) in large samples than in small samples. Intuitively this is what one would expect as one would place greater reliance on an estimate from a large sample than a small sample – other things being equal such as the quality or randomness of the data. (In statistical terms the sample size, N, is the denominator in calculating the standard error, so the larger the N the smaller the standard error and the larger the z or t, which in turn leads to a smaller p value.) The implication of this is that two studies might get the same value for a coefficient, b, but one might be significant and the other not, purely on the basis of the sample size. In practice, if I analyse data from the Labour Force Survey (LFS) I find most of my results are significant simply because the sample size is so large (individuals living in approximately 60,000 households). Consider the scenario where due to my modest means I am only able to carry out a small study of people's employment status. As a result I obtain the same value of b as that obtained from the LFS. However, my b is not significant at the 5% level, whereas the LFS analysis indicates significance. How should I interpret my result? I would conclude that I have obtained confirmatory evidence to that obtained in the LFS. (I appreciate that statisticians will tell me that my null hypothesis should have been that my b is no different from that obtained from the LFS and that I should have constructed my test accordingly – but I hope you take my point.)

Not only will sample size affect the p value but significance may also be influenced by the number of tests carried out. If 100 tests are carried out, 5 can be expected to be significant at the 5% level by chance regardless of any underlying relationship.

All the above qualifications have led some to denigrate the notion of significance but this seems to be equally as absurd, if not more so, than rigidly adhering to the 5% rule. The level of significance is one piece of useful information and guides the interpretation of statistical models. However, what it tells us has to be set in the context of the research question and the hypotheses generated, the size and quality of the data on which the tests are conducted and the findings from other research. Even if we obtain statistical significance, is the result of substantive significance in aiding our understanding? What is just as important is the size or magnitude of the effect we obtain. We might for example find the odds ratio between men and women is 1.1 on some outcome and this to be statistically significant. But is it telling us anything other than men and women are very similar?

3.5 Categorical explanatory variables; dummy variables; reference or base category

When discussing data in section 2.4, a distinction was drawn between continuous and categorical variables. Many variables in social research are categorical, including ethnicity, religion and occupation, to mention but a few. It is almost always the case that categorical variables will need to be incorporated within the model in Equation (1.1) alongside continuous variables such as age or income. A problem arises in that having no natural measurement scale or metric, it makes no sense to think of the effect of a unit increase in religion or ethnicity as it would for age (being a year older) or income (earning £1000 more). However, we can constructively think of the effects of being in a particular ethnic or religious group as opposed to being in another ethnic or religious group. Following this approach we can transform a categorical variable into a set of dummy variables which indicate whether or not a person has a particular characteristic. Dummy variables are also referred to as indicator variables, a term favoured by Stata.

Consider the variable *religion*, which for the purposes of this illustration we will consider to have four categories. They have been coded as follows:

Christian   1
Jew   2
Hindu   3
Muslim   4

The numbering is arbitrary, the four religions could have been put in a different order and different numbers could have been assigned to them.

This variable can be transformed into four dummy variables: *Christian, Jew, Hindu, Muslim*. A Christian would be coded 1 on the variable *Christian* and 0 on *Jew, Hindu* and *Muslim*. A Jew would be coded 0 on the variable *Christian*, 1 on *Jew* and 0 on *Hindu* and *Muslim*. Similarly a Hindu would be coded 1 on *Hindu* and 0 on the other three and a Muslim 1 on *Muslim* and 0 on the other three variables.

Having constructed these four variables, they can be entered as explanatory variables in the model. However, for the technical reason of multicollinearity (discussed in section 3.6) not all the four variables can be entered into the model together. One at least must be omitted. The dummy variable omitted is known as the reference category (which Stata calls the base category). Supposing we are interested in examining the effects of religion on some dependent variable y and there are no other independent variables of interest that need to be taken into account. Furthermore, if we choose *Christian* to be our omitted dummy variable, that is, our reference category, the model is:

$$y = b_0 + b_1(Jew) + b_2(Hindu) + b_3(Muslim)$$

The effect on y of being a Christian is b_0, because the value of all the other variables is 0 (and $b \times 0 = 0$).

The effect on y of being a Jew is $(b_0 + b_1)$, because *Jew* = 1 and the rest of the variables are 0.

Thus the effect of being a Jew *as opposed* to a Christian is b_1. Similarly the effect of being a Hindu as opposed to a Christian is b_2 and a Muslim b_3. Thus being a Jew, Hindu or Muslim can be considered by way of reference to being a Christian, that is, the additional affect, b_p, to being a Christian b_0. Note that it does not matters which of the four is chosen to be the reference category. Had we chosen say *Muslim* to be the reference category, b_0 would change, as it is now the affect of being a Muslim, and the three b_ps would change as they are now determined in relation to being a Muslim. But, the estimated differences between any of the religions would be exactly the same.

Handling categorical data in SPSS

Unfortunately SPSS is not consistent in its treatment of categorical variables (or even in the terms used to describe them). We shall see that the multiple regression module does not have a facility to enter categorical explanatory variables. No distinction is made between continuous and categorical variables; all are put together under the generic term independent variables. The researcher has to construct dummy variables for categorical variables prior to undertaking regression. In the logistic regression module (for binary response variables), independent variables have been relabelled covariates but there is an option to separately identify any of the covariates as categorical. With the multi-nomial logistic regression module (for multinomial response variables) and the ordinal logistic regression (for ordered response variables) continuous variables are entered in the box labelled Covariates and categorical variables are entered into the box labelled Factors. The advantage of the logistic, multinomial and ordinal modules, which permit categorical variables to be specifically identified, is that SPSS will convert the variables into dummy variables and automatically drop one which it calls the reference category. The default is to select the last (that is the level with the highest code – in the above example Muslim) as the reference category.

When needed, dummy variables are easily constructed in SPSS. Taking the example of the variable *religion* above choose:

> Transform → Compute

and in the box create a new variable name under Target Variable. For the dummy variable for whether or not a person is a Muslim, we could create the variable name *muslim*. Under the box Numeric Expression we would type *religion* = 4. A new variable muslim will then be added to the data file and everyone coded 4 on *religion* will be coded 1 on *muslim* and all others (Christians, Jews and Hindus) will be coded 0. This procedure would have to be repeated for the other three religious groups with the variable names and codes changed accordingly.

Handling categorical data in Stata

Stata is more consistent in its approach, the same procedure being followed for every type of model being fitted.

Stata offers two options. First, indicator variables (adopting Stata terminology) can be created as permanent variables and added to the database.

> Tab religion, generate (religion)

This command would produce a frequency (one-way table) of *religion*, showing the number in the sample belonging to each religious group, and at the same time, produce four indicator variables, one for each religion. The researcher then chooses which to enter into a model.

Indicator variables can also be produced 'on the fly', that is temporarily for the purpose of fitting the model. When specifying a model, the researcher informs Stata that some variables are to be treated as indicator variables and also which variables are to be treated in this way. For example, if the focus of the research was the way in which religious affiliation was related to income, a regression analysis could be specified as follows:

> xi: reg income i.religion

xi forewarns Stata that some variables are to be converted to indicator variables, and i.religion states that *religion* is to be treated in this way. Stata will automatically convert *religion* into four indicator variables and include the first three, making the fourth (Muslim) as the reference (or in Stata terminology, the base category).

It is always advisable to consider which level of a categorical variable will be chosen by the computer software to be the reference category. Often in a dataset the highest code is given to a numerically small and largely uninteresting group called 'other'. For example, in a study of voting behaviour we may have four levels: 1 Conservative, 2 Labour, 3 Liberal Democrat, 4 Other. The computer, unless indicated otherwise, would choose Other as the reference category and the three main parties would be compared with it. However, we are probably more interested in a comparison between Conservative and Labour. We shall find later that it is still possible to compare Conservative and Labour even if Other is the reference category, but nevertheless, it would still be more appropriate to choose either Conservative or Labour as the reference category so that the model fitted gives a direct comparison between the two.

3.6 Multicollinearity

Problems arise with the model if the explanatory variables are themselves highly inter-correlated. Recall that the coefficients of the model represent the partial effect of their corresponding variables after taking into account the other variables in the model. In the extreme case, where two variables are perfectly correlated ($r = +1$ or -1) it is impossible to attribute the partial effect of each variable.

The same problem arises if variables are perfectly related. For example, if the variable total income is formed from adding the variable income from employment to all other income, the three variables are related in that total income is the sum of the other two. Or income from employment is total income minus all other income, and so on. It is for this reason that not all dummy variables can be included in a model as taken together they are perfectly related. In the example of religion cited previously, if a person is not a Christian, Jew or Hindu then they must be a Muslim (assuming our population consists of only people with those four religious backgrounds).

Unless we are dealing with dummy variables or derived variables and their constituents, it is unlikely that we will confront the problem of perfect collinearity. But at what point do problems arise? Allison (1999) says he 'worries' if correlations reach a level of $\pm.8$. I would put the threshold lower, at .6.

What is the nature of the problem? If variables are highly collinear the coefficients are unaffected but their standard errors will be large. If the standard error increases t will be smaller (because $t = b/(\text{s.e. } b)$) and the smaller the value of t the greater the probability and the lesser chance of obtaining a statistical significant result. Hence the effect of multicollinearity is to reduce the chance of getting a significant result and some relationships which exist will be missed.

How can multicollinearity be detected? Inspection of the correlation matrix can identify high intercorrelations between continuous variables which help diagnose potential problems. Similarly cross-tabulations between categorical variables will establish associations.

However, there are two statistics, which can be calculated and will be produced by SPSS and Stata if requested.

Tolerance (which is $1 - R^2$):

One should be concerned if tolerance is below .40.

Variance inflation factor (VIF):

> One should be concerned if VIF is above 2.5. (A VIF of 2.5 is equivalent to a tolerance of .4.)

The interpretation of VIF is such that the square root of VIF tells you how much larger the standard error is compared with what it would be if the variable was uncorrelated with other variables.

What can be done about multicollinearity? As it is invariably the case that the collinear variables are alternative measures of the same concept (often a latent concept like deprivation or intelligence etc.) there are three main options:

1 delete all but one of the collinear variables from the model, leaving one to represent, or be a proxy for, the underlying concept;
2 combine the variables into an index by adding them up or multiplying them or by some other means;
3 estimate a latent variable by principal component analysis or factor analysis (described in Chapter 10).

3.7 Interaction terms

So far we have considered the partial effects of each explanatory variable, that is, each variable's effect on the dependent variable after controlling for other variables in the model. However, on occasion, it is the case that the effect of one explanatory variable may change according to the values of another explanatory variable.

Consider the following examples. In arriving at the sentence to be awarded, a court will give consideration to the offender's age and his or her previous criminal history (along with other characteristics of the offender and the offence). However, the combination of being young and having a very extensive criminal career may lead the court to impose a sentence greater than it would have done based on age and previous criminal history separately. If this is the case we would say that there is an interaction effect; the combination of age and previous criminal history affect sentence (the dependent variable) over and above age and previous criminal history on their own.

To give a further example, there has been much recent discussion concerning the problems faced by Afro-Caribbean boys in schools. Evidence suggests that they greatly underachieve compared with other groups of school pupils. This suggests a possible interaction effect: the combination of being both Afro-Caribbean and a boy affects educational attainment over and above what might be expected from being Afro-Caribbean and from being a boy.

If we hypothesise or suspect evidence of an interaction effect we will wish to incorporate the effect in our model. This is possible but first we need to create an interaction term by simply multiplying the two variables together.

In the first example, age is multiplied by the number of previous offences to produce a new variable, which might be called 'interaction of age and previous criminal history'.

In our model to explain sentencing outcomes we would specify the model:

y *(sentence)* $= b_0 + b_1$ *(age)* $+ b_2$ *(previous history)* $+ b_3$ *(interaction of age and previous criminal history)* $+$ *(any other variables)*

We can then fit the model as before and assess the output produced in the same way as we have done up to now.

In situations where an interaction term is included it is common to describe the variables age and previous criminal history as the *main effects* of age and previous criminal history and the interaction term as the *interaction effect* of age and previous criminal history. (This terminology stems historically from analysis of variance.)

In the same way that the bs change when new variables are included (because they represent the partial effects of the variables taking account of other variables) so in the model above b_1 and b_2 will change from the main effects model (the model without the interaction term) once the interaction term has been added.

Interaction terms can be found to be very important in increasing the explanatory power of the model. However, they complicate the interpretation of the model. What now is the impact of previous criminal history on sentences awarded? It has an effect b_2 but also (with age) an effect b_3.

The example above created an interaction variable from two continuous variables. But interactions can be created in just the same way from a continuous variable and a categorical variable. Suppose one of the explanatory variables affecting sentencing is the type of offence committed, which has three categories, 'violence offence', 'property offence' and 'motoring offence'. To incorporate these in the regression model we would need to create three dummy variables (and omit one – to be regarded as the reference category). Now suppose we wish to include an interaction effect between age and type of offence. We would simply multiple age by each of the dummy variables, giving us three interaction terms, any two of which we could include in our model.

Interaction effects can be created from two categorical variables. First, each has to be converted into dummy variables then the dummy variables are multiplied together.

It is not thought to be good practice to add an interaction term if the main effects are not themselves significant. With interactions we are looking for additional contributions from the variables over and above what they are contributing individually. On the other hand, the main effects should be retained in the model even if one or other is no longer significant once the interaction term is added. In fact, it is not uncommon to find that including an interaction term leads the main effects of one or other of the variables to no longer be significant. One need not be unduly concerned, but the main effects are needed (like the constant term) to estimate predicted values.

Creating interaction variables in SPSS and Stata

SPSS is inconsistent. With multiple regression the researcher has to create interaction terms prior to the analysis, which can be a little time consuming and tedious. However, with logistic, ordinal and multinomial logistic regression SPSS has the facility to automatically create interaction terms specified by the researcher.

In Stata, interaction variables need to be created prior to the analysis using the generate command.

3.8 Incorporating nonlinear relationships

It was pointed out when introducing the general linear model (section 1.3) that the model is only linear in the bs, that is in the coefficients of the model. It is the fact that the bs are added together (albeit after being multiplied by a variable x) that is the requirement for linearity. The xs themselves need not be linear, they can take any form, including a nonlinear form. The response variable y can also be transformed. Thus in practice the general linear model can be a very flexible tool for analysing a range of nonlinear as well as linear relationships. Here we outline some of the common methods adopted to incorporate nonlinear relationships.

A common transformation of the response variable y, favoured by economists when analysing monetary values such as income and prices, is $\log(y)$. The theoretical justification for this transformation is that a variable such as income does not increase by a fixed amount with, for example, age, but increases by a fixed or constant *percentage* with age. Substituting $\log(y)$ for y in the model better captures this percentage increase effect. We shall return to this in section 4.4.

Another common transformation when y is a categorical response variable is to transform the response to $\text{logit}(y)$, that is, the log of the odds. This transformation was discussed in section 3.1 and, as we shall see, underpins the logistic family of models (logistic, multinomial logistic, and ordinal logistic regression).

Continuous explanatory variables, x, can take any form such as $\sqrt{x}$, x^2, x^3, $\log x$ and so on. Of the options, x^2 has certain attractions. As Allison (1999) points out, it can reflect a wide range of nonlinear relations and can be used where the explanatory variable is measured on an interval scale as well as for those measured on a ratio scale. Most other transformations are only appropriate where the variable is measured on a ratio scale. Allison's practical advice is to include x^2 (together with x) in the model. If the coefficient of x^2 is significant this provides evidence of a nonlinear relationship which might require further exploration.

An alternative and useful approach to transforming a continuous explanatory variable when the relationship is not linear is to convert the continuous variable into a categorical variable and enter it in the model as a set of dummy variables. For example, if income is different at different ages during a working life, then age could be categorised into separate age groups, young to old. Entering these groupings as dummy variables will result in a different coefficient, b, for each group, reflecting the different effects at different ages.

Finally, it should be noted that interaction terms (discussed in section 3.7) are also nonlinear explanatory variables and are yet another means of incorporating nonlinear relationships within the framework of the general linear model.

3.9 Residuals

Residuals were introduced in section 1.4 where they were defined as the difference between the actual value of y and the value of y, $\hat{y}$, estimated or predicted by the model. Examination of residuals is important as it provides information on the adequacy of the model: how well the model fits the data and whether the assumptions of the model, including linearity, are met. Exceptional residuals also indicate whether, and if so which, data points are outliers, which may be exerting an undue influence on the model. But what is considered to be exceptional? The size of a residual will depend in part on the units of measurement such that if the response variable is income we might get a residual of £1000. On the other hand if our response variable is binary, taking a value of 0 or 1, the predicted value of y is a probability between 0 and 1 and hence a residual can be no greater than 1. Rather than consider absolute residuals, it is the convention to analyse standardised residuals, that is, the residual divided by its standard error. Evoking statistical theory, the standardised (or studentised) residuals will have a normal or t distribution with mean 0 and variance 1 and we can interpret them in the same way as z and t statistics, discussed in section 3.3. Thus we would expect 95% of the residuals to lie within ±1.96, 1% within ±2.58 and so on.

A more important consideration than whether a subject is an outlier, is whether it exerts an undue influence on the model, in particular on the estimates of the coefficients or parameters, b. Various statistics have been proposed to measure influential observations and they are discussed and applied in sections 4.8 and 5.6.

When the response variable is categorical, a different approach is required. In such situations we can conceive the model as a multiway contingency table and for each combination of explanatory variables compare the actual number falling within that combination with the number predicted or expected by the model within that combination. This is analogous to the calculation of chi-squared in section 3.3. If we divide the difference between the observed and expected number by its standard error we obtain what is known as the Pearson residual or the chi-squared residual. The Pearson residual is approximately normally distributed and can be interpreted in the same way as standardised residuals.

An alternative when the response variable is binary is to divide the sample into groups according to their predicted probabilities and compare the number predicted with the actual number. This is the basis of the Hosmer–Lemeshow test which is described in section 5.6.

Having calculated the standardised or Pearson residuals, they should be inspected to see if any exceed a value of ±2.0 or ±2.5. Obviously under the normal distribution we can expect 5% to be greater than 2 (or less than −2) but we should become concerned if a higher percentage exceed the percentage expected or if we encounter standardised residuals greater than 3.

What would one do if the results of the residual analysis indicted problems? Possible errors in the data would be my first thought and I would examine each of the offending cases. Examination may suggest other reasons why some are different, but the exact reason will be specific to the subject matter and context of the research. Having corrected any errors, if outliers remained I would next request and examine leverage statistics in order to see what influence the subjects were having on the model, in the hope that while some may be outliers, not all were having an undue influence on the model. In addition, I would fit the model with and without the outliers and influential observations and compare the models obtained. With large datasets and a small number of outliers I invariably find the models to be similar.

If a large proportion of the sample have standardised residuals greater than 2.0 then a different approach is required. My initial thought should this situation occur is that the dataset comprises samples from more than one underlying population. I would thus explore the different characteristics between the two groups (those with standardised residuals less than 2.0 and than those with standardised residuals greater than 2.0) in the hope of identifying the nature of the underlying problem. The investigation may lead me to analyse the groups separately or to include other variables which reflect the differences between the groups.

SPSS and Stata will, if requested, calculate predicted values, residuals and standardised residuals and add these as variables to the original data file. It is then possible to plot these new variables in any way the researcher wishes in order to gain further insights into the adequacy of the model and to assess whether the assumptions are being met. One option is to produce a histogram or stem-and-leaf plot to see if the residuals are normally distributed, as they should be. Other options include a normal probability plot which plots the cumulative distribution of the standardised residuals against the expected normal distribution. The points should lie along a straight line and any deviation reveals how the standardised residuals differ from normality. A further useful diagnostic is to plot the standardised residuals against the standardised predicted values; there should be no evident pattern – the standardised residuals should fluctuate around zero for all values of the standardised predicted values.

Examples of residual analysis, including examples of graphical presentations discussed above, will be given in subsequent chapters of this book when models are developed and fitted.

3.10 Unobserved variables and unobserved heterogeneity

It was stated in section 1.4 that an initial stage in developing a model is to specify which explanatory variables to include and the selection of variables will be guided by theory or previous research. As we shall see, however, statistical models never fit the data perfectly; there always remains some unexplained variation. This may arise through random variation as variables are never measured with total accuracy. Models can be improved by including additional explanatory variables (perhaps not initially considered) and/or by increasing the contribution of those already included; by transforming them or by considering interaction terms (discussed in sections 3.8 and 3.7 respectively). However, it may not be possible to include some important variables because they are not themselves measured. This is known as the problem of unobserved variables or unobserved heterogeneity. The following example illustrates the problem.

In section 9.5 data is analysed to examine the factors associated with being employed or not employed and in Chapter 13 we present data from an evaluation of an initiative aimed at helping people who have been unemployed for a long period of time return to employment. In both examples, important variables that lead people to being in work or returning to work include age, educational qualifications, previous employment and so on. However, there is still some heterogeneity even amongst people who share the same explanatory characteristics. People of the same age and the same educational qualifications are not all employed or unemployed. Some heterogeneity may be due to other observed characteristics, such as a person's health, information on which, having been recorded, can be included in the model. But some of the heterogeneity may be due to unobserved characteristics, such as a person's motivation to seek work or their confidence in seeking employment. Having been unemployed for a long time, a person may be de-motivated, thinking there is little prospect of employment, or may lack the confidence to apply for work or to present themselves to best effect at interview. In behavioural terms, long-term unemployment may lead to 'inertia' or in statistical terms the phenomenon may be described as 'state dependency'; being in the state unemployed may lead to a greater prospect of remaining unemployed regardless of other characteristics.

Unobserved variables, or unobserved heterogeneity, can lead to erroneous inferences, if the unobserved variables are related to both other included explanatory variables and the response variable. Technically, one or more of the included explanatory variables x are correlated with the error term, e, violating one of the assumptions of the model. In such cases, the included explanatory variables may appear more or less important than they are because they are reflecting, in part, the contribution of the unobserved (and omitted) variables. Whether they appear more or less important depends on the nature of the relationship between the three sets of variables (the response variable, the explanatory variables and the unobserved variables).

Unfortunately it is not always possible to overcome the problems caused by unobserved heterogeneity, but the researcher should always have the problem in mind when specifying or interpreting a model. At the data collection stage it may be possible to anticipate the problem and perhaps collect proxy variables which could substitute for the unobservable variables.

Another approach, often favoured by economists, is to identify and include an instrumental variable. Essentially, if we can find a variable which can be measured and which is both correlated with the error term but uncorrelated with the explanatory variables, x, we could include this in the model. The instrumental variable then acts to remove the bias in the estimation of the effects of the xs. However, it is not always straightforward to identify a variable that can serve as an instrumental variable. We adopt this approach in section 11.3 but any reader interested in pursuing the theory and application of the method of instrumental variables should consult a standard econometric text, such as Wooldridge (2003).

It is also common practice for economists to include a lagged dependent variable as an explanatory variable. So, if the dependent variable is y_t (that is, y measured at some point in time), y_{t-1} or y_{t-2} etc. (y measured at an earlier point in time) would be included as an explanatory variable. On the assumption that many conditions remain relatively stable over time, the lagged variable will encapsulate past history, including conditions that cannot be measured.

Longitudinal research designs are considered superior as they are better able to take account of the sequence of events, previous states and duration (the time a person has been in a state). We shall also see in Chapter 12 that certain models which can be fitted to panel data can remove the effects of some unobserved variables, namely those unobserved variables that do not change over time.

However, longitudinal data, including panel data, may not always be available, and it may not be possible to include a proxy variable or to identify an instrumental variable. In order to ameliorate the problem caused by unobserved variables, it is often good practice to include explanatory variables which take into account previous experience or duration in states, such as the length of time previously unemployed. Or, to provide another example, when modelling offending it is important to include the number of previous offences an offender has committed, as previous offending is highly related to future offending and represents the extent to which a person is confirmed in their criminal career.

The reader may be interested to note the availability of SABRE (specialist statistical software) which was developed at the University of Lancaster as part of an Economic and Social Research Council (ESRC) methods programme. SABRE incorporates techniques for handling unobserved heterogeneity and is freely available, together with instructions on how to use it, at the Teaching Resources and Materials for Social Scientists (TRAMSS) website, http://tramss.data-archive.ac.uk.

4   Multiple regression for continuous response variables

4.1 Introduction

Multiple regression is the oldest and most well established of the modelling techniques and is appropriate when the dependent variable is continuous. Explanatory (independent) variables can be continuous and/or categorical. Multiple regression is closely related to analysis of variance (ANOVA) and analysis of covariance (ANCOVA). In fact ANOVA and ANCOVA are alternative but complementary ways of presenting the same information and, carried out on the same data, will give exactly the same inferences as multiple regression. ANOVA is appropriate when all the independent variables are categorical and ANCOVA is appropriate when the independent variables are both categorical and continuous. As they are alternative ways of presenting the same results, most statistical computer packages, including SPSS and Stata, present analysis of variance results as part of the output from multiple regression. As multiple regression more readily conforms to the formulation of the general linear model (see Equation (1.1)) I feel that for most applications multiple regression is preferable. However, one or two statistics presented as part of the ANOVA results are helpful in interpreting the regression model.

4.2 Example: Determinants of pay

In order to explain multiple regression, let us begin by considering an example where the focus of interest is the amount of pay received by persons in employment. In particular we shall investigate what factors contribute to the amount received and, specifically, whether women are paid less than men. To investigate this issue, a small subset of data was drawn from the 2002 Labour Force Survey (LFS; a large survey conducted quarterly in Great Britain and the main source of information on employment and unemployment). The advantage of a small dataset is that all the observations can be shown graphically. To be precise, the first 150 individuals were selected from the LFS Teaching Dataset at the UK Data Archive but those individuals who were not in work or for whom data was missing on any of the variables were excluded. This resulted in 77 persons (38 males and 39 females) available for analysis. In addition to hourly pay (measured in pounds sterling) and gender, four other variables were chosen; age, age the person completed continuous education, the number of years the person had been in his or her current job and his or her occupation.

In the first instance it may be hypothesised that the rate of hourly pay is related to the employee's age and our objective is to explore the form and strength of that relationship. A starting point is to produce a scatterplot of the two variables and this is easily done in SPSS and Stata. As pay is the focus of interest it is the dependent variable, *y*, which is represented on the *y* (vertical) axis of the scatterplot. Age is the explanatory variable and is represented on the *x* (horizontal) axis. The plot from SPSS is shown in Figure 4.1 (click Graphs → Scatter/Dot and specify the variables).

A visual inspection of the scatterplot suggests evidence of a positive relationship between the two variables: older employees seem to receive a higher hourly rate of pay. However, this relationship does not appear to be strong as there is considerable variation in the pay people receive at all ages. Further evidence of a weak relationship comes from the correlation coefficient between the two, which is found to be $r = .26$. However, it is statistically significant at the 5% level.

Regression enables us to express the form of the relationship between age and hourly pay. In graphical terms a linear relationship is equivalent to a straight line representation of the data. Intuitively, the best straight line to represent the relationship between the two variables is one that in some sense comes closest to all the individual data points. Ordinary Least Squares (OLS) is a fitting procedure for deriving the equation that defines such a line.

The scatterplot shown in Figure 4.2 is the same as Figure 4.1 but with the fitted regression line included. The ordinary least squares regression line is the one that minimises the sum of the squared differences between the line and each of the observed data points. The differences between some of the points and the regression line are shown as vertical lines in the plot. Why squared differences? Because if the differences were not squared, some differences would be positive (the distance from the line to those points above it) and some would be negative (the distance from the line to those points below it). The positive differences and the negative differences would cancel each other out resulting in a sum of zero – not a very useful measure of the distance of the points from the line. However, the squared differences are all positive and so when summed, result in a positive measure. The OLS line minimises the squared differences in that any other line drawn between the observed points would result in a larger sum

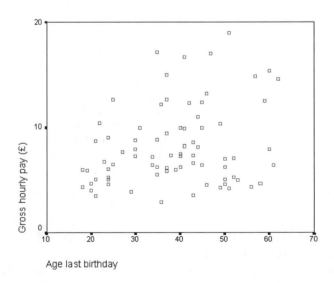

Figure 4.1 SPSS output, scatterplot of gross hourly pay and age last birthday.

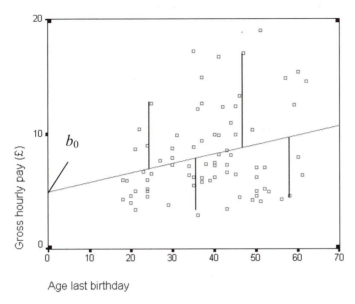

Figure 4.2 SPSS output, scatterplot with the fitted regression line.

when the squared differences are added together. Thus the OLS regression meets the objective of coming closest to all the observed points and summarises, or provides an average of, the relationship between age and the hourly rate of pay. In this context, the correlation coefficient measures the spread of the data points around the straight line.

In mathematical notation, the straight line depicted in Figure 4.2 is of the form:

$$y + b_0 + b_1 x_1 \tag{4.1}$$

which is the general linear model introduced in section 1.3. b_0 is a constant and its value is the value of y where the regression line meets the y axis. It is thus the value of y when $x = 0$. It is also known as the intercept as it is the point where the line intercepts the y axis.

4.3 Fitting a multiple regression model in SPSS

Running the linear regression module in SPSS (click Analyze → Regression → Linear) brings up the screen below at Figure 4.3.

Hourpay (gross hourly pay) has been specified as the dependent variable and age (age last birthday) as the independent variable. SPSS produced the output shown in Figure 4.4. (That element of the output that simply lists the variables considered has been omitted.)

In terms of our regression equation (Equation (4.1)), the coefficients are listed in the last box labelled Coefficients in the column headed Unstandardized coefficients B. (The standardized coefficients are explained later.) b_0 is designated (Constant), the b_ps are given in the column adjacent to their variables.

The regression equation can be written as:

$$y = 4.964 + .082 \ (age\ last\ birthday)$$

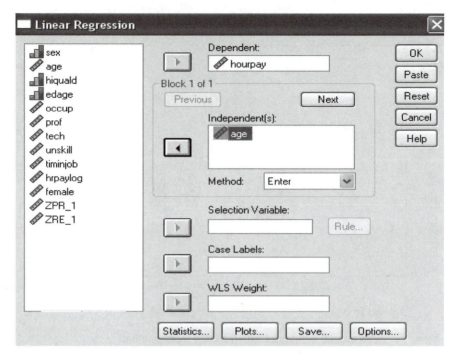

Figure 4.3 SPSS dialogue box for multiple regression.

Model Summary

Model	R	R Square	Adjusted R Square	Std. Error of the Estimate
1	.263[a]	.069	.057	3.63293

a. Predictors: (Constant), Age last birthday

ANOVA[b]

Model		Sum of Squares	df	Mean Square	F	Sig.
1	Regression	73.690	1	73.690	5.583	.021[a]
	Residual	989.862	75	13.198		
	Total	1063.552	76			

a. Predictors: (Constant), Age last birthday

b. Dependent Variable: Gross hourly pay (£)

Coefficients[a]

Model		Unstandardized Coefficients		Standardized Coefficients	t	Sig.
		B	Std. Error	Beta		
1	(Constant)	4.964	1.408		3.525	.001
	Age last birthday	.082	.035	.263	2.363	.021

a. Dependent Variable: Gross hourly pay (£)

Figure 4.4 SPSS output, regression model.

Thus for every additional year in age, after taking into account other variables in the model (in this case there aren't any – but that will change), the hourly rate of pay increases by £0.082 (or 8.2 pence).

Given a person's age, their hourly rate of pay can be predicted. Thus for a person who was 50 last birthday, their predicted hourly rate of pay is:

$$y = 4.964 + .082(50)$$

$$= 4.964 + 4.1$$

$$= £9.64$$

Variables in a regression analysis are usually measured in different units, age in years, price in pounds sterling, distance in miles and so on, and the bs represent the change in y given a unit change in the variable. Because of the different units it is difficult to compare bs, and hence the relative importance of the different variables. Standardized coefficients, Beta, go some way to overcoming this problem as they reformulate the coefficients in terms of standard deviations in order to put them on a comparable scale. A standardized coefficient is thus the number of standard deviations y changes as a result of one standard deviation change in x, controlling for the other variables in the model. Formulating coefficients in terms of standardized coefficients removes the requirement for a constant and it can be seen that there is no value in the (Constant) row in the Beta column.

Standardized coefficients are occasionally cited in research reports and scientific papers and it is the convention to present them in path analysis diagrams (see section 11.2) so it is important to be aware of them. They can also be useful in providing a rank order of the relative importance of the independent variables in a model. However, conceptually it is difficult to think in terms of standard deviations of age, a change of one year is more meaningful. Furthermore, standardised coefficients are inappropriate for a binary variable – how should a standardised coefficient of gender be interpreted? In any case a rank order of the importance of variables in a model is often provided by comparing t values.

4.4 How good is the regression model?

Having fitted the model and estimated the parameters (the coefficients), how good a model is it and what inferences can we draw?

Recall from section 1.4 that there are three ways that we can assess a model. The first is to consider the model in its entirety and against other models. One such other model is to have no model at all, that is, to assess how our understanding is improved by having the model compared with our understanding in the absence of any model. Consider the absence of a model and the only information available for the 77 individuals in the sample is their hourly rate of pay. If required to predict a person's pay, the best guess would be the average or mean pay for the sample, that is, $\bar{y}$ (pronounced 'y bar') which is calculated to be £8.14. The prediction would be wrong in each case depending on how that person's pay differed from the mean for the group – and we saw from the scatterplot (Figure 4.1) that there is significant variation in pay. In the same way that we can calculate the squared differences from the regression line, we can calculate the squared differences from the mean of *y*. Graphically the mean would be a horizontal line as indicated in Figure 4.5, and the differences would be the vertical distances from each point to the line.

Squaring these differences and adding them together we call the total sum of squares (TSS) total to signify all the variation that exists, in this case in hourly pay, around the mean.

Fitting a regression line improves our understanding. Now if asked to predict a person's pay we can take into account their age by inserting it into our regression model and arrive at a more accurate estimate. Although we have improved our prediction we will still incur some error. There is variation between our regression estimates and the observed values (as pointed out in Figure 4.2). The sum of squared differences between the observed points and the regression line, the vertical lines depicted in Figure 4.2, is known as the unexplained sum of squares or the residual sum of squares and represents what variation is left over once the regression has been fitted. The difference between the total sum of squares and the residual sum of squares can be regarded as the amount of the variation that has been explained by the regression model. This component is known as the explained sum of squares or the regression sum of squares (SPSS) or the model sum of squares (Stata). Furthermore:

$$\frac{\text{Regression / model sum of squares}}{\text{Total sum of squares}} = \frac{\text{the proportion of the variance}}{\text{explained by the regression model}}$$

The values of the various sums of squares are contained in the analysis of variance component (ANOVA) of the regression output. In the output at Figure 4.4, the total sum

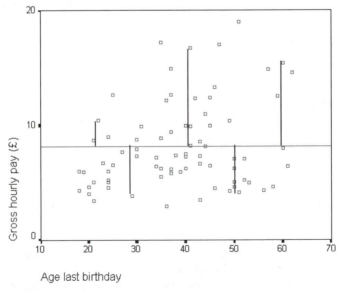

Figure 4.5 SPSS output, scatterplot with line depicting mean of *y*.

of squares is 1063.552 and the regression model explains 73.690 sums of squares. Expressed as a proportion, the fitted regression model explains:

$$\frac{73.690}{1063.552} = .069 \text{ or } 6.9\% \text{ of the variance}$$

Note that the proportion explained, .069, is exactly the same as the value of R Square given in the Model Summary component of the SPSS output at Figure 4.4. R^2 is defined to be the proportion of variance explained by the model and it is also known as the coefficient of determination. R (the square root of R^2), often known as Multiple R (to emphasise that it is a statistic from multiple regression), is .263, which is exactly the value of the correlation coefficient, r, between hourly pay and age. Where there is only one explanatory variable in the regression model R is equivalent to r. However, when there is more than one explanatory variable in the model this equivalent relationship does not hold.

SPSS (and Stata) calculate and present an Adjusted R Square value. The adjusted R^2 attempts to correct for the fact that R^2 can be affected by the number of variables included in the model. It can be helpful when assessing the worth of similar but competing models, but I have always found R^2 to be an informative and satisfactory measure.

Tests of significance

Does the fitted regression model truly add to our understanding? In this example, are we in a better position to explain hourly rates of pay knowing the age of employees, or could the relationship simply be a chance occurrence? In order to answer this question a test of the null hypothesis is needed. The *F*-test is a global test, which tests the significance of the model in its entirety. The details of the *F*-test need not concern us but it stems from the analysis of variance formulation of the model and the relevant values can be found in the ANOVA component of the computer output at Figure 4.4. In the last column, headed Sig, a value of .021 appears. This figure is the probability of obtaining that regression model by chance, that is, if age last birthday had no effect on, or had no relation with, y, hourly pay. In this model, .021 is less than .05 so the regression can be said to be significant at the 5% level, the threshold commonly adopted as indicative of identifying evidence of a true relationship.

In addition to testing the model in its entirety, we also wish to test each explanatory variable individually to see if it contributes to the model by having an independent effect on the dependent variable (over and above the other variables included in the model). The *t*-test provides a procedure for testing each variable. To be precise the t statistic tests whether the coefficient b is significantly different from zero. Following the conventions of statistical tests discussed in section 3.3: $b/(\text{s.e.}b) = t$.

The relationship between t and z scores was also reviewed in section 3.3. A value of t of 2.0 (or 1.96 to be more precise) is significant at the 5% level. In the example above SPSS provides the values of b (B), the standard error of b (Std. Error), t (t) and the probability of obtaining that t value (Sig.). For the regression fitted, which included age, b is .082 and the standard error .035 and $t = (.082/.035) = 2.363$ which has a probability of occurrence of .021 (i.e. less than 5%).

Note that the significance of t in this example is exactly the same as the significance of F (both .021). In the situation where only one variable is included in the model, F and t are essentially testing the same effect. The t statistic is testing the contribution of age whereas F is testing the entire model. However, as the entire model only includes age, F and t should give the same inference, which, reassuringly, they do.

4.5 Expanding the model

The analysis so far indicates that age is significantly related to hourly pay but explains very little of the variance in hourly pay, merely 6.9%. Much remains to be explained and the next step seeks to identify other models that might explain some of the residual variance. Models can be expanded by including new variables which we turn to later but first we develop the model with age as the only explanatory variable. The model above assumes a linear relationship between age and income such that for every additional year the hourly rate increases by a constant 8.2 pence regardless of the age of the employee. Thus a 19-year-old can expect 8.2 pence more per hour than an 18-year-old; similarly a 36-year-old can expect 8.2 pence more than a 35-year-old, a 56-year-old more than a 55-year-old and so on. However, those who study wage rates would hypothesise that wages do not increase by a fixed absolute amount but are more likely to increase by a constant percentage. A model that (approximately) captures this effect is to transform the dependent variable y (hourly pay) to $\log(y)$ and most economists analysing pay/income/salary/wages data would adopt $\log(y)$ as the response variable (see section 3.8). The coefficient for age with $\log(y)$ as the response variable was .009, suggesting that for each additional year of age, income increases by approximately 0.9%. However, the model with log(hourly rate) as response did not fit as well as the model presented above with hourly rate as response. The R^2 for the log(hourly rate) model was 5.8%, less than the 6.9% obtained previously.

So far the assumption has been that pay increases with age, either by a fixed amount or by a fixed percentage. But the relationship between income and age may not be linear. It is often found that income increases with age at younger ages, is then relatively constant thereafter and subsequently declines in older life. If faced with this or any other nonlinear pattern, economists capture it by including both age and age^2 as explanatory variables. Furthermore, as pointed out in section 3.8, Allison's (1999) advice is to test the significance of x^2 as evidence of a nonlinear relationship. Inspection of the scatterplot did not suggest a markedly nonlinear relationship so it was not altogether surprising that including both age and age^2 in the model did not increase R^2 dramatically; only by 1% to nearly 8% (and it did not matter whether the response variable was hourly pay or log(hourly pay)).

Neither adopting $\log(y)$ as the response variable nor including age^2 had much effect in this example, perhaps because of the small sample and the fact that the response variable was hourly pay rather than annual pay. Nevertheless, over and above their substantive importance in many applications, $\log(y)$ and age^2 are also examples of how non-linear relationships can be incorporated within the framework of the linear model. Recall from sections 1.3 and 3.8 that linearity stems from the addition of the effects of the variables not from the linearity of the variables themselves.

In one sense the approach to modelling as presented so far, in which one variable, age, was selected, is somewhat artificial. It was adopted principally to explain least squares estimation procedures and hence how certain statistics are derived and interpreted. In reality one would hypothesise at the outset several explanatory variables that might all be related to the dependent variable. In the dataset drawn from the LFS two other continuous variables, the age at which a person completed continuous full-time education and the number of years an employee had been in the current job, might also be thought to affect the rate of hourly pay. The longer a person stayed in continuous education, the more highly qualified they are likely to be and hence the more likely they are to be engaged in a higher paid job. Similarly, the longer in a job the more likely a person is to be promoted, receive annual increments on a pay scale and so on.

With several variables it is not possible to produce scatterplots in multidimensional space. (Although one should separately produce, in turn, a scatterplot for each of the explanatory variables under consideration with the dependent variable. But they are not shown here.) Other empirical evidence would be sought from considering the correlation between these variables and the dependent variable. The correlation matrix at Figure 4.6, produced by SPSS (click Analyze → Correlate → Bivariate), does indicate a positive and significant relationship between hourly pay and age, age completed education and length of time in the current job. All the relationships are positive, which is in the hypothesised direction: namely the older the employee, the longer time spent in education and the greater the time in the present job, the higher the hourly pay.

In addition to the two further continuous variables, two categorical variables are available: occupation and sex. Occupation has been recoded into three categories: professional or managerial (*prof*); technical/administrative/skilled (*tech*), and unskilled or manual (*unskill*). Sex has two categories: male and female. Both categorical variables need to be converted into sets of dummy variables as described in section 3.5. *Prof* and *unskill* were included in the model together with *female*. (Recall from section 3.5 that one dummy variable at least has to be omitted from the model and the omitted dummy variable is the reference category.)

Given that several explanatory variables are now to be included in the model, and in view of the significant correlations between them (as indicated in Figure 4.6), collinearity diagnostics were requested (by checking the Collinearity diagnostics box in Statistics). The results of the regression analysis are shown in Figure 4.7.

This model performs much better than the previous model in that the R^2 for the model was found to be .506 or the model explained 51% of the variance in hourly pay (compared with only 6.9% in the previous model, which only included age as an explanatory variable).

Note several matters when comparing this model with the previous one. First the coefficient of age has changed (from .082 in the previous model to .036 in this model). The reason for the change is because the coefficients, *b*, are the amount of change in *y* following a unit change in *x* (in this case age) *after taking into account the other variables in the model*. There are different variables in this model so the partial effect of age will be different. The same is true of the constant term, which also changes from model to model depending on what variables are included. In this example the constant has even changed to a negative value in this model, from a positive value in the previous model. The value of the constant term is the value of *y* when all the variables are equal to 0. The constant is often meaningless; in this case no individual is observed to be naught years of age, left continuous education at naught and has spent naught years in their current job. The constant only has meaning when taken together with the other coefficients.

The *F*-test (not shown) indicates that the model as a whole is significant ($p < .001$),

Correlations

		Gross hourly pay (£)	Age last birthday	Age completed continuous full-time education	Number of years in current job
Gross hourly pay (£)	Pearson Correlation	1	.263*	.295**	.473**
	Sig. (2-tailed)		.021	.009	.000
	N	77	77	77	77
Age last birthday	Pearson Correlation	.263*	1	-.241*	.556**
	Sig. (2-tailed)	.021		.034	.000
	N	77	77	77	77
Age completed continuous full-time education	Pearson Correlation	.295**	-.241*	1	-.190
	Sig. (2-tailed)	.009	.034		.099
	N	77	77	77	77
Number of years in current job	Pearson Correlation	.473**	.556**	-.190	1
	Sig. (2-tailed)	.000	.000	.099	
	N	77	77	77	77

*. Correlation is significant at the 0.05 level (2-tailed).

**. Correlation is significant at the 0.01 level (2-tailed).

Figure 4.6 SPSS output, correlation matrix.

Coefficients[a]

Model		Unstandardized Coefficients		Standardized Coefficients	t	Sig.	Collinearity Statistics	
		B	Std. Error	Beta			Tolerance	VIF
1	(Constant)	-2.395	2.918		-.821	.415		
	Age last birthday	.036	.033	.115	1.091	.279	.631	1.585
	Age completed continuous full-time education	.486	.138	.320	3.512	.001	.851	1.175
	Number of years in current job	.190	.044	.442	4.312	.000	.671	1.491
	prof	1.126	.805	.140	1.398	.167	.701	1.427
	unskill	-1.827	.779	-.235	-2.346	.022	.706	1.416
	female	-1.130	.641	-.152	-1.763	.082	.949	1.054

a. Dependent Variable: Gross hourly pay (£)

Figure 4.7 SPSS output, multiple regression model.

but what is the contribution of each of the variables included? It can be seen that the two new continuous variables are both highly significant. The age the employee left full-time education has a t value of 3.512 and a corresponding p value < .001 (i.e. less than .1%). Similarly, the number of years in the current job is also highly significant ($t = 4.312$, p value < .001).

Interestingly, however, in this model age is not found to be making a significant contribution. The value of t is only 1.091 with a p value of 0.279. It is not unusual when fitting models to find that a variable significant in one model is not found to be significant in other models. There are two reasons for this. One may simply reflect the problem of multicollinearity, which was discussed in section 3.6. However, from the output above, multicollinearity does not appear to be of extreme concern here, for none of the explanatory variables are the values of tolerance below .4 nor are any values of VIF above 2.5 (the threshold values given in section 3.6). The second reason stems from the fact that the model is only including the partial effect of age, having taken into account the other variables in the model. The new variables are more important in determining hourly pay and once their effects have been taken into account, age adds little in explaining pay. Looking back at the correlation matrix it can be seen that age and the number of years in a job (while not leading to problems of multicollinearity) are highly correlated, $r = .556$. Not surprisingly, older people tend to have been in their current job longer than younger people. Hence knowing how long a person has been in their current job also tells us something about their age. The coefficient for time in current job thus contains indicative information on age, thereby limiting any additional information that might come from also knowing an employee's age.

Consider now the effects of occupation as represented in the model by the two dummy variables: *prof* (professional or managerial) and *unskill* (unskilled or manual). Whether a person's occupation is professional or managerial does not appear significant in determining hourly pay (once other characteristics of the person are taken into account) but an occupation that is unskilled or manual is highly significant. However, care needs to be exercised when interpreting dummy variables. Recall that *tech* (technical/administrative/skilled) has been omitted from this model and is thus the reference category. The model is not saying that being a professional (or a manager) does not significantly influence one's hourly pay, only that being a professional compared with being a technician/administrator/skilled worker does not significantly affect pay. But being unskilled or manual compared with being a technician/administrator/skilled worker does significantly reduce one's pay (by £1.827 per hour). Including *tech* and *unskill* in the model (instead of *prof* and *unskill*) would lead to the same inference, in that *unskill* would be significant (and the coefficient negative) compared to *prof* – which is now the reference category – but *tech* would not be significant, compared with *prof*. Finally, if *prof* and *tech* are included – with *unskill* becoming the reference category – both are found to have a positive effect (compared to *unskill*) on pay and both are statistically significant.

Consider the final explanatory variable in the model, *female*. The coefficient for *female* is −1.130, suggesting that after controlling for other variables, women are paid on average £1.13 per hour less than men. Is the result significant and is there thus evidence that women indeed get paid less than men? How do we interpret this result? The p value is given as .082 or 8.2%, above the conventional 5% level. However, recall the discussion of significance tests in section 3.4. If the hypothesis had been (as it might well have been, given previous research and debate) that women are paid less than men, the significance test would be directional and hence one-tailed. On this basis a p value of .082 is statistically significant leading to the conclusion that women are indeed paid less than men even after controlling for other factors that influence pay. (The purpose here is not to resolve the issue of differential pay between men and women, merely to highlight issues in statistical modelling and significance testing. If resolving this issue was the objective of the research, all the LFS data would have been analysed and other variables would have been considered when developing the model – something we pursue further in section 11.2.)

In the model, the dummy variable *female* was included making *male* the reference category (coded 0). Had *male* been included rather than *female* the *p* value (.082) would have been exactly the same and the coefficient would have the same numerical value (1.13) but would be positive not negative, indicating that men are paid £1.13 per hour more than women.

4.6 Adding interaction terms

Interaction terms were introduced and described in section 3.7 and here we consider introducing an interaction term to the model. A common way of modelling interaction is to derive an interaction term by simply multiplying together two variables. In this example there are three continuous explanatory variables; age, age completed education and number of years in the current job. Interaction terms could be formed by multiplying any two (or all three) together if prior knowledge or theory dictated that an interaction term should be included in the model along with the original variables. Allison (1999) found from his data a significant interaction between age and number of years spent in education, such that the differential in income between those who had been in school longer (and were thus better qualified) and those people who had left education earlier (and were thus less well qualified) increased with age. This finding reflects the fact that salaries of better educated, professional people tend to rise and continue rising more sharply than salaries of less well educated and unskilled people which tend to be relatively flat. In this dataset there was no evidence of a significant interaction effect between age and length of time in education but there was some evidence of this underlying relationship in an interaction between age and the dummy variable *unskill* (whether the person was unskilled or not).

In order to illustrate the nature of the interaction effect we first remove all other explanatory variables from the model and include only the main effects of *age* and *unskill*. The model is given below (see Figure 4.8).

It can be seen from the above model that both *age* and *unskill* are highly significant. Recall that if the person is unskilled they are coded 1 on *unskill* and if they are not unskilled (for convenience we call them skilled) they are coded 0. Thus if we consider the hypothetical situation where a person's age is 0, a skilled person's hourly income will be $(5.8 + (-3.3 * 0)) = £5.8$ and the unskilled person's hourly income will be $(5.8 + (-3.3 * 1)) = £2.5$. For each additional year of age, hourly income is expected to rise by £0.9 and this rise is the same whether a person is skilled or unskilled. This relationship can be represented graphically as shown in Figure 4.9.

From Figure 4.9 it can be seen that the difference between the skilled and unskilled is

Coefficients[a]

Model		Unstandardized Coefficients		Standardized Coefficients		
		B	Std. Error	Beta	t	Sig.
1	(Constant)	5.805	1.291		4.497	.000
	Age last birthday	.090	.032	.289	2.859	.006
	unskill	-3.288	.787	-.422	-4.177	.000

a. Dependent Variable: Gross hourly pay (£)

Figure 4.8 SPSS output, regression model with *age* and *unskill*.

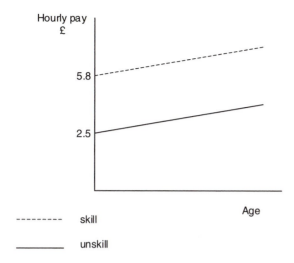

Figure 4.9 Graphical representation of the main effects model.

the constant or intercept. The effect of age is the same, hence the parallel lines. The slope of both lines is the same (.09), the coefficient of age. (The slope of the lines has been exaggerated here to emphasise the increase in hourly rate with age – if drawn to scale both lines would appear almost horizontal.)

The interaction term *unskage* was constructed by multiplying the dummy variable *unskill* with *age* and added to the above model. The model with the interaction term is given below in Figure 4.10.

Comparing the two models, it can be seen that adding the interaction term has had a marked effect. While the interaction term is close to the 5% significance level, the effect of *unskill* is now no longer significant and its coefficient has changed from negative to positive. One need not be alarmed by this; it is not uncommon for the main effects not to be significant once the interaction term is added. However, the main effects (in this case *unskill*) should be retained in the model as all the variables are required for explanatory purposes and in order to make accurate predictions. The change in sign has also to be considered in context, the effect of being unskilled is, in this model, mediated through the main effect *unskill* and also through the interaction term *unskage*. So how do we interpret the model?

Considering the effects of age on hourly pay, for skilled people (that is for those where *unskill* = 0 and *unskage* = 0) hourly pay increases by £0.132 for each additional year of age. For unskilled people *unskage* = 1, thus the effect of *age* is £0.132 + (–£0.128) = £0.004. For the unskilled the interaction term is the additional effect of *age*. The pay of the skilled is increasing by £.132 each year as they get older, whereas the pay of the unskilled is remaining relatively constant and is only increasing at £0.004 for each additional year of age. The unskilled notionally start with a higher rate of hourly pay. The model indicates that at age = 0 the unskilled receive £1.716 more per hour than the skilled (£5.9 compared with £4.2). But of course no person is aged 0 and in employment. The differential effect of age on the two groups indicated by the model is shown graphically in Figure 4.11.

In Figure 4.11 the gradients of the line for skilled people has been exaggerated to

Coefficients[a]

Model		Unstandardized Coefficients		Standardized Coefficients	t	Sig.
		B	Std. Error	Beta		
1	(Constant)	4.197	1.515		2.770	.007
	Age last birthday	.132	.038	.424	3.497	.001
	unskill	1.716	2.695	.220	.637	.526
	unskage	-.128	.066	-.692	-1.938	.056

a. Dependent Variable: Gross hourly pay (£)

Figure 4.10 SPSS output, regression model including interaction term.

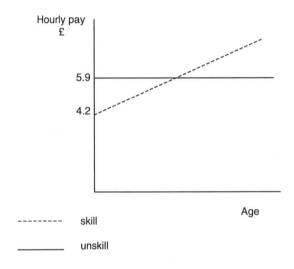

Figure 4.11 Graphical representation of the interaction model.

emphasise that hourly pay is increasing with age, and considerably faster than for the unskilled.

4.7 Automated model selection procedures

It was stated in section 1.5 that SPSS can be tasked to identify the 'best' model. (So far I have specified the model and the explanatory variables to be included.) In the multiple regression dialogue box exhibited in Figure 4.3 it can be seen that next to Method, Enter is indicated. This is the default option and simply means that all the variables I include as Independent(s) are entered into the model. However, there are alternatives to Enter which request SPSS to follow a procedure to select the 'best' fitting model. A forward procedure, Stepwise, was chosen (see the discussion in section 1.5). Details of the fitted model are not shown here but the best model found by SPSS included the three variables, age completed full-time education, number of years in current job and whether the employee was unskilled or not. The inclusion of these three variables is not surprising as they were found to be highly significantly related to hourly pay. Nor is it surprising that age and whether the employee was in a professional or managerial position were excluded from the model as under any criteria they were not found to be significant to hourly pay. However, consider the plight of gender. The variable *female* was not selected by SPSS because its significance did not reach 5%, but in the model I fitted *female* attained a significance level of 8.2% which is significant on a one-tailed test. This finding highlights another potential limitation of allowing the computer to fit the model, in that by applying rigid criteria some possible inferences may be missed. (To be fair to SPSS, the criteria for including variables can be changed and information is provided on the variables excluded as well as those included.)

4.8 Diagnostics: Analysis of residuals

So far the model has been judged in its entirety and the contribution of each explanatory variable has been considered. However, a third criterion for assessing a model, as highlighted in section 1.4, is to examine how the model fits each of the individual data points. A good way of doing this is to examine residuals, which were the subject of section 3.9. In this example a residual is the difference between the actual value of hourly pay and the value of hourly pay predicted by the model. If the model fits well then the residuals should be small. The pattern of the residuals will also help assess potential problems, in particular whether the underlying relationship is in fact linear, whether the assumptions of multiple regression hold and whether extreme cases, or outliers, are present which could have an undue influence or distort the estimates. Each is considered in turn.

Although SPSS will provide the actual value of the residuals, understanding is aided by considering standardised residuals (see section 3.9). Standardised residuals can be calculated for each case and stored as a variable on the data file. (This is accomplished by clicking Save and checking Residuals, Standardized.) Once saved (as a variable labelled *ZRE*) further analysis can be undertaken.

Linearity

If the relationship between *y* and the explanatory variables is linear then there should be no relationship between the predicted values of *y* and their corresponding residuals. Thus, a useful diagnostic is to plot the standardised residuals against the standardised predicted values. This is shown at Figure 4.12.

If the assumption holds there should be no evident pattern between standardised residuals and standardised predicted values; the standardised residuals should fluctuate around zero for all values of the standardised predicted values. Reassuringly this plot suggests that the assumption of linearity is not violated. If the plot had provided evidence of a nonlinear relationship we would need to consider the options for incorporating nonlinear relationships set out in section 3.9.

Regression assumptions

Allison (1999) discusses the various assumptions underlying multiple regression, the most important of which is that the error term, *e*, is unrelated to the explanatory variables *x*. If they are related the estimates of the coefficients are likely to be biased. Unobserved variables or unobserved heterogeneity is a likely cause of this assumption being violated. Unfortunately, there is no simple diagnostic test to gauge whether this

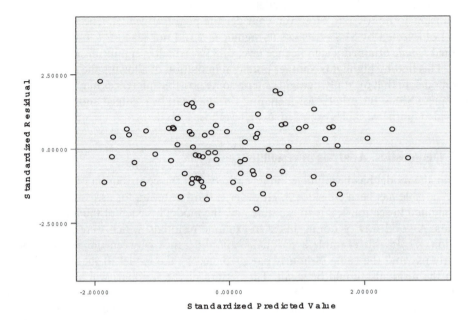

Figure 4.12 SPSS output, residual plot.

assumption holds or not and the researcher is left to draw on his or her substantive knowledge of the subject under investigation. Unobserved variables or unobserved heterogeneity is discussed in more detail in section 3.10.

Another assumption of regression (although, as Allison points out, often the least important) is that the residuals are normally distributed and a stem-and-leaf plot (or a histogram) can be plotted to see if the assumption holds. The stem-and-leaf plot is shown at Figure 4.13.

Reassuringly, the residuals do appear to be normally distributed, but the stem-and-leaf plot also identifies two outliers (discussed below).

One widely recommended option is to produce a normal probability plot which plots the cumulative distribution of the standardised residuals against the expected normal distribution. The points should lie along a straight line and any deviation reveals how the standardised residuals differ from normality. A normal probability plot was requested by checking the appropriate box within Plots. The resulting plot is given at Figure 4.14.

It can be seen that the points are close to the line throughout its length.

A further assumption of multiple regression is that the variance of *e* should be the same for all values of *x*; this is known as homoscedasticity. If we look back at the original scatterplot, Figure 4.1, we see evidence of heteroscedasticity (unequal variance) as the data on incomes is more spread out for older people than for the younger people. This is a common phenomenon with income data as younger people tend to have more similar incomes than older people or, to put it another way, the variation in income increases with age. Our assumption of homoscedasticity seems to be violated. Heteroscedasticity does not lead to bias in the estimates of the coefficients, *b*, but does lead to bias in the estimates of the standard errors (leading to incorrect

```
Standardized Residual Stem-and-Leaf Plot

 Frequency     Stem &  Leaf

      4.00        -1 .  5778
      8.00        -1 .  00111111
     13.00        -0 .  5566677899999
     15.00        -0 .  011111122233444
     15.00         0 .  000112333344444
     11.00         0 .  55556777788
      7.00         1 .  1122334
      2.00         1 .  89
      2.00 Extremes      (>=2.6)

 Stem width:    1.00000
 Each leaf:        1 case(s)
```

Figure 4.13 SPSS output, stem-and-leaf plot.

Normal P-P Plot of Regression Standardized Residual

Dependent Variable: Gross hourly pay (£)

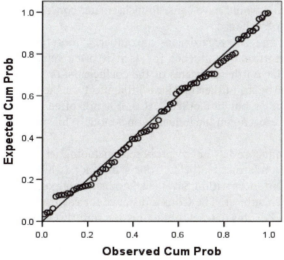

Figure 4.14 SPSS output, normal probability plot.

t and probability values – and hence possibly erroneous inferences). However, Allison states that heteroscedasticity has to be severe to cause serious bias in the estimates of the standard errors. One way of overcoming the problem is to calculate *robust standard errors* (first mentioned in section 3.3), which is an option in Stata and pursued in section 4.9.

With the exception of the concerns regarding homoscedasticity, the residual analysis conducted so far provides reassurance of the adequacy of our model. Although not shown, similar plots and graphs were produced for the model with log(hourly pay) as the response variable. Interestingly they gave clear evidence that the latter model was markedly inferior to the model with hourly pay as the response variable. The standardised residuals deviated from normality, as indicated by a histogram and a normal probability plot.

Outliers and influential observations

Outliers are observations (cases or subjects) that have large residuals and standardised residuals; although what is large is a matter of degree. Nevertheless, it is good practice to examine standardised residuals above 2.0 or 2.5 and especially above 3.0. Casewise diagnostics can be requested (by checking the Casewise diagnostics box within Statistics in the SPSS dialogue box at Figure 4.3) which proceeds to identify all cases that might be considered as outliers. Casewise diagnostics were requested and the threshold for defining outliers was set at 2.5 standard deviations in order to highlight cases that were in the 1% tail of the normal distribution. The following output was obtained (see Figure 4.15).

From Figure 4.15 it can be seen that two cases, located at rows 17 and 67 in the data file, had standardised residuals greater than 2.5. (These are the same two cases as identified in the stem-and-leaf plot.) However, in both cases, the standardised residual is not much greater than 2.5 and may not be considered extreme. (And it should be remembered that for every 100 cases, one with such a value can be expected.) Standardised residuals greater than 3 would have caused much greater concern as they are rare and very unlikely to occur by chance.

However, while a case may be regarded as an outlier, a more important issue is whether it has a disproportionate influence (or as it is often referred to, leverage) on the model, in particular on the estimates of the coefficients, or parameters, b. An observation (subject) can be an outlier but have little effect on the model, or it may affect one or some of the bs but not others. Also, but not often in my experience, extreme observations can exert an undue influence on a model while not being regarded as outliers.

Various measures of influence have been proposed, including leverage, Cook's distance, dfit, dfbeta and standardised dfbeta. Cook's distance (which is obtained by checking Cook's under Distances within Save) is a good starting point as it provides a summary measure for each subject. The Cook's distance for each subject is stored on the data file as a variable. For this dataset, obtaining descriptive statistics revealed that Cook's distance had a mean of .015 and a standard deviation of .04. A plot of Cook's distance against the identifier (*id*) for each subject is shown at Figure 4.16.

From the graph it can be seen that eight subjects had a high value of Cook's distance

Casewise Diagnostics[a]

Case Number	Std. Residual	Gross hourly pay (£)	Predicted Value	Residual
17	2.560	17.03	10.0155	7.01447
67	2.657	17.16	9.8787	7.28127

a. Dependent Variable: Gross hourly pay (£)

Figure 4.15 SPSS output, casewise diagnostics.

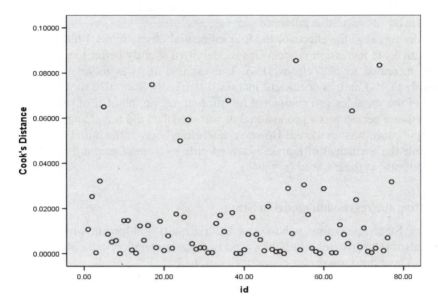

Figure 4.16 SPSS outputs, plot of Cook's distance.

and are exerting a disproportionate influence on the model. I identified the eight cases and then interrogated the effect they were having on the coefficients of the model. For this I requested standardised dfbetas (by checking Standardized DfBeta(s) in Save in the dialogue box at Figure 4.3) which estimates the effect an observation is having on each of the coefficients b_p of the model. The standardised dfbetas are added to the data file, one for each coefficient (variable) included in the model and one for the constant (or intercept). In this example seven dfbetas were added to the data file, one for the intercept and one for each of the six variables in the model.

The rule of thumb adopted is to judge a dfbeta as large is if its absolute value exceeds

$$\frac{2}{\sqrt{N}} \quad \text{or} \quad \frac{3}{\sqrt{N}}$$

For this data $N = 77$, thus $\sqrt{N} = 8.77$ and

$$\frac{2}{\sqrt{N}} = .23 \quad \text{and} \quad \frac{3}{\sqrt{N}} = .34$$

Similar plots to the one above for Cook's distance can be produced for each dfbeta, but with a small dataset it was possible to inspect the dfbetas by eye, and in particular to inspect the eight subjects identified by Cook's distance. From inspection it did not appear that the eight cases were unduly influencing just one coefficient; rather that their effect(s) were dissipated across several coefficients. Not all cases were affecting all coefficients. Furthermore, some cases were only having a small effect on several coefficients but not a major effect on any one. From this analysis, and by setting a cut-off of Cook's distance at .065 (the mean plus two standard deviations), I concluded that four of the cases were having an undue influence.

In order to gauge the effects of the four influential observations, I filtered them out and re-fitted the regression model. This model fitted slightly better than the previous one, R^2 increased to 57% (from 51%). The variable age was more significant than previously (7.4%) and its coefficient increased markedly from .036 to .055. The coefficients of the variables, age completed full-time education, number of years in current job, whether a person was a professional or was unskilled did not change as much and their significance was unaltered. However, interestingly given the initial research question, while the coefficient of female increased only by a small amount, to −1.2, it was now significant at the 5% level ($p = .048$).

4.9 Fitting the regression model in Stata

On entry, Stata opens four windows, a Stata Results window, in which results are displayed (not shown here), a Variables window, a Review window and a Stata Command window. These three are shown below at Figure 4.17.

Any of the windows can be enlarged or moved around the screen or closed to suit the researcher's preferences. Others can be opened, such as the data editor for inputting or editing the data file. The Review window above shows that two regression analyses have been fitted this session, the first with just age as an explanatory variable and the second with six variables (that is, the same two regressions as fitted in SPSS previously).

The output from the second regression is presented at Figure 4.18.

The first line (beginning with a full stop) gives the command issued to perform the regression analysis. This can be entered as a command or by point and click and drop-down menus (in this example, Statistics, Linear regression and related, and then

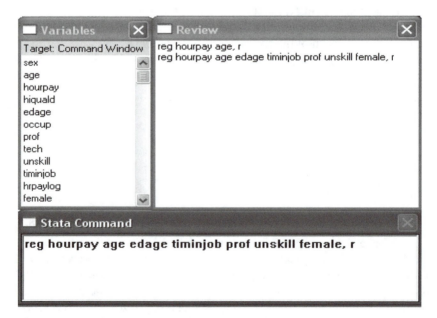

Figure 4.17 Stata window, specifying regression model.

```
. reg hourpay age edage timinjob prof unskill female, r

Regression with robust standard errors            Number of obs =      77
                                                  F( 6,    70) =   11.73
                                                  Prob > F      =  0.0000
                                                  R-squared     =  0.5058
                                                  Root MSE      =  2.7403

------------------------------------------------------------------------------
             |              Robust
     hourpay |    Coef.   Std. Err.      t    P>|t|     [95% Conf. Interval]
-------------+----------------------------------------------------------------
         age |  .0360194   .031729     1.14   0.260    -.027262     .0993009
       edage |  .4858051   .1376186    3.53   0.001     .2113335    .7602767
    timinjob |  .1903678   .0449076    4.24   0.000     .1008025    .2799331
        prof |  1.126011   .9189985    1.23   0.225    -.7068738    2.958896
     unskill | -1.826507   .6916871   -2.64   0.010    -3.206034   -.4469808
      female | -1.130051   .6382893   -1.77   0.081    -2.403079    .1429771
       _cons | -2.394657   2.794807   -0.86   0.394    -7.968723    3.179409
------------------------------------------------------------------------------
```

Figure 4.18 Stata output, multiple regression.

entering the variable names and selecting any options wanted). Note that *r* has been added (after the comma) at the end of the command to request robust standard errors.

The next segment is the ANOVA output (although it is not headed that). However, note that Stata calls the sums of squares attributable to the regression Model (sums of squares). The values of the coefficients are exactly the same as estimated by SPSS but the estimates of the standard errors are different. That is because robust standard errors were requested. As the standard errors are different, the values of *t* are different (because $t = b/s.e.\ b$) and hence the probabilities, *p*, are also different. In this instance the inferences are the same; in no case would we change our view of the significance of the variables.

The output from Stata is more compact and provides 95% confidence intervals for the coefficients as part of its standard output, but not standardised coefficients. Standardised coefficients (Beta) can be requested and they will be given in the output instead of the 95% confidence intervals.

Further regression models are fitted using Stata in Chapter 11 which considers simultaneous equation models.

4.10 Tobit model

Before leaving multiple regression, readers may wish to be aware of the tobit model which is often thought to be more appropriate when a large proportion of the sample has a value of *y* at one end of the range of possible values of *y*. For example, the annual Smoking, Drinking and Drug Use Among Young People survey asks a sample of school pupils how many cigarettes they smoked and how many units of alcohol they drank in a previous period. A large proportion of the sample state that they did not smoke or drink during the period, resulting for them in a value of $y = 0$ while the remainder reported a value of 1, 2, 3, etc. Thus in the case of drinking and smoking, the response variable y is continuous and positive but zero for a significant proportion. At the other extreme we may, for example in another study, ask people their income. However, for those with exceptionally high incomes we may not know the exact income, only that it is at or above a certain value. The response variable y is thus truncated at a certain upper value.

In each of the above examples we could proceed and fit a multiple regression model and in many cases the regression may be adequate. However, the problem arises if we wish to predict as the regression model may produce unreliable estimates at the extremes, even resulting in negative values of the number of cigarettes smoked and units of alcohol drunk in the first example. The tobit model overcomes these problems, which explains why it is preferred in these situations. The tobit model is, however, more complex and more difficult to interpret. It is not discussed further here but details can be found in Wooldridge (2003).

Further reading

P. A. Allison has written an exemplary, accessible and readable text on multiple regression which is highly recommended (Allison 1999).

The Tobit model is also fully explained in Long (1997).

5 Logistic regression for binary response variables

5.1 Introduction

Binary response variables (where the outcome can take one of only two values) are surprisingly common, occurring naturally in many research projects. Examples include being employed or not, reoffending or not, passing or failing an examination and so on. When the response variable is binary, multiple regression should not be used, but logistic regression should be used instead.

If the dependent variable, y, is binary, coded 0 if the event does not occur and coded 1 if the event does occur, and substituted in (Equation (1.1)) we would effectively be modelling the probability, p, of the event occurring. However, including such a binary dependent variable in multiple regression causes problems as the assumptions underpinning multiple regression are violated. First, the least squares estimation procedure does not produce the most efficient estimates of the coefficients b, and, second, the model can produce predicted probabilities less than 0 (negative in value) or greater than 1 – both of which are outside the range of a probability, 0 to 1.

With regard to the second problem, matters are improved by replacing p, the probability of the event occurring, by the odds of the event occurring. Odds were explained in section 3.1 where their properties were outlined. To recap, one advantage of odds is that whereas the probability p ranges from 0 to 1, odds range from 0 to ∞ (infinity). Furthermore, taking the natural logarithms of the odds changes the odds scale from 0 to ∞, to $-\infty$ to $+\infty$ centred on zero. Odds less than 1 have negative values of log odds whereas odds greater than 1 have positive log odds.

Adopting the log of the odds, or log odds, or logit, of p as the dependent variable gives rise to the name logistic regression.

The logit is defined as:

$$\log_e \frac{(p)}{(1-p)}$$

We will see that although the model is fitted in log odds, the output is also converted back to odds (the anti-log, see section 3.2) for our convenience and ease of interpretation.

So far we have overcome the problem of a binary variable by transforming p to the logit. However, the inefficiency of least squares needs to be addressed.

To overcome the problems caused by least squares, logistic regression models are fitted by the estimation procedure known as maximum likelihood, briefly described in section 1.4. We do not need to be concerned with the mathematical details of maximum likelihood estimation procedures, but should be comforted by knowing that this is the best option available and is the method used by SPSS and Stata.

5.2 Example: Victim of car crime

To illustrate the application of logistic regression and the interpretation of the results, we consider data from the British Crime Survey (BCS) for the year 2000. The focus of interest is whether or not a household has been the victim of vehicle crime. Experience of any incidence of a stolen vehicle, theft from a vehicle or criminal damage to a vehicle is recoded 1 on the variable *victcar* and 0 if the household has not experienced any of these crimes. Obviously, to be at risk of vehicle crime, a household must possess a vehicle – so all households who did not have a vehicle were omitted from the sample available for analysis. The effective sample size was 15,081 of whom 3396 or 22.5% were the victim of a vehicle crime.

The BCS is a complex survey (for an explanation of a complex survey design, see section 2.3). However, as the design features are not recorded as variables in the data file, the data has been analysed as if the BCS was a simple random sample.

A subset of five independent variables was selected from the many variables within the BCS data file. Three variables recorded individual characteristics, namely the respondent's sex, age and ethnicity. There are limitations in using individual variables to explain household crimes as only one member of the household aged 16 or over, selected at random, answers on behalf of the household. Characteristics of the interviewee may not reflect vehicle ownership. An older person may have sons and daughters in the household who each own a vehicle. A 16-year-old respondent cannot (legally) drive. Unlike other individual variables, the ethnicity of the respondent may be a more reliable indicator of the ethnicity of the household. Notwithstanding these concerns, the main purpose here is to explain logistic regression and not to address the substantive issue of vehicle crime.

Two household variables were chosen, the number of vehicles in the household and tenure of the accommodation. Other things being equal, the more vehicles the household owns, the greater the chance that at least one will be stolen, vandalised or have something taken from it. The number of cars has been recoded such that a household with more than four vehicles has been collapsed into the category '4 or more cars'. Tenure of the household has been dichotomised into 'rented accommodation' and 'all other' – which comprises mainly owner-occupied accommodation but not exclusively so. Owner-occupied households are more likely to have a garage than households living in rented accommodation and reflects a higher level of security, at least while the vehicle is not in use. But tenure also acts as a proxy for the type of area in which the household lives.

The five independent variables together with the dependent variable are summarised in Table 5.1. Prior to analysis many were recoded from the originals. (An 'r' at the end of the variable name is my convention of distinguishing recoded variables from their originals.)

It can be seen from Table 5.1 that *victcar* is a 0,1 response variable. Of the independent variables, *sex*, *agegpr*, *ethnicr* and *tenurer* are categorical variables and three have two levels whereas *agegpr* has three levels. *Numcarr* is a continuous variable but has been truncated at 4.

Table 5.1 Variables available for analysis

Dependent variable	
victcar	1 if victim of vehicle crime; 0 if not
Independent variables	
sex	1 male; 2 female
agegpr	1 16–44; 2 45–54; 3 55 and over
ethnicr	1 white; 2 all other
numcarr	Number of vehicles in household, 1, 2, 3, 4 or more
tenurer	1 not rented; 2 rented

5.3 Undertaking logistic regression in SPSS

Click: Analyze → Regression → Binary Logistic

This brings up the following dialogue box.

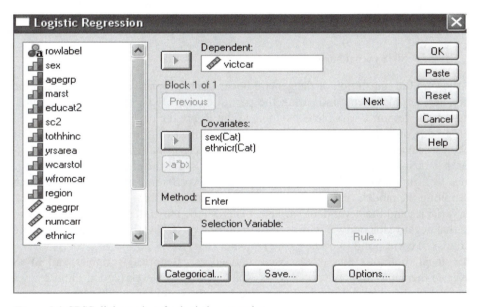

Figure 5.1 SPSS dialogue box for logistic regression.

Victcar has been declared as the dependent variable and the first logistic regression included *sex* and *ethnicr* as independent variables. Note that unlike multiple regression, SPSS has called the independent variables covariates. Furthermore, this module of SPSS allows the researcher to distinguish categorical variables from continuous variables. This is accomplished by clicking the Categorical . . . button; SPSS lists the covariates and invites the researcher to nominate categorical variables. Both *sex* and *ethnicr* have been declared as categorical variables and are indicated as such by (Cat) after them. The purpose of identifying a variable as categorical is that SPSS automatically converts it to dummy variables and includes all but one of the dummy variables in the model. The default in SPSS is to drop the last (highest coded) category which in effect becomes the reference category. (Recall that at least one dummy variable has to be omitted when fitting a model – see section 3.5.) However, it is possible to change the reference category from the last to the first by highlighting the categorical variable, which lights up Change Contrast, then check First then Change. (Always remember to click on Change as countless times I have thought I had changed the reference category to the first and then been bemused by the output – only to realise some time later I had not authorised the change by clicking Change.) Why SPSS does not distinguish categorical variables in multiple regression and makes the researcher construct dummy variables but performs these operations for the researcher in logistic regression is a mystery.

The fitted model is shown in Figure 5.2.

Variables in the Equation

		B	S.E.	Wald	df	Sig.	Exp(B)
Step 1 a	sex(1)	.070	.039	3.208	1	.073	1.072
	ethnicr(1)	-.233	.086	7.392	1	.007	.793
	Constant	-1.053	.086	151.674	1	.000	.349

a. Variable(s) entered on step 1: sex, ethnicr.

Figure 5.2 SPSS output, logistic regression model.

Following the convention of the general linear model, Equation (1.1), the *B*s are the parameters or coefficients indicating the partial effects of the explanatory variables. However, the response variable is the logit so the *B*s are the partial effects of the *x*s on the log odds of being a victim of car crime, which is not intuitively meaningful. But SPSS also calculates and presents the anti-logs, Exp(*B*), that is, it converts the coefficients to be interpretable in terms of the odds. The *B*s are therefore important when it comes to fitting (and testing) the model but the Exp(*B*)s are more important when interpreting the model, that is, when describing the relationships between the explanatory variables and the dependent variable. (This will be illustrated shortly below.) Also note that negative log odds (*B*) correspond to odds, Exp(*B*), less than 1, whereas positive log odds (*B*) correspond to odds, Exp(*B*), greater than 1.

As stated, both *sex* and *ethnicr* were defined as categorical variables and SPSS converted them into dummy variables. As each had only two levels (coded 1 and 2) level 1 was included and level 2 (the highest coded level) was omitted and became the reference category. An important part of the output is a table titled Categorical Variables Codings which defines how SPSS has labelled the variables and which it has taken as the reference category. An example is given later but here *sex(1)* is male and *ethnicr(1)* is white.

Interpreting the model thus becomes:

> After taking account of other variables in the model (in this case ethnicity), being a male rather than a female increases the odds of being a victim of vehicle crime by 1.072. Thus, the odds of being a victim of car crime are 7.2% greater for men than women.

> After taking account of other variables in the model (in this case gender), being

in ethnic category white compared with any other ethnic group reduces the odds of being a victim of vehicle crime by .793.

Of course, if it aids explanation one can always express the odds the other way. For example, one might wish to say that after taking account of gender, being from an ethnic minority background increases the odds of being a victim of vehicle crime by 1.26 (that is, 1/.793).

Two tips regarding presentation. First if one anticipates expressing the odds in terms of ethnic minorities as opposed to white, it is preferable to code them or change the reference category such that the odds in the text relate to the presentation of the model. It is confusing to be given one set of odds in the text and another set in the model. Second, when presenting odds in a report at most two decimal places would suffice. Here, in order that the reader can relate the text to the output, the odds in the text have been given to the same three decimal places as the output.

Tests of significance

Having fitted a model, we wish to assess whether it improves our understanding in any significant way or whether the results are within the bounds of a chance occurrence. As in the case of multiple regression, we wish to test whether the model in its entirety is significant and whether any (and if so which) of the explanatory variables are significantly related to the dependent variable. There are analogous tests for logistic regression and they are described in turn.

To judge an entire model, one option is to test the model which includes explanatory variables against the baseline model, that is, a model with no variables included, only the constant. This is exactly the procedure followed for multiple regression, which resulted in the *F*-test. In logistic regression the analogous procedure is to compare −2Loglikelihood statistics (the statistic that results from estimating models by the method of maximum likelihood) for the two models, the model with and without the explanatory variables. Recall from section 3.3 that −2Loglikelihood has a chi-squared distribution and that the difference between two chi-squareds is also a chi-squared. The difference between the −2Loglikelihoods provides a straightforward and convenient test of the collective contribution of the explanatory variables. SPSS automatically makes this comparison and the resulting chi-squared test is given in the box Omnibus Tests of Model Coefficients – see Figure 5.3.

Omnibus Tests of Model Coefficients

		Chi-square	df	Sig.
Step 1	Step	10.405	2	.006
	Block	10.405	2	.006
	Model	10.405	2	.006

Figure 5.3 SPSS output, omnibus test of model.

SPSS proceeds by fitting what it calls a Block 0: Beginning Block at Step 0 which is the model without the variables specified but just the constant term with 1 degree of freedom. (Block 0 is not shown here.) It then proceeds to Block 1 (at Step 1) which fits the model including the variables specified (in this case *sex* and *ethnicr*). The first results are the omnibus tests. Here the step, the block and the model are all the same (with the two variables included). The table says that entering the two variables *sex* and *ethnicr* reduces the –2Loglikelihood by 10.405 which is distributed as chi-squared with 2 degrees of freedom (df). This is significant at the .006 level, which implies that including the two variables *sex* and *ethnicr* adds to our understanding or explanation of the odds of being a victim of vehicle crime.

SPSS always provides the relevant degrees of freedom so the researcher need not be concerned about how they are determined. However, one degree of freedom is lost for every coefficient in the model. In the two-variable model shown in the Variables in the Equation output above there are 3 degrees of freedom, one for each coefficient of the two variables and one for the constant. The Omnibus Tests of Model Coefficients above shows 2 degrees of freedom not 3. This is because it is comparing the fitted model with the base model in Block 0 which had 1 degree of freedom for the constant term. Recall what was said earlier that chi-squareds and their degrees of freedom can be subtracted. The Omnibus Tests is the difference in chi-squared so its corresponding degrees of freedom are the difference between the degrees of freedom of the two chi-squareds, that is 3 – 1 = 2.

A model summary follows next as shown below.

Model Summary

Step	-2 Log likelihood	Cox & Snell R Square	Nagelkerke R Square
1	16029.343[a]	.001	.001

a. Estimation terminated at iteration number 4 because parameter estimates changed by less than .001.

Figure 5.4 SPSS output, model summary.

The value of the –2Log-likehood need not be of concern. More important are the chi-squared tests resulting from the difference between –2Loglikelihoods, as described above.

In an attempt to produce a statistic analogous to R Square for multiple regression, two statistics have been produced, Cox and Snell and Nagelkerke statistics, and are presented in the model summary box. These should be interpreted with caution as neither has quite the same intuitive appeal as the R Square in multiple regression (which can be interpreted as the proportion of variance explained). They are invariably low in value but this does not mean that the models themselves are of little value.

So far the tests have considered the model in its entirety. We also need to assess whether the individual variables, sex and ethnicr, make a significant contribution. What is needed is an equivalent to the *t*-test in multiple regression and this is provided by the Wald test, which is given in the 'Variables in the Equation' box above – the first element of the output that we considered.

The Wald test was described in section 3.3 (where it was pointed that it is equal to z^2 or t^2) and is distributed as chi-squared with 1 degree of freedom. The value of the Wald test, its degrees of freedom, and the significance level are all given as part of the model.

In the model fitted above it can be seen that *ethnicr(1)* has a *p*-value (Sig.) of .007

(or 0.7%) whereas *sex(1)* on the other hand has a *p*-value of .073 (or 7.3%). We conclude that ethnicity is highly significant but sex much less so, not quite reaching the 5% threshold level.

A good model will accurately predict whether a person, given their characteristics on the explanatory variables, is likely to be a victim of car crime or not. Thus comparing predicted and actual outcomes will provide an indication of the adequacy of a model and Hosmer and Lemeshow have formulated a test (available within Options) based on this comparison. Further details are given later when this test is applied to the expanded model.

5.4 Expanding the model

By any standards the model with sex and ethnicity does not perform well (and in all honesty had I been analysing this data for real I would probably not have started here). The next model fitted included all five explanatory variables in Table 5.1. Fitting this model illustrates how to compare models and how to interpret the model, in terms of odds and predicted probabilities, when continuous variables and categorical variables with more than two levels are included. Blocking is also explained.

Four of the five explanatory variables were declared to be categorical and SPSS reports how it has constructed dummy variables and how it has included them in the model. This is shown in the Categorical Variables Codings shown in Figure 5.5.

Categorical Variables Codings

			Parameter coding	
		Frequency	(1)	(2)
Age recoded	16 to 44	7200	1.000	.000
	45 to 54	2784	.000	1.000
	55 and over	4934	.000	.000
Accommodation recoded	not rented	12437	1.000	
	rented	2481	.000	
Ethnic group recoded	white	14184	1.000	
	BME	734	.000	
Sex	Male	7323	1.000	
	Female	7595	.000	

Figure 5.5 SPSS output, categorical variable coding.

From this box it can be seen that *agegrpr(1)* is the dummy variable for the 16 to 44 age group, that is, those aged 16 to 44 have been coded 1 and those outside that age group have been coded 0 on the variable *agegpr(1)*. *Agegpr(2)* is the dummy variable for the 45-to 54-year-olds as those in that age group have been coded 1 and those not in that age group have been coded 0. The 55 and over age group has been taken as the reference category and no dummy variable has been created for that group. For the other categorical variables it can readily be seen that dummy variables have been created for *not rented*, *white* and *male*. Thus *rented*, *BME* and *female* are reference categories. It is important to clarify from the Categorical Variables Codings box how the dummy variables have been constructed by SPSS and which have been included in the model. Confusion can arise, especially if the reference category is changed from last to first. (Why SPSS cannot label the dummy *male* instead of *sex(1)* is another mystery.)

With all five explanatory variables included, the model fitted is:

Variables in the Equation

		B	S.E.	Wald	df	Sig.	Exp(B)
Step 1[a]	sex(1)	.085	.040	4.503	1	.034	1.089
	ethnicr(1)	-.055	.088	.386	1	.534	.947
	agegrpr			252.488	2	.000	
	agegrpr(1)	.791	.050	249.667	1	.000	2.205
	agegrpr(2)	.482	.063	59.353	1	.000	1.620
	tenurer(1)	-.528	.051	107.311	1	.000	.590
	numcarr	.345	.028	148.261	1	.000	1.413
	Constant	-1.837	.108	290.808	1	.000	.159

a. Variable(s) entered on step 1: sex, ethnicr, agegrpr, tenurer, numcarr.

Figure 5.6 SPSS output, logistic regression model with all explanatory variables included.

Interpreting the model: Odds and odds ratios

The first point to note is that a coefficient represents the partial effects of the variable, dependent on what other variables are included in the model. Thus having added three new variables the coefficients of *sex* and *ethnicr* have changed. The additional variables have also changed the relative importance of *sex* and *ethnicr*; *sex* is now significant at the 5% level and *ethnicr* no longer is. However, although *sex* is significant, the difference between men and women in their odds of being the victim of vehicle crime is not marked (being close to 1 – a mere 1.089). This is an example of a point raised in section 3.4, namely that in large samples variables can be significant but of little substantive importance. *Sex* would not be a strong candidate for retention in the final model. However, the three new variables are all highly significant.

The number of vehicles the household has (*numcarr*) is a continuous variable, the unit being a vehicle. Thus the model is indicating that for each additional vehicle the household possesses, the odds of the household being the victim of vehicle crime (that at least one of the vehicles is stolen, vandalised or had something stolen from it) increases by 1.413. Owning three cars increases the odds of victimisation by a factor of 2.8 (= $e^{.345 \times 3}$).

Tenure of the accommodation also has a dramatic effect on vehicle crime. For those not living in rented accommodation (mainly owner occupiers – many with a garage) the odds are only .590 in comparison with households that do live in rented accommodation.

Age has been grouped into three levels, so SPSS has created three dummy variables and dropped the highest coded level from the model, making this the reference category. As there are more than two levels a Wald test is provided for the entire effect of *agegpr* (which indicates that *agegpr* is highly significant). However, although *agegpr* is significant some of the individual age groups (levels) may not be, but in this case they are. The omitted category is the older age group (age 55 and over).

The interpretation of the model is that after taking account of other variables in the model, the odds of being a victim of vehicle crime is 2.205 greater for those aged 16 to 44 than for those aged 55 and over. Similarly, the odds of being the victim of vehicle crime is 1.620 greater for those aged between 45 and 54 than for those aged 55 and over. So how do the risks for 16- to 44-year-olds compare with the risks faced by 45- to 54-year-olds? This can be calculated from the model as they are both referenced to the older age group. Thus the odds for the two groups are simply (2.205/1.620) = 1.36; the odds of being a victim of crime are 1.4 greater for 16- to 44-year-olds compared with 45- to 54-year-olds. In general we can compare any two categories by the ratio of their odds (as the odds for the reference category is set to 1).

What conclusions can be drawn about ethnicity, which was significant in the first model but is not found to be significant in the five-variable model? I suspect multicollinearity. Cross-tabulating ethnicity with tenure and ethnicity with age indicates that ethnic minority respondents were more likely to live in rented accommodation and, even more striking, ethnic minority respondents were disproportionately represented in the youngest age group. My theory (common sense?) tells me that it is not ethnicity that is important as the offender does not know the ethnicity of the owner of an unoccupied car unless he (and it is invariably a male) has a personal vendetta against the owner. Young car owners own different kinds of cars (perhaps less secure) and use their cars in different ways to older car owners; they use them late at night where they are parked in public places and their cars may be more likely to contain more desirable items attractive to young offenders. I tested my assumptions by re-running the model excluding tenure and found ethnicity still to be significant but less so. However, when I omitted age (but included tenure) ethnicity was no longer significant. I conclude that ethnicity per se is not related to being a victim of car crime but that other characteristics of ethnic minority communities predispose them to car crime.

Interpreting the model: Predicted probabilities

So far the model has been interpreted in terms of odds and odds ratios. Odds are often the most straightforward and intelligible way to convey the relationships between the variables. On other occasions, however, one may want to interpret the model in terms of predicted probabilities. One reason for developing statistical models expressed in section 1.2 is in order that we might predict events or identify groups that are at high risk. In this example we might use the model to identify people who are at greatest risk of car crime and the insights gained could guide a crime prevention or intervention strategy. From the logistic regression model the predicted probability of an event can be estimated from:

$$\text{Predicted probability, } p = \frac{\exp{(b_0 + b_1 x_1 + b_2 x_2 + \ldots)}}{(1 + \exp{(b_0 + b_1 x_1 + b_2 x_2 + \ldots)})} \tag{5.1}$$

Predicted probabilities can be calculated following the same procedure as for multiple regression, by substituting a subject's characteristics into Equation (5.1).

So for a white male, aged 60, living in his own house (that is, not rented) and having two cars, his risk of car crime from the model above is:

$$(-1.837) \text{ constant} + .085 \ (male) - .055 \ (white) + 0 \ (age)$$
$$- .528 \ (not \ rented) + .345*2 \ (cars)$$

Note that this subject is in the reference category on the variables age and tenure and hence his value on these variables is zero. He has two cars and the coefficient was .345 for each car.

The score for this subject is: $- 1.645$, and $\exp (-1.645) = .193$

Thus the predicted probability $= \dfrac{.193}{1.193} = .16$

As a second illustration we estimate the risk of car crime for a young black female aged 25, living in rented accommodation, owning one car. Her score from the model is:

$$(-1.837) \text{ constant} + 0 \ (female) + 0 \ (bme) + .791 \ (age) + 0 \ (rented) + .345*1 \ (car)$$

The score for this subject is: $-.701$, and $\exp (-.701) = .496$

Thus the predicted probability $= \dfrac{.496}{1.496} = .33$

Of course, an alternative way of obtaining predicted probabilities for the two subjects cited above (and for any other subject) is to request SPSS to estimate predicted probabilities (by checking Probabilities in Save . . .) which are then added as a variable *PRE* to the data file. The subjects of interest can then be selected from the data file and their value of *PRE* extracted.

When presenting predicted probabilities it is helpful to present a range of probabilities for typical combinations of explanatory variables which illustrate how risks vary for key groups within the population.

Assessing the overall model

The statistics for the overall model are given in Figure 5.7.

The Model Summary states the -2Loglikelihood for the model and reveals it has only a modest explanatory power as indicated by either R Square statistic. However, the omnibus tests show that the model is very highly significant, the chi-squared statistic being 599.923 with 6 dfs. What do the Step and Block chi-squared statistics convey? It was stated earlier that subtracting the -2Loglikelihoods of different models provides a chi-squared test for the additional variables in one model but not in the other. To circumvent having to undertake this by hand, SPSS offers the researcher the opportunity to specify alternative models as what it calls Blocks. This procedure was followed here. Block 1 included *sex* and *ethnicr* (as before), Block 2 included *sex* and *ethnicr* plus *agegpr*, *tenurer* and *numcarr*. What the omnibus test reveals is that the Block adding the three new variables increased chi-squared by 588.942. With

Omnibus Tests of Model Coefficients

		Chi-square	df	Sig.
Step 1	Step	588.942	4	.000
	Block	588.942	4	.000
	Model	599.923	6	.000

Model Summary

Step	-2 Log likelihood	Cox & Snell R Square	Nagelkerke R Square
1	15325.959[a]	.039	.060

a. Estimation terminated at iteration number 4 because parameter estimates changed by less than .001.

Figure 5.7 SPSS output, logistic regression omnibus test and summary statistics.

4 dfs this is a very significant improvement. If the three new variables contributed 588.942 to take the chi-squared for the model to 599.923 then the two previous variables, *sex* and *ethnicr*, together must have contributed 599.923–588.942 which equals 10.98. This figure is virtually the same as the chi-squared value we obtained when considering the two-variable model – the only difference stems from the fact that a few cases with missing data have been dropped prior to fitting the five-variable model.

Blocking can be useful as it saves keeping note of which −2Log-liklihood relates to which model and so on. However, it is not a requirement to follow this procedure and I find that blocking itself can cause confusion when sorting through output or comparing models.

Before leaving this section, the model could have been expanded further by including interaction terms (see sections 3.7 and 4.6). Unlike multiple regression, in logistic regression SPSS can create interaction terms and this is achieved by clicking on one of the variables to be part of the interaction term (which is highlighted) and while holding down the control key highlighting the second variable. Highlighting both variables illuminates the button to the left of the Covariates box, >a*b> (see initial dialogue box, Figure 5.1). Click on this button and the interaction term is created and entered in the list of covariates. All possible interactions were created amongst the four significant variables (that is, excluding ethnicity) and entered into the model one at a time. However, none were found to be even close to significance at the 5% level and did not add to the main effects model shown above.

5.5 Automated model selection procedures

Just as SPSS could be set to select the best fitting model in multiple regression, so it can be tasked to select the best fitting logistic regression model. Three forward and three backward selection procedures are available; referring back to the initial dialogue box (Figure 5.1), the researcher clicks Method and substitutes one of the alternatives for Enter. The results at each step are reported in the output.

When the Forward: Wald model selection procedure was chosen it resulted in four of the five explanatory variables being included in the final model. The variable omitted was *ethnicr* – not surprisingly given the analysis so far conducted.

5.6 Diagnostics: Analysis of residuals

In order to test how well the model fitted the individual data points, diagnostic tests were requested and residuals examined.

The predicted probability of being a victim of car crime can also be compared with the actual outcome of respondents who were or were not the victim of car crime. A good model would produce a close correspondence between the two, such that only a small proportion of those respondents with a low predicted probability of becoming a victim actually were a victim and, conversely, a higher proportion of respondents with a high predicted probability were victims. The Hosmer–Lemeshow goodness-of-fit test (within Options – see initial dialogue box at Figure 5.1) is based on this comparison. The sample is divided into groups (usually ten groups) according to the predicted probability of (in this example) being a victim of car crime. Within each group the actual number of victims is compared with the expected number for that group. The table showing the observed and expected numbers within each of the ten groups is shown in Figure 5.8.

The expected number is simply the sum of the predicted probabilities for the members of the group. It can be seen from the table that the numbers observed and expected in each group are similar.

A composite statistic is produced for all the groups which approximates to a chi-squared distribution with (the number of groups – 2) degrees of freedom. For this model the Hosmer–Lemeshow test was found to be 11.5 with 8 df. The *p*-value

Contingency Table for Hosmer and Lemeshow Test

		Victim of car crime = not victim car crime		Victim of car crime = victim car crime		
		Observed	Expected	Observed	Expected	Total
Step 1	1	1354	1352.133	168	169.867	1522
	2	1349	1327.483	160	181.517	1509
	3	1366	1364.284	259	260.716	1625
	4	1019	1029.540	245	234.460	1264
	5	1095	1093.153	301	302.847	1396
	6	1371	1402.971	449	417.029	1820
	7	697	718.230	257	235.770	954
	8	1022	998.056	369	392.944	1391
	9	888	883.224	374	378.776	1262
	10	1393	1384.926	782	790.074	2175

Figure 5.8 SPSS output, Hosmer and Lemeshow test.

was .175 which is not significant and indicates that the model provides an adequate fit to the data.

Within Options the Casewise listing of residuals box was checked which led SPSS to list all cases with standardised residuals greater than 2 (the default – which was accepted). In addition, within Save Standardized residual can be requested and added as a variable to the data file. In total 330 cases were listed as being above the threshold value. Under a normal distribution 5% can be expected to have standardised values greater than 2 so to find 330 out of a sample of just under 15,000, or 2.2%, is not surprising. Furthermore, on inspection, none of the 330 cases had standardised residuals exceeding 3.0, which would have been the cause of some concern. In fact the highest standardised residual was found to be 2.82.

As a further check on the data, Cook's statistic was requested (by checking Cook's under Influence within Save). Strictly Cook's is not the same as Cook's distance in multiple regression (see section 4.8) but an analogue has been developed for binary outcomes available for logistic regression and serves the same function: identifying the extent to which individual cases influence the model. Details are not given here but Cook's estimates were plotted and from this a threshold value was set and subjects with values above that threshold were filtered out, some 360 in total. The model was then refitted on the reduced data file, which turned out to be very little different to the model presented above in all respects (the overall fit, the values and significance of the parameters).

The diagnostic tests did not, therefore, seem to indicate any extreme problems in this example.

5.7 Fitting the logistic regression model in Stata

The following Stata command (which could be issued directly or generated through accessing dialogue boxes) would fit the above logistic regression model:

xi: logit victcar i.sex i.ethnicr i.agegrpr i.tenurer numcarr, or

Recall that Stata calls categorical variables indicator variables. xi: alerts Stata to the fact that some variables are to be treated as indicator (categorical) variables. logit specifies that a logistic regression is to be fitted, and *victcar* is the dependent variable. The categorical variables are prefixed with i. and Stata automatically converts them to sets of dummy variables. The absence of any prefix to *numcarr* means it is treated as a continuous variable by Stata – which it indeed is. By adding the option or, odds are given in the output, not log odds.

Output from the model is not given here but an example of Stata output from the closely related multinomial logistic regression is given in the next chapter.

5.8 Probit model

An alternative to the logistic transformation of *y* is the probit transformation leading to the probit model. The probit model was developed before logistic regression and still finds favour in some disciplines and applications. The probit model was developed initially to model binary outcomes resulting from dosage levels of a particular drug. However, as Agresti (1996) points out, the two models are virtually indistinguishable and invariably result in the same inferences. The parameters (coefficients) of the probit model are more difficult to interpret than those of the logistic model, which can be readily interpreted as odds and odds ratios – as we have seen. As a result the logistic model is now much more popular and more widely used. Personally I have never applied the probit model in any analysis I have undertaken and cannot envisage a reason for doing so.

Further reading

A more theoretical discussion of logistic regression (and the probit model) can be found in Agresti (1996) and Long (1997). Long and Freese (2006) cover much of the material in Long (1997) but also explain how to fit models in Stata.

6 Multinomial logistic regression for multinomial response variables

6.1 Background

In many applications the categorical response variable has more than two categories. An example here is the type of sentence awarded by the court, and in the data presented in Table 3.1 there were four sentences: custody, community penalty, fine and discharge. Another example from political science is the vote for a political party and later we examine the preference expressed at the 1997 general election between the three parties, Conservative, Labour and Liberal Democrat.

When faced with a categorical response variable with more than two categories the researcher has several options. First, the researcher could simply dichotomise the response variable into two categories and fit a logistic regression. This may be satisfactory in certain circumstances but is not generally recommended especially if there is no clear rationale for merging categories. In the above example, if the prime interest is to understand the circumstances in which custody is imposed, a logistic regression model could be fitted to the response variable custody versus all other sentences. But imposing an artificial dichotomy can distort the model as well as ignoring other important inferences about the imposition of the full range of sentences. In the past, when there were limited options, one may have needed to dichotomise the response variable but recent developments have removed that necessity.

The 1970s and 1980s witnessed the advent of loglinear models which became very popular during that period. Loglinear models grew out of a very different tradition which was concerned with understanding the associations amongst categorical variables arranged as multi-way contingency tables. Their separate development has led to different notation and presentation which makes loglinear models more difficult to specify, understand and interpret. I personally would not advocate the use of loglinear models, especially where there is a clear response variable – which is the case in the overwhelming majority of research applications (and certainly all the applications I have ever been involved in). Better options are now available, but, for completeness (and because one may still come across them in the research literature), loglinear models are described in Chapter 7.

In situations where there is a clear response variable (with more than two categories) the loglinear model has been superseded by multinomial logistic regression, which became available in SPSS and Stata in the 1990s. In fact, where there is a response variable, the loglinear model and the multinomial arrive at equivalent results. As the name implies, multinomial logistic regression is an extension of binary logistic regression, described in Chapter 5, and thus requires little additional investment in time and knowledge to become familiar with it. The multinomial is simpler to apply than the loglinear model, more straightforward to interpret and can easily accommodate continuous explanatory variables. In addition, being more recently incorporated within SPSS, it has many desirable features which will become apparent when multinomial logistic regression models are explained later. Furthermore, if the data is in the form of a multi-way table, the tabular data can easily be weighted and analysed as if it were an individual, subject, level dataset. The procedures for handling tabular data are explained in Appendix 2. Thus, other than in exceptional circumstances, which are explained in Chapter 7, I would always favour the multinomial over the loglinear model.

If the categories of the response variable form a natural order, as is often the case with attitudinal or preference data, the researcher can fit ordinal logistic regression models. These are the subject of Chapter 8.

6.2 Fitting the multinomial in SPSS to data on sentences awarded by the court

Multinomial logistic regression is an extension of logistic regression, having the same conceptual framework of fitting the logit and comparing the odds of one event occurring, rather another event occurring (in the case of logistic regression the other event being not occurring).

Consider the response variable sentence imposed by the court. In this example an offender can be sentenced in one of four ways: to custody, to a community penalty, by being fined or by receiving a discharge. Multinomial logistic regression proceeds by fitting all the alternative logistic regressions simultaneously, that is, by comparing:

- custody against community penalty
- custody against fine
- custody against discharge
- community penalty against fine
- community penalty against discharge
- fine against discharge.

As we shall see, not all the six logistic regressions above need be fitted, one can be taken as the reference category and logistic regressions fitted for the other three sentences against the reference sentence. The other three logistic regressions not fitted can be derived from those that are fitted.

The multinomial logistic regression routine in SPSS is superior to logistic regression; categorical variables do not have to be separately identified (something I continually forget to do in logistic regression and then spend a considerable amount of time wondering why the results don't make sense).

In sections 3.1 and 3.3 we considered how the sex of the offender was related to the sentence awarded and found significant differences between men and women in the types of sentence imposed. But when deciding upon a sentence, judges and magistrates will also be influenced by the offender's previous criminal record, as indicated by the number of previous times he or she has appeared in court. The number of previous court appearances is a continuous variable but here it has been recoded to be a categorical variable (*pappfact*), coded 1 no previous court appearances, 2 one to four previous court appearances, 3 five or more previous court appearances. *Sex* is coded 1 male and 2 female. The response variable (*sentgpr*) is sentence with the four possible options defined above, coded 1 custody, 2 community penalty, 3 fine, 4 discharge. The sample comprises 2860 adults aged 21 and over, found guilty of a shop theft offence. This data is set out as a multi-way table in Appendix 2 where it appears to illustrate procedures for weighting tabular data.

Analyze → Regression → Multinomial Logistic ... brings up the following dialogue box.

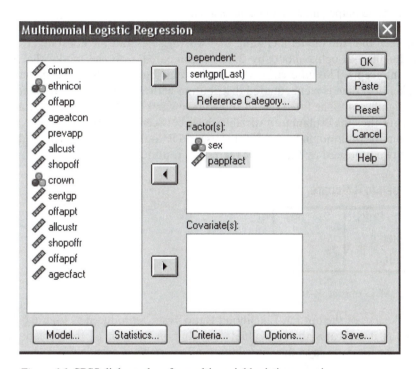

Figure 6.1 SPSS dialogue box for multinomial logistic regression.

Sentgpr is entered as the dependent variable and the last level (the one with the highest numerical code) discharge becomes the reference category by default. However, by clicking Reference Category it is possible to change the reference category to the first or any other category (by clicking Custom and entering the code of the chosen category).

There are two boxes to designate explanatory variables. Categorical variables are entered in Factor(s) and continuous variables in Covariate(s).

The first element of the output (not shown here) is Case Processing Summary which, helpfully, gives the frequency distribution for each categorical variable and records the number of missing cases. The second element (reproduced at Figure 6.2) is Model Fitting Information which shows the contribution of the two explanatory variables taken together.

Model Fitting Information

Model	Model Fitting Criteria	Likelihood Ratio Tests		
	-2 Log Likelihood	Chi-Square	df	Sig.
Intercept Only	405.939			
Final	113.984	291.955	9	.000

Figure 6.2   SPSS output, model fitting information.

It can be seen that the model including the two variables and the constants (inter-cepts) reduces the −2Loglikelihood by 291.955 compared with the model that just includes the intercepts. This difference, which is the contribution of the two explanatory variables taken together, is a chi-squared distribution with 9 degrees of freedom and is very highly significant. (The fitted model shown below has 12 dfs but three are for the three intercepts, thus the explanatory variables have between them 9 dfs.)

Output from the multinomial records three pseudo R-Squares – McFadden has been added to the two produced by the logistic regression routine in SPSS.

Pseudo R-Square

Cox and Snell	.097
Nagelkerke	.104
McFadden	.037

Figure 6.3   SPSS output, R-squares

The next element of the output, Likelihood Ratio Tests, reproduced at Figure 6.4, is very helpful as it indicates the individual contribution of each of the explanatory variables. As the footnote says, the contribution of a variable is calculated by compar-ing the full model (with all explanatory variables – two in this case) with the model omitting that variable but including the other explanatory variables (in this case the other one). The chi-squared thus indicates the additional contribution of the variable once account has been taken of the others (see Figure 6.4 opposite).

It can be seen that both explanatory variables make a significant contribution to the model.

The final element of the output is the model itself. Note that there are three models. The output helpfully reminds the researcher that discharge is the reference category so the first section of the output compares custody with discharge, the second compares community penalty with discharge and the third fine with discharge.

The layout of the model is shown in Figure 6.5 and is very similar to the layout for logistic regression.

Considering the results for custody, the model indicates that after adjusting for the other variables in the model (in this case *sex*) first offenders and offenders with one to four previous court appearances (*pappfact* = 1 and *pappfact* = 2) are much less likely to receive a custodial sentence than a discharge than offenders with five or more previous

Likelihood Ratio Tests

Effect	Model Fitting Criteria	Likelihood Ratio Tests		
	-2 Log Likelihood of Reduced Model	Chi-Square	df	Sig.
Intercept	113.984[a]	.000	0	.
sex	176.515	62.532	3	.000
pappfact	299.052	185.069	6	.000

The chi-square statistic is the difference in -2 log-likelihoods between the final model and a reduced model. The reduced model is formed by omitting an effect from the final model. The null hypothesis is that all parameters of that effect are 0.

a. This reduced model is equivalent to the final model because omitting the effect does not increase the degrees of freedom.

Figure 6.4 SPSS output, likelihood ratio tests.

Parameter Estimates

sentence awarded - four categories[a]		B	Std. Error	Wald	df	Sig.	Exp(B)
custody	Intercept	-.206	.142	2.113	1	.146	
	[sex=1]	.992	.145	46.790	1	.000	2.696
	[sex=2]	0[b]	.	.	0	.	.
	[pappfact=1.00]	-1.423	.174	66.493	1	.000	.241
	[pappfact=2.00]	-1.344	.157	73.108	1	.000	.261
	[pappfact=3.00]	0[b]	.	.	0	.	.
community penalty	Intercept	.159	.123	1.687	1	.194	
	[sex=1]	.272	.124	4.818	1	.028	1.313
	[sex=2]	0[b]	.	.	0	.	.
	[pappfact=1.00]	-1.089	.164	43.896	1	.000	.336
	[pappfact=2.00]	-.335	.131	6.557	1	.010	.715
	[pappfact=3.00]	0[b]	.	.	0	.	.
fine	Intercept	-.351	.129	7.358	1	.007	
	[sex=1]	.706	.126	31.116	1	.000	2.025
	[sex=2]	0[b]	.	.	0	.	.
	[pappfact=1.00]	-.305	.147	4.324	1	.038	.737
	[pappfact=2.00]	.084	.129	.429	1	.512	1.088
	[pappfact=3.00]	0[b]	.	.	0	.	.

a. The reference category is: discharge.

b. This parameter is set to zero because it is redundant.

Figure 6.5 SPSS output, model estimates.

court appearances (odds of .24 and .26 respectively). *Sex* = 1 is male, so the odds for males compared with females are 2.7 greater of receiving a custodial sentence than a discharge.

Similar inferences can be made about an offender's chance of receiving a community penalty as opposed to a discharge, except that the odds are generally reduced. Men are twice as likely to receive a fine rather than a discharge compared with women. However, being a first offender (*pappfact* = 1) as opposed to having five or more previous court appearances reduces the odds of being fined (and increases the odds of being discharged) but having one to four previous appearances as opposed to having five previous court appearances makes little difference. *Sex* though is still important.

Often in sentencing studies the interest is not in comparing custody with discharge but in understanding what determines a custodial sentence rather than a community penalty. The two can be compared from the model. For example, if the particular interest is in understanding the sentencing of men and women, the model indicates that the odds ratio of men to women custody to discharge is 2.696 and the odds ratio of men to women community penalty to discharge is 1.313. Thus the odds ratio of men to women custody to community penalty is (2.696/1.313) = 2.05. However, if comparing custody with community penalty is of prime importance it would be advisable to make either the reference category and rerun the model. Then one would not only obtain the odds between the two sentences but also the Wald statistics and the significance levels.

6.3 Diagnostics: Analysis of residuals

How good is the model in fitting the data? We can assess this in two ways. One of the Statistics . . . options available in SPSS is Classification table which compares the actual sentence received by an offender with the sentence predicted by the model. The classification table was requested for this model and is shown below.

Classification

Observed	Predicted				
	custody	community penalty	fine	discharge	Percent Correct
custody	543	67	107	23	73.4%
community penalty	383	88	154	93	12.3%
fine	365	44	230	107	30.8%
discharge	258	65	171	162	24.7%
Overall Percentage	54.2%	9.2%	23.1%	13.5%	35.8%

Figure 6.6 SPSS output, classification table.

It will be recalled from Table 3.1 that approximately one-quarter of the sample received each of the four sentences, yet from the above classification table the model predicts over one-half to be sentenced to custody. It predicts about one-quarter to be fined but only 14% and 9% to be discharged and to be given a community penalty respectively. The model is also more accurate at predicting custodial sentences.

From this table we can estimate how much the model improves prediction. As a baseline we can consider the number of correct and incorrect predictions that would be obtained without fitting a model (that is, without knowing how the explanatory variables affected the outcome). Without a model, the best prediction of sentence would be to predict all offenders received the sentence that was most frequently imposed. From

Table 3.1 it can be seen that fine was the sentence most often awarded, to 746 offenders. If fine was predicted for all offenders, 746 (or 26%) would be correct and 74% in error. It can be seen from the table above that the model improves on the baseline by correctly predicting the sentence for 35.8% of offenders. An alternative, often-adopted measure is to estimate the percentage reduction in errors. At baseline, without the model, predictions would be in error for 2114 offenders (2860 – 746). However, using the model to predict sentence, 1023 (543 + 88 + 230 + 162) sentences would be correctly predicted and there would be 1837 (2860 – 1023) prediction errors. Thus the model has reduced prediction errors by

$$\frac{(2114 - 1837)}{2114} = .13 \text{ or } 13\%$$

A further, more detailed, breakdown can be requested by checking Cell probabilities (also within Statistics) and SPSS outputs the observed and predicted values together with Pearson residuals for all combinations of the explanatory variables. The output is shown in Figure 6.7.

Inspection of the table suggests that the model fits well in that the predicted number in each cell is similar to the observed number. As pointed out in section 3.9, Pearson

Observed and Predicted Frequencies

number of previous court appearances factor	gender of offender	sentence awarded - four categories	Frequency Observed	Frequency Predicted	Pearson Residual
no previous court appearances	male	custody	44	41.312	.459
		community penalty	46	40.455	.955
		fine	82	82.121	-.016
		discharge	70	78.113	-1.115
	female	custody	12	14.688	-.736
		community penalty	24	29.545	-1.131
		fine	39	38.879	.022
		discharge	83	74.887	1.293
1 to 4 previous court appearances	male	custody	63	56.897	.870
		community penalty	108	109.430	-.159
		fine	148	154.255	-.633
		discharge	101	99.418	.182
	female	custody	11	17.103	-1.535
		community penalty	69	67.570	.208
		fine	68	61.745	.933
		discharge	79	80.582	-.220
5 or more previous court appearances	male	custody	543	551.791	-.466
		community penalty	383	387.115	-.242
		fine	365	358.624	.384
		discharge	258	251.470	.450
	female	custody	67	58.209	1.305
		community penalty	88	83.885	.544
		fine	44	50.376	-.999
		discharge	65	71.530	-.904

The percentages are based on total observed frequencies in each subpopulation.

Figure 6.7 SPSS output, cell counts and residuals.

residuals greater than 2 (or less than –2) warrant further inspection but the values here seem well within acceptable bounds.

Unfortunately, unlike multiple regression and logistic regression, methods for detecting outliers and influential observations are not as well developed nor are they readily available for multinomial logistic regression (or for ordinal logistic regression – the topic of Chapter 8).

6.4 Expanding the model

In addition to the sex of the offender and the number of previous occasions the offender has committed crime and appeared in court, sentencers will also take into account the offender's age and the number of shop offences the offender is found guilty of at that court hearing. Both these variables are continuous but thought was given to how they should appear in the model. To include them as continuous variables assumes a linear relationship in that every additional year of age has the same incremental effect on sentence regardless of the age of the offender. A cross-tabulation of age and sentence indicated this not to be the case. Inspection of the table revealed that the chances of receiving a custodial sentence were approximately constant until middle age and then fell markedly. In view of this, age was dichotomised into those aged 21 to 44 and those aged 45 and above and this variable (*agefact2*) entered into the model as a factor.

The number of offences at the court appearance was similarly considered but it did appear to exhibit a linear relationship with sentence. The variable *offappt* was included as a continuous variable (or Covariate(s) in the SPSS dialogue box).

The expanded model improved the fit of the previous model. The likelihood ratio chi-squared statistic was very highly significant, being 977.2 with 15 dfs, $p < .001$. Both new variables were highly significant and the Cox and Snell pseudo R^2 increased to .29. The model is shown as Figure 6.8, opposite.

It can be seen from the model that younger offenders are more likely to receive a custodial sentence or a community penalty than a discharge. Each additional offence at the court appearance also increased the odds of a more severe sentence. However, these characteristics are not important in determining the decision to impose a fine or a discharge.

Having conducted a good deal of research on sentencing, these results are in line with my expectations. Women, older offenders and those committing fewer offences (either at the same court appearance or previously) are more likely to receive a discharge. Young male persistent offenders are more likely to receive more severe sentences. There is often not much to choose between a fine and a discharge (as indicated by the model) except that men are more likely to be fined. A fine is often felt to be inappropriate for women as they may not have the means to pay or they may have dependent children who would be adversely affected by the imposition of a fine.

The classification table for this model is shown at Figure 6.9. Compared with the previous model (at Figure 6.6) the expanded model improves prediction. The overall percentage correct predictions has risen to 43.8% (compared with 35.8%). This model is much better at predicting fines, slightly better at predicting community penalties and discharge but not so good at predicting custody.

Following the methodology in section 6.3 in respect of the previous model, the percentage reduction in error obtained with the four-variable model was 24%.

Parameter Estimates

sentence awarded - four categories [a]		B	Std. Error	Wald	df	Sig.	Exp(B)
custody	Intercept	-2.449	.285	73.749	1	.000	
	offappt	.811	.056	212.472	1	.000	2.251
	[sex=1]	.997	.159	39.264	1	.000	2.709
	[sex=2]	0[b]	.	.	0	.	.
	[pappfact=1.00]	-1.317	.190	48.259	1	.000	.268
	[pappfact=2.00]	-1.397	.173	65.036	1	.000	.247
	[pappfact=3.00]	0[b]	.	.	0	.	.
	[agefact2=1.00]	.538	.239	5.093	1	.024	1.713
	[agefact2=2.00]	0[b]	.	.	0	.	.
community penalty	Intercept	-1.587	.258	37.850	1	.000	
	offappt	.616	.055	125.350	1	.000	1.852
	[sex=1]	.256	.129	3.914	1	.048	1.291
	[sex=2]	0[b]	.	.	0	.	.
	[pappfact=1.00]	-1.040	.170	37.291	1	.000	.354
	[pappfact=2.00]	-.325	.137	5.656	1	.017	.723
	[pappfact=3.00]	0[b]	.	.	0	.	.
	[agefact2=1.00]	.655	.224	8.508	1	.004	1.925
	[agefact2=2.00]	0[b]	.	.	0	.	.
fine	Intercept	-.269	.224	1.447	1	.229	
	offappt	-.055	.067	.682	1	.409	.946
	[sex=1]	.708	.127	31.140	1	.000	2.029
	[sex=2]	0[b]	.	.	0	.	.
	[pappfact=1.00]	-.302	.147	4.235	1	.040	.739
	[pappfact=2.00]	.089	.129	.475	1	.491	1.093
	[pappfact=3.00]	0[b]	.	.	0	.	.
	[agefact2=1.00]	-.006	.179	.001	1	.972	.994
	[agefact2=2.00]	0[b]	.	.	0	.	.

a. The reference category is: discharge.

Figure 6.8 SPSS output, model estimates.

Classification

Observed	Predicted				
	custody	community penalty	fine	discharge	Percent Correct
custody	465	65	178	32	62.8%
community penalty	277	107	234	100	14.9%
fine	102	28	484	132	64.9%
discharge	72	36	351	197	30.0%
Overall Percentage	32.0%	8.3%	43.6%	16.1%	43.8%

Figure 6.9 SPSS output, classification table.

Pearson residuals were requested and examined. However, when fitting a model with many explanatory variables, especially if any are continuous, the numbers in many of the cells (representing the combinations of the explanatory variables) become very small. Many cells are likely to have expected values less than 5, which is invariably regarded as the minimum for reliable estimates, and that was found to be the situation here. Nevertheless, the Pearson residuals for the vast majority of cells were within acceptable limits; those that were not were for rare combinations of explanatory variables. As there seemed to be no discernable pattern to the high Pearson residuals (other than small numbers in the cell), I concluded that the diagnostic tests had not identified any serious inadequacies with the model.

The expanded model can be seen to have many parameters and it is not uncommon for multinomial models to be extensive and complex. If the real world that the model is attempting to represent is complex then a complex model is inevitable. Nevertheless, a more parsimonious model is desirable and more straightforward to interpret so it is worth considering whether the multinomial can be simplified. There are two possibilities. First, if the response variable is ordered, an ordinal logistic regression can be fitted. Ordinal regression is the subject of Chapter 8. Second, if none of the explanatory variables affect the odds of one outcome rather than another, the two outcomes can be combined. However, I have never come across such a situation where combining categories was a viable option. While the explanatory variables might not alter the odds between some outcomes, I find that there is always one explanatory variable that does. In the above example, many of the explanatory variables do not affect the odds of fine rather than discharge, but sex of the offender and having never appeared in court before do affect the odds of a fine rather than discharge. If one did face the option of combining two outcomes, it is best to test beforehand that all the coefficients of the explanatory variables are 0 by fitting a binary logistic regression on the reduced sample comprising only those subjects that received the two outcomes.

Adding interaction terms

The multinomial routine will create interaction terms and follow an automated stepwise procedure if requested. To perform either, click on the 'Model . . .' bar in the dialogue box that appeared in Figure 6.1. This brings up the box shown at Figure 6.10, opposite.

Custom/Stepwise must first be checked and this 'lights up' the box. In order to follow a stepwise procedure the variables to be considered need to be entered in the Stepwise Terms: box and a stepwise method selected – Forward entry being the default option. Here we are not interested in allowing SPSS to select the model (a practice which I would generally discourage), rather we wish to demonstrate how to create an interaction term, in this example, between age and sex. All the four variables to be included in the model are copied into the Forced Entry Terms: box. The interaction term is created by clicking on *sex*, holding the down the control key and clicking on *agefact2* then clicking on the Build Terms arrow – the interaction term appears as *agefact2*sex*. This interaction term was not found to be significant. In fact all possible interaction terms between the four explanatory variables were created but none were found to be significant.

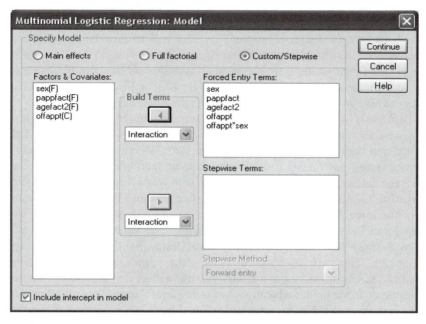

Figure 6.10 SPSS dialogue box to create interaction terms.

6.5 Relationship between SPSS logistic and SPSS multinomial

If the multinomial is an extension of the logistic (in situations where there are more than two possible outcomes on the response variable) the multinomial should fit the same model as the logistic when there are only two outcomes – and this is the case, but with one proviso. Consider the analysis in the previous chapter which examined the probability of being a victim of car crime. Non-victims were coded 0 and victims 1. The logistic, 'knowing' there are only two outcomes, fits the model to show the odds of being a 1 (victim) as opposed to a 0 (non-victim). The multinomial does not operate that way. Expecting any number of outcomes it looks for the highest coded and drops that – to become the reference category. In the case of a 0,1 variable it will make the '1' the reference category and estimate the odds of being a 0 compared with a 1. Thus the multinomial will estimate the odds of not being a victim compared with being a victim. Hence all the chi-squared, likelihood and Wald statistics, together with their significance levels will be exactly the same in the logistic and the multinomial but the odds (the Exp(B)s) will be the inverse of each other. Obviously either odds can be obtained by inverting the odds produced by the model or by rerunning the model and changing the reference category.

6.6 Fitting the multinomial in Stata to voting data, incorporating complex design factors

Section 2.3 discussed complex samples and emphasised the importance of taking into account sampling design factors when developing statistical models. Essentially the point was made there that ignoring complex design features, and treating the data as if it was from a simple random sample, would produce the wrong standard errors for the coefficients (*b*) in the model. While it depends on the design features pertaining in each study, it is invariably the case that standard errors will be underestimated if the complexity of the sample design is ignored, *t* values will thereby be overestimated and *p* values smaller, resulting in possible erroneous inferences. So long as the various aspects of the design features are recorded as variables on the data file, Stata has the facility to estimate correct standard errors. The British Election Survey (BES) 1997 contains the relevant information and is used to illustrate the procedures.

The BES 1997, like all other surveys in the series conducted at the time of a general election, asked a range of questions on whether respondents voted, for which party if they voted and their reasons for choosing that party. We are not interested here in any substantive issues, but merely to demonstrate some methodological points. For these purposes the dataset has been reduced to those who voted for the three political parties, Conservative, Labour and Liberal Democrat. The response variable is *vote* (indicating which of the three parties the respondent voted for). Only four explanatory variables are considered, *sex*, *hedqualb*, *leftrigh* and *libauth*. The variable *sex* was transformed into two dummy variables, *male* and *female*, following the procedures explained in section 3.5. The variable *hedqualb* reflects the highest educational qualification obtained and has been reduced to a binary variable with code 1 indicating that the voter has a degree or other higher educational qualification, 0 represents all other qualifications or that the voter has no educational qualifications. *leftrigh* is measured on a continuous scale (from 1 to 5) indicating whether a respondent leans to the left or the right of the political spectrum and a similarly constructed variable *libauth* (on a scale from 1 to 6) indicates whether a person has libertarian or authoritarian values. Both variables are latent variables and are described in more detail in section 10.2.

Assuming that the data is from a simple random sample, the command for the multinomial logistic regression in Stata is:

mlogit vote female hedqualb leftrigh libauth, rrr

This command has the same structure as the commands for other models presented earlier. Prefixing the command xi: is not needed in this case because female is a dummy variable so Stata is not required to create one. rrr stands for relative risk ratios and requests Stata to report odds rather than the coefficients on the log scale. The output is given in Figure 6.11 overleaf.

Note that Stata does not present −2Loglikelihood but the Loglikelihood. Nevertheless, the LR chi2(8) = 984.21 shown in the output is the difference between the −2Loglikelihoods for the model above and the base model, and is thus the chi-squared attributable to the model. It can be seen that the chi-squared value (with 8 degrees of freedom) is very highly significant.

The default in Stata is to select the numerically largest category of the response variable as the reference category (base category). This is a sensible strategy as it avoids routinely designating the last category, which is often small in number and of little interest (for example, 'other'), as the reference category. Any category can be designated as the reference category but as Labour is the largest category and either it or Conservative would have been selected in any case, the default was accepted.

The effect of the *leftrigh* scale and the *libauth* scale are in the expected direction. For every unit increase on the *leftrigh* scale, that is towards the right end of the scale, a voter is nearly 20 times more likely to vote Conservative rather than Labour. Similarly,

```
. mlogit vote female  hedqualb leftrigh libauth,rrr

Iteration 0:   log likelihood = -2247.6198
Iteration 1:   log likelihood = -1802.9175
Iteration 2:   log likelihood = -1758.4153
Iteration 3:   log likelihood = -1755.5371
Iteration 4:   log likelihood = -1755.5169

Multinomial logistic regression            Number of obs   =       2223
                                           LR chi2(8)      =     984.21
                                           Prob > chi2     =     0.0000
Log likelihood = -1755.5169                Pseudo R2       =     0.2189

------------------------------------------------------------------------------
        vote |      RRR    Std. Err.      z    P>|z|     [95% Conf. Interval]
-------------+----------------------------------------------------------------
Conservative |
      female |  1.440896    .181356      2.90   0.004    1.125894    1.844029
    hedqualb |  1.575181    .232955      3.07   0.002    1.178814    2.104822
    leftrigh |  19.71705   2.760731     21.29   0.000    14.98507    25.94329
     libauth |  2.762165   .3385657      8.29   0.000    2.172279    3.512235
-------------+----------------------------------------------------------------
Liberal De~t |
      female |  1.106082   .1318776      0.85   0.398    .8755863    1.397255
    hedqualb |  2.716404   .3560918      7.62   0.000    2.100927    3.512189
    leftrigh |  2.466255   .2921712      7.62   0.000    1.955232    3.110841
     libauth |  1.129719   .1226578      1.12   0.261    .9131712    1.397618
------------------------------------------------------------------------------
(Outcome vote==Labour is the comparison group)
```

Figure 6.11 Stata output, multinomial logistic regression.

for every unit increase towards being more authoritarian than libertarian a voter is 2.8 times more likely to vote Conservative rather than Labour. Females and respondents with a higher educational qualification are also about one and a half times more likely to vote Conservative than Labour. All variables are highly significant. Note that Stata presents z statistics (or as will be seen in the next output, t statistics) rather than Wald statistics which are favoured by SPSS. Nevertheless, whichever are given the inference will be the same (recall that z, t and Wald are related – see section 3.3).

Contrasting Liberal Democrat voters and Labour voters, Liberal Democrat voters tend to be to the right in their political outlook as measured by the left–right scale, but far less pronounced than Conservative voters (odds being 2.5 rather than 20). The odds of those with higher educational qualifications voting Liberal Democrat rather than Labour are more pronounced than in the case of Conservative voters. However, there is no significant difference between Liberal Democrat voters and Labour voters on gender or on a libertarian or authoritarian values – the odds being close to 1.

Had our interest been in more substantive issues we would have also compared Conservative and Liberal Democrat voters. However, here the interest is in taking account in the analysis of survey design factors. Referring back to section 2.3, the first stage of the survey was to select a sample of postal sectors which are thus the primary sampling units (*psu*). In the data file the variable *isspc* records the postal sector. The sample was stratified and the strata from which the psu was selected is noted in the variable *stratno*. The weight calculated to adjust for the differential probability of being selected is the variable *wtallgb*.

The design factors can be added to Stata commands every time an analysis is performed. However, a better way of proceeding is to declare and set these factors at the outset by the set survey command, svyset. For the BES the command is:

svyset [pw = wtallgb], psu (isspc) strata (stratno)

Having defined the design features of the survey (which can be set at any time and are stored permanently – unless reset), they are automatically incorporated by prefixing the mlogit command by svy. This is shown below together with the results of the multinomial logistic regression.

```
. svymlogit vote female  hedqualb leftrigh libauth,rrr

survey multinomial logistic regression

pweight:  wtallgb                              Number of obs   =      2223
Strata:   stratno                              Number of strata =       80
PSU:      isspc                                Number of PSUs  =       211
                                               Population size  = 1820.8964
                                               F(  8,    124)  =     60.43
                                               Prob > F         =    0.0000

------------------------------------------------------------------------------
        vote |     RRR    Std. Err.      t     P>|t|     [95% Conf. Interval]
-------------+----------------------------------------------------------------
Conservative |
      female |  1.386548   .1977045    2.29   0.023    1.045761    1.838388
    hedqualb |  1.65196    .2545665    3.26   0.001    1.217886    2.240744
    leftrigh | 18.32093   2.706873    19.68   0.000   13.67766    24.54048
     libauth |  2.658714   .3187004    8.16   0.000    2.097426    3.370207
-------------+----------------------------------------------------------------
Liberal De~t |
      female |  1.085879   .151681     0.59   0.556     .8237074   1.431496
    hedqualb |  2.321927   .3386454    5.78   0.000    1.739987    3.098496
    leftrigh |  2.231199   .2967452    6.03   0.000    1.715041    2.902699
     libauth |   .9491322  .1410316   -0.35   0.726     .7074037   1.273462
------------------------------------------------------------------------------
(outcome vote==Labour is the comparison group)
```

Figure 6.12 Stata output, multinomial logistic regression incorporating complex design factors.

It can be seen that Stata helpfully reminds the researcher of the design variables as these might have been set some time previously. Stata also states the number of strata and psus. These are slightly different from the original survey due to missing data and the fact that only a subset of the data are being analysed here.

The more important point to note, however, is the effect of the design features on the coefficients of the model and in particular the standard errors which together affect the *p* values. Of the eight *p* values, four remain unaltered, one has reduced (although only at the level of the third decimal place). On the other hand, three have increased substantially: Conservative *female* from .004 to .023, Liberal Democrat *female* from .398 to .556 and Liberal Democrat *libauth* from .261 to .726. In this example, the inferences that might be drawn have not changed materially. No variable has changed from being thought significant to non-significant or vice versa. Nevertheless, the comparison does serve to underlie the need to adjust estimates to take into account the complexities of study design.

Note that *t* statistics are given in svymlogit while *z* statistics are given in mlogit!

Note also that multistage clustered samples can be viewed as hierarchical or multi-level data, and can be analysed within a multilevel modelling framework (discussed in Chapter 9).

SPost and the odds-ratio plot

As we have seen, multinomial regression models can generate a large number of parameters and time and care is needed in understanding the complex set of results. Long (1997) proposed various ways, including graphical methods, for presenting results as an aid to interpretation. Long and Freese (2006) have since compiled a suite of Stata commands, called SPost, to produce output and graphs originally proposed by Long (op. cit.). SPost can be downloaded and installed within Stata (and can be found by typing net search SPost). Details of how to implement these commands, together with examples of the outputs and their interpretation, can be found in Long and Freese (op. cit.).

One useful graphical presentation is the odds-ratio plot and an illustration is given below. Unfortunately the SPost command does not appear to work with svymlogit so the plot shown has been derived from the model based on the simple random sample, which is the first model presented at Figure 6.11.

From Figure 6.13, it can be seen that each of the four independent variables in the model, the two binary variables *female* and *hedqualb* and the two continuous variables, *leftrigh* and *libauth* are represented as a separate row in the plot. The lower horizontal axis is the log odds scale (B) and the upper horizontal axis is the corresponding odds scale (ExpB). The letters correspond to the outcomes. However, to avoid the confusion of both Labour and Liberal Democrats being denoted by the letter L, the category label for Liberal Democrats was reversed to Democrat Liberal, which resulted in that party being indicated by the letter D in the plot.

Labour has been chosen as the reference (base) category as in the model, but either of the other parties could have been selected instead. Significance can be requested and a line connecting any two letters indicates that the log odds (or the odds) between the two outcomes is *not* significant. If a letter is to the right of another letter it indicates that a change or increase in the independent variable makes the outcome denoted by the letter to the right more likely. The distance between the letters indicates the magnitude of the effect.

The odds-ratio plot dramatically and visually portrays the results of the model. For example, the plot shows that there is no significant difference between Labour and

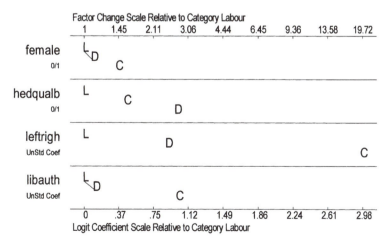

Figure 6.13 Odds-ratio plot.

Liberal Democrats on gender and the extent to which voters are libertarian or authoritarian. Voters to the right on the left–right scale are much more likely to vote Conservative. Furthermore, while voters who have a higher education qualification are more likely to vote Conservative than Labour, they are even more likely to vote Liberal Democrat. All the results depicted in the odds-ratio plot can be obtained from the model (and the coefficients in the model can be seen to accord with the position of the letters on the two scales), but the plot makes the relationships in the model more distinctive and easier to assimilate.

SPost has many other options, in particular commands to calculate predicted probabilities for individuals with specified characteristics of the independent variables. It was stated in section 5.4 that calculating predicted probabilities is an important way of interpreting any form of a logistic model and assessing the effects of the independent variables. SPost makes the task of calculating predicted values much easier.

SPost can also undertake and present, for each explanatory variable, odds and log odds for comparisons among all pairs of outcomes, that is, without having to refit the model with an alternative base category.

Further reading

Agresti (1996) and Long (1997) provide a more theoretical and comprehensive review of multinomial logistic regression. Long and Freese (2006) covers much of the material in Long (1997) but also explains how to fit models in Stata.

7 Loglinear models

7.1 Introduction

In section 6.1, I said that I would always choose to fit a multinomial logistic regression in preference to a loglinear model in analyses where there is a clear response variable. However, for completeness, loglinear models are described in this chapter.

Loglinear models developed from the analysis of categorical data set out as multi-way contingency tables, and we approach loglinear models from that viewpoint. Essentially, loglinear modelling partitions chi-squared into its constituent parts to test for associations between the different categorical variables included in the analysis. At this point none of the variables are considered to be a response variable. All variables are treated equally, the purpose being to identify any associations between them.

We begin by considering the cross-tabulation between sentence and sex, which was set out in Table 3.1, and recap what was said about chi-squared in section 3.3. Chi-squared compares the number observed in a cell with the number that might be expected under the null hypothesis of no association between (in this case) sentence and sex. Expected cell counts can be obtained by Equation (3.1a), which is repeated here for ease of reference:

$$N \times \text{row marginal prob (custody)} \times \text{column marginal prob (male)} \quad \text{Equation (3.1a)}$$

We see that Equation (3.1a) has three terms multiplied together. This can be converted to an additive model by taking logarithms (see section 3.2). Because logs have been taken to produce an additive model, this model is called a *loglinear model*.

To avoid confusion that arises by using S for sentence and S for sex, in the models that follow G (gender) will used to denote sex. If we denote μ (the Greek letter mu) as the number in the cell, the formula for the expected number in each cell can be written as:

$$\log \mu = \lambda + \lambda^S + \lambda^G \quad (7.1)$$

The model states that the log of the expected number in a cell is made up of three components added together:

λ (the Greek letter lambda) – a constant – common to all cells
λ^S – the row effect of sentence (in the case of the first cell, custody)
λ^G – the column effect of gender (in the case of the first cell, male)

The model presented in Equation (7.1) is similar in form to the other linear models presented in earlier sections. The difference is that the dependent variable in the loglinear model is the cell count – the number in the cell. Because Equation (7.1) predicts the expected cell count under the null hypothesis of no association, it is known as the *loglinear model of independence* for two-way contingency tables.

The loglinear model for the observed cell count is:

$$\log \mu = \lambda + \lambda^S + \lambda^G + \lambda^{SG} \tag{7.2}$$

Equation (7.2) is the same as Equation (7.1) (the model for the expected cell count under the null hypothesis) with the addition of λ^{SG}, which is the effect of the association or interaction of sentence and gender. Alternatively, subtracting the model in Equation (7.1) from the model in Equation (7.2) is equivalent to measuring the effect of λ^{SG} – the association between sentence and gender. The chi-squared test for two-way tables, which compares observed cell counts with expected cell counts, is in effect testing whether the association term, λ^{SG}, is zero.

Equation (7.2) contains all possible terms (constant, all one-way main effects and all two-way interactions) that contribute to the observed cell count. As Equation (7.2) perfectly defines the cell count, if this model was applied to the data it would merely reproduce the observed cell counts. Because all possible terms are included, Equation (7.2) is called the *saturated model*.

At this point it could be asked why have we gone to the trouble of reformulating the simple chi-squared of two-way tables into what appears to be a more complicated loglinear model? The reason is that it simplifies the analysis when we include additional factors in the model. Let us now consider doing that by returning to the analyses in the previous chapter which introduced multinomial logistic regression.

7.2 Three-factor model

We now add a third variable previous criminal history (P) to the analysis together with sentence (S) and sex (G). These three variables were the subject of the model fitted in section 6.2. As before, the continuous variable number of previous convictions has been recoded to form a categorical variable (factor) with three levels, 'no previous convictions' (that is a first offender), 'one to four previous convictions' and 'five or more previous convictions'.

Previous convictions is very highly related to both gender and the sentence awarded. Males are much more likely to have an extensive criminal record; 70% of males had five or more convictions compared with 41% of females. The association between the two variables was found to be highly significant; chi-squared 189.4, df 2; likelihood ratio 183.1, df 2.

As expected, an extensive criminal career was more likely to lead to a custodial sentence. Of offenders with five or more previous convictions, 34% were sentenced to custody but only 14% of first offenders received a prison sentence. On the other hand, first offenders were more likely to be given a discharge, 38%, and only 18% were sentenced to custody. The association between previous convictions and sentence was highly significant; chi-squared 220.2, df 6; likelihood ratio 229.4, df 6.

The three variables can be displayed as a three-way table. It is not given here but appears in Appendix 2, Table A.2.

The observed cell count for each cell of the three-way table sentence (S) by gender (G) by previous convictions (P) is determined by the saturated model:

$$\log \mu = \lambda + \lambda^S + \lambda^G + \lambda^P + \lambda^{SG} + \lambda^{SP} + \lambda^{GP} + \lambda^{SGP} \tag{7.3}$$

It can be seen that Equation (7.3) includes every conceivable term, constant, all main effects of sentence, gender and previous convictions, all two-way interactions between each pair of factors and an interaction between all three.

7.3 Expanding the model

The loglinear model can be expanded to include any number of other categorical variables. In section 6.4, age (A) was also found to be important and can be added to the model. (Age was dichotomised into a categorical variable: 1 age 21 to 45, 2 age 45 and over.) We now have four categorical variables, S, G, P and A and the saturated model for the observed cell counts is given by the model:

$$\log \mu = \lambda + \lambda^S + \lambda^G + \lambda^P + \lambda^A + \lambda^{SG} + \lambda^{SP} + \lambda^{SA} + \lambda^{GP} + \lambda^{GA} + \lambda^{PA} + \lambda^{SGP}$$
$$+ \lambda^{SPA} + \lambda^{SGA} + \lambda^{GPA} + \lambda^{SGPA} \tag{7.4}$$

It can be seen that Equation (7.4) contains all possible one-, two-, three- and four-way terms. As models including many variables contain many terms a short-hand convention is adopted. Equation (7.4) can be written as SGPA, which specifies a model which includes the four-way term and all possible lower order terms.

In section 6.4 the number of offences at the court appearance (O) was also important, resulting in five variables S, G, P, A and O. The saturated model could be written out extending Equation (7.4), but this would result in many terms – hence the advantage of the shorthand notation. The saturated model for five variables is:

SGPAO   (7.5)

Because the saturated model (Equation (7.2) in the case of two-way tables, Equation (7.3) for three-way tables, Equation (7.4) for four-way and Equation (7.5) for five-way) includes all possible terms, the cell count it predicts is, in fact, the observed value. Thus under the saturated model the observed cell count equals the expected cell count. Thus the difference between observed and expected is zero and the chi-squared for the saturated model is zero, that is non-significant. The saturated model perfectly fits the data.

Thus we know that we can always fit a saturated model including all possible terms that will fit the data perfectly (and result in a non-significant chi-squared value of zero). The approach in loglinear modelling is, in effect, to identify reduced models with fewer terms that fit the data equally as well as the saturated model. If the terms that are dropped make an insignificant contribution to the cell count, the reduced model will be as almost as good as the saturated model (its chi-squared will not be zero but it will not be significant). However, it is not the convention to add or drop terms at random. If the starting point is the saturated model (the approach followed by SPSS) the highest order interactions are assessed first. If these are not significant and can be omitted, the interactions at the 'next level down' can be tested. In the case of Equation (7.4), for example, the four-way interaction λ^{SGPA} is considered first, and if this is found not to be significant and can be omitted the four three-way interactions are considered, and so on until one arrives at the most parsimonious model that is not significant. An ordered approach to assessing terms, starting with the highest, has led some to refer to this procedure as *hierarchical loglinear modelling*.

One other point to note, that sometimes leads to confusion, is that in loglinear modelling the researcher is looking for non-significant simplified models. This is different from the other modelling approaches that have been discussed where the researcher is seeking the most significant model. There is no contradiction, just a different way of proceeding. In most cases one starts, as it were, at the beginning with the constant and no other terms, and then proceeds to make the model more complex by adding significant terms. In loglinear modelling, one starts, conceptually at least, at the other extreme with all the terms notionally included and then proceeds by deleting terms that are not significant. In both cases one is trying to find the most parsimonious model between the two extremes (of no variables and all variables) that adequately explains the data.

7.4 Loglinear models specifying a response variable

In the loglinear models presented so far, all variables were treated equally, that is, no distinction was made between them in terms of being a dependent (or response) variable or an explanatory variable. Loglinear modelling, as applied so far, considers them *all* to be response or *all* to be explanatory variables (it does not matter which). Because all variables are treated equally, this approach is sometimes described as *symmetrical*.

But in the sentencing example there is a clear response variable, sentence (S) and loglinear models can be specified in such a way that designates one of the variables to be a response variable. Consider the five-factor model with sentence (S), sex (G), number of previous convictions (P), age (A) and number of offences (O). Here the interest is in how G, P, A and O affect the response S. We are not interested in the association between G, P, A and O, nor in the main effect of S which need to be eliminated or controlled for before the relationship between S and the other variables are considered. The base (or minimal model) is, using the shorthand notation:

$$S + GPAO \tag{7.6}$$

And these terms must always be included in any subsequent model. Starting with the model in Equation (7.6), terms are added such as SG, SP and SA to assess whether G (sex) or P (previous convictions) or A (age) is associated with sentence. If these terms do not result in an adequate (non-significant) model, higher order terms, such as SGP or SGA are added. Loglinear models specified in this way are equivalent to multinomial logistic regression models. In section 6.4, the multinomial model found all the explanatory variables to be significant but did not find any interactions to be significant. Thus, the equivalent loglinear model is:

$$S + SG + SP + SA + SO + GPAO \tag{7.7}$$

Strictly the multinomial of section 6.4 and Equation (7.7) are not equivalent as O in the multinomial was included as a continuous variable (covariate) whereas in the loglinear model in Equation (7.7), O is included as a categorical variable.

Thus when one variable is to be treated as a response variable, the loglinear model is specified in such a way as to be equivalent to the multinomial. This prompts the question, why specify a loglinear model as above when the equivalent model can be fitted more easily as a multinomial (especially when the loglinear procedure in SPSS is so unwelcoming)? Why indeed? I would always opt for the multinomial.

Having said that, one possible advantage of loglinear models over the logistic and the multinomial, which should be noted, is in situations where the researcher has more than one response variable. Loglinear models can be specified with several response variables included in the same model. Consider the hypothetical example where there are four variables A, B, C and D, in which A and B are considered as response variables and C and D as explanatory variables. The base, or minimal, model is:

$$AB + CD \tag{7.8}$$

We would then add terms such as ABC and ABD to assess the effects of C and D on A and B.

Agresti (1996) fitted a model with three response variables to data from a survey of students who were asked whether they had ever smoked cigarettes, drank alcohol or taken marijuana. These three variables were simultaneously considered as response variables, gender and race were included as explanatory variables. However, such models are complex to interpret and an alternative approach would have been to consider each of the three response variables separately.

Further reading

Agresti (1996) explains the theoretical underpinnings of loglinear models in more detail.

Fielding and Gilbert (2006) provide a further example of fitting hierarchical loglinear models to four categorical variables related to social mobility.

8   Ordinal logistic regression for ordered categorical response variables

8.1 Introduction

If the categories of the response variable form a natural order, the researcher has the option of fitting an ordinal logistic regression model. Ordinal variables, as they are known, arise in different contexts. Some may simply be less fine gradations of an underlying continuous variable, such as ten-year age bands. A very common way of generating ordered variables is to elicit people's attitudes, beliefs or levels of satisfaction about a particular issue or product where views may be ranked from strongly negative to strongly positive. In such situations, as with many latent variables, there may be an underlying continuous variable but we do not know the metric, that is, the distance between adjacent levels. Other variables have a natural order but no clear metric. Examples here included educational attainment, which can range from no educational qualifications to obtaining a higher degree. Sentence awarded (and the subject of analysis in sections 3.1 and 6.2) might be considered to reflect a scale of severity of punishment, with discharge as the least severe and custody as the most severe penalty. Although subsequent analysis (not reported here) indicated that sentence should not be regarded as an ordered but a multinomial variable.

Compared with nominal variables, ordered variables contain additional information, namely how one category stands in relation to another, it being 'more' or 'less' than the other. How can we capitalise on this additional information? Essentially we adopt the framework of the familiar logit models (logistic and multinomial logistic regression) and compare the odds of being in one category with being in others but taking the order of the levels into account. We shall see that ordinal logistic regression is simpler (having fewer coefficients) and potentially more powerful (in the sense of being more likely to detect significant relationships) than multinomial logistic regression.

Several different approaches can be followed, the most common is what is known as the *proportional odds model*, and this is the model that SPSS fits in its module Regression → Ordinal and the model Stata fits with its command ologit. (Other possible approaches are described in Agresti, 1996 and Long, 1997.) The proportional odds model is introduced by way of the following example.

8.2 Example: Ability to influence local political decisions

In the Citizenship Survey, conducted on behalf of the Home Office in 2001, approximately 10,000 people were interviewed about what it means to be a good citizen, the extent to which they were active in their local communities and neighbourhoods and

Table 8.1 Agreement with ability to influence local political decisions

	Number of respondents	Proportion of respondents	Cumulative proportion of respondents	Cumulative odds
Definitely disagree	2407	.25	.25	.33
Tend to disagree	3086	.32	.57	1.33
Tend to agree	3119	.33	.90	9.0
Definitely agree	962	.10	1.0	
Total	9574	1.0		

the extent to which they volunteered, and so on. One question asked respondents to state the extent to which they agreed with the proposition that it was possible to influence political decisions in their local area. Their responses are given in Table 8.1.

Four possible responses were available, from definitely disagree to definitely agree, which are shown in Table 8.1. Each could be treated as a separate level of a categorical variable and a multinomial logistic regression fitted as before (one level being the reference category). However, as the responses clearly form an ordinal scale we can introduce the concept of 'less than' or 'more than' a particular point on the scale (an option not available when the levels are nominal). In effect we can consider cumulative logits, the log odds of being above or below a particular 'cut point' of the scale. In this example we can compare the probability of 'definitely disagree or less' (there isn't a lesser position one could take), .25, with taking a more positive view ('tend to disagree', 'tend to agree' and 'definitely agree' or .32 + .33 + .10), .75 or (1 − .25). The odds is thus .25/.75 = .33.

Similarly, the proportion of those who at least 'tend to agree' is .9 and the proportion holding stronger views is .1. The cumulative odds are thus 9.0.

Suppose we have k ordered levels of our categorical variable (in the example above $k = 4$). Then the proportional odds model is:

$$\log \frac{p_1 + p_2 + \ldots + p_i}{p_{i+1} + \ldots + p_k} = b_{0k} + b_1 x_1 + b_2 x_2 + \ldots + b_p x_p \tag{8.1}$$

The response variable is the log of the probability of being in a category up to and including the ith category divided by the probability of being in the categories above the ith, that is, categories $i + 1$ to the final category k.

On the right-hand side of Equation (8.1) there is only one coefficient for each explanatory variable (e.g. b_1 for x_1). What this means (and it is the basic underlying assumption of the model) is that the effect of each explanatory variable is the same for all k categories of the response variable. So, for example, if x_1 is a continuous variable such as age (in years), the model would say that for each additional year the log odds of being above a point on the scale compared with being below that point on the scale would change by b_1 regardless of the point on the scale.

However, note b_{0k}. This says that there is a different constant for each level of the ordered variable. The constant 'fixes' the model in the sense that it is needed to predict the probability of being above a particular level.

At this point the reader may wish to compare ordinal regression with multiple regression, logistic regression and multinomial logistic regression. In multiple regression and logistic regression there was one constant, one coefficient (*b*) for each continuous variable, and a coefficient for each level (bar the reference category) of each categorical variable. At the other extreme, with the exception of the reference category, for each level of the response variable, multinomial logistic regression had a separate constant *and* a different coefficient for each explanatory variable. In the case of multinomial logistic regression this level of complexity is necessary because each level is a different entity. Ordinal regression is in between these two extremes. The fact that the response variable can be considered on some underlying continuum means that the explanatory variables can reflect how one progresses along that continuum. However, as the continuum is not measured on an interval scale (with equal units along the scale) but on a cruder, ranked scale, a different constant is needed to reflect where the subject is on the scale.

An alternative way of conceptualising ordinal regression is as parallel regression lines. Consider the case with just one continuous explanatory variable, x_1. The ordinal model is thus:

$$\log \frac{p_1 + p_2 + \ldots + p_i}{p_{i+1} + \ldots + p_k} = b_{0k} + b_1 x_1$$

For multiple regression the model could be represented as a straight line. Ordinal regression can also be represented as a straight line but a separate straight line is needed for each level of the response variable. However, the lines are parallel because they have the same slope (b_1). This is depicted diagrammatically in Figure 8.1, below.

If an underlying assumption is that the lines are parallel, it is important to test that this assumption is not violated when fitting a proportional odds ordinal logistic regression model.

One point to note is that it does not matter which way round the levels are numbered. If the order is reversed the coefficients will have the same absolute values but the signs will change (from positive to negative or vice versa). An additional important attribute of the proportional odds model is that any collapsing of the ordinal variable (by merging adjacent levels) will result in virtually the same coefficients b_i and the same inference and conclusions.

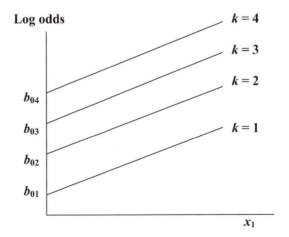

Figure 8.1 Graphical representation of the proportional odds ordinal logistic regression model.

8.3 Fitting the ordinal logistic regression model in SPSS

To illustrate the method, a model was fitted to data from the Citizenship Survey described above. The response variable was the variable presented in Table 8.1; the extent to which respondents felt they could influence local political decisions, *inflpol.* With all ordered variables it is important to know how the scale has been coded. Here definitely agree was coded 1 and definitely disagree was coded 4. The explanatory variables were the number of years a person had lived in the neighbourhood (*timeneig*), education (*educat*) (those with higher degrees coded 1 and those with no qualifications coded 4), whether respondents read the local newspaper (*locnews*) (coded 1 if they did) and whether respondents had participated in civic activities (*partciv*) (coded 1 if they had).

To fit an ordinal regression model in SPSS the steps are, Analyze → Regression → Ordinal. The dialog box is shown below.

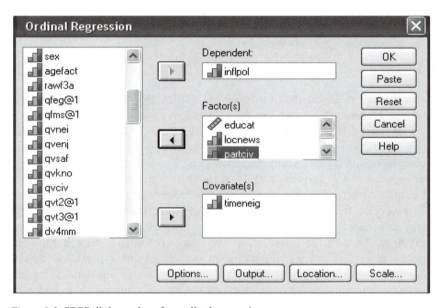

Figure 8.2 SPSS dialogue box for ordinal regression.

It can be seen that this module readily distinguishes between factors and covariates and the researcher is not asked to give the minimum and maximum level of each factor. Under Location (a curious title) one can click on Custom and specify interaction terms. Under Options it is possible to request Test of parallel lines, which is important in assessing the underlying assumptions of the model.

Not all the output is presented. As with other modules, SPSS feeds back information on the variables and the number of valid cases used in the analysis. The chi-squared attributable to the model was 699.7 and with 6 degrees of freedom, is very highly significant (p < .001). The main output giving the parameter (coefficient) estimates is reproduced in Figure 8.3 overleaf.

It can be seen that all four explanatory variables are highly significant. However, when it comes to describing the model we note a disappointing omission. Only the coefficients on the log scale (*B*) are given, not the odds (Exp(*B*)). This means that the

Parameter Estimates

		Estimate	Std. Error	Wald	df	Sig.	95% Confidence Interval	
							Lower Bound	Upper Bound
Threshold	[inflpol = 1.00]	-2.981	.064	2140.901	1	.000	-3.107	-2.855
	[inflpol = 2.00]	-1.007	.056	319.245	1	.000	-1.117	-.896
	[inflpol = 3.00]	.462	.056	69.084	1	.000	.353	.571
Location	timeneig	.007	.001	38.449	1	.000	.005	.009
	[educat=1.00]	-.951	.053	318.522	1	.000	-1.056	-.847
	[educat=2.00]	-.637	.064	98.512	1	.000	-.763	-.512
	[educat=3.00]	-.434	.049	78.550	1	.000	-.530	-.338
	[educat=4.00]	0ᵃ	.	.	0	.	.	.
	[locnews=1.00]	-.248	.044	32.114	1	.000	-.333	-.162
	[locnews=2.00]	0ᵃ	.	.	0	.	.	.
	[partciv=1.00]	-.429	.039	120.331	1	.000	-.505	-.352
	[partciv=2.00]	0ᵃ	.	.	0	.	.	.

Link function: Logit.

a. This parameter is set to zero because it is redundant.

Figure 8.3 SPSS output, model estimates.

odds have to be calculated independently by a calculator that can estimate e^B. For example, B for whether a person has participated in civic activities, *partciv*, is − .429. Thus the odds are $e^{-.429}$ which equals .65. Holding all other variables constant, this can be interpreted as the odds of a person who has participated in civic activities definitely disagreeing as opposed to the combined outcomes of tend to disagree, tend to agree and definitely agree with the question that it is possible to influence local political decisions are .65 compared with a person who has not participated in civic activities. Similarly, for someone who has participated in civic activities, the odds of their combined responses definitely disagreeing or tending to disagree as opposed to agreeing or definitely agreeing with the question are .65 compared with a person who has not participated in civic activities. Furthermore it is the same odds when comparing the combined outcomes definitely disagree, tend to disagree and tend to agree with definitely agree. Remember the order in which the scale is constructed in which code 1 was 'definitely agree' and code 4 was 'definitely disagree'. So to be higher on the scale means more towards the disagree end of the scale. Thus respondents who participate in civic activities are less likely to disagree, and, therefore, more likely to agree that it is possible to influence local political decisions.

The test for parallel lines was requested and the results are given below:

Test of Parallel Linesᵃ

Model	-2 Log Likelihood	Chi-Square	df	Sig.
Null Hypothesis	6954.350			
General	6892.712	61.638	12	.000

The null hypothesis states that the location parameters (slope coefficients) are the same across response categories.

a. Link function: Logit.

Figure 8.4 SPSS output, test of parallel lines.

The null hypothesis is that it is safe to assume a common b_i across all levels. The significant chi-square value rejects this assumption and says that different b_is are needed for each level. This implies that the explanatory variables have differential effects on the odds of moving from one level to another depending on the levels one is moving between. What does one do in such situations? The evidence can be ignored if it is felt that the model still provides a useful representation of the relationships between the variables, but this is not recommended, especially if the test proves highly significant. Another option is to treat the response variable as nominal, not ordinal, and fit a multinomial logistic regression. However, a further option is to collapse some adjacent levels and repeat the test to gauge whether the reduced variable satisfies the basic assumption. (Recall that collapsing the scale by amalgamating adjacent levels does not affect the inferences to be drawn.) The last option was adopted: the first level 'definitely agree', which contained relatively few cases, was merged with the level 'tend to agree' and coded 1, 'tend to disagree' became level 2 and 'definitely disagree' became code 3. The collapsed response variable was renamed *inflpolr*. The results are given below.

First note that the test of parallel lines is not significant. This collapsed model does not violate the underlying assumptions of the proportional odds model.

Test of Parallel Lines[a]

Model	-2 Log Likelihood	Chi-Square	df	Sig.
Null Hypothesis	5232.728			
General	5226.448	6.279	6	.393

The null hypothesis states that the location parameters (slope coefficients) are the same across response categories.

a. Link function: Logit.

Figure 8.5 SPSS output, test of parallel lines.

The parameter estimates are:

Parameter Estimates

		Estimate	Std. Error	Wald	df	Sig.	95% Confidence Interval	
							Lower Bound	Upper Bound
Threshold	[inflpolr = 1.00]	-.998	.057	304.053	1	.000	-1.110	-.886
	[inflpolr = 2.00]	.471	.056	69.515	1	.000	.360	.581
Location	timeneig	.008	.001	46.712	1	.000	.006	.010
	[educat=1.00]	-.969	.055	311.622	1	.000	-1.077	-.862
	[educat=2.00]	-.663	.066	101.145	1	.000	-.792	-.534
	[educat=3.00]	-.447	.050	81.302	1	.000	-.545	-.350
	[educat=4.00]	0[a]	.	.	0	.	.	.
	[locnews=1.00]	-.268	.045	35.747	1	.000	-.356	-.180
	[locnews=2.00]	0[a]	.	.	0	.	.	.
	[partciv=1.00]	-.378	.040	87.701	1	.000	-.457	-.299
	[partciv=2.00]	0[a]	.	.	0	.	.	.

Link function: Logit.

a. This parameter is set to zero because it is redundant.

Figure 8.6 SPSS output, model estimates.

The second model above was also highly significant, $\chi^2 = 673.4$, 6 df, $p < .001$. Comparing the two models it can be seen that the second model has two constants whereas the original model had three. However, the coefficients (the b_is) are very similar in each model. This model is fitted again by Stata in section 8.4. As Stata provides odds ratios, interpretation of the model is left until section 8.4.

Diagnostics

The fit of the ordinal logistic regression can be assessed in the same way as the multi-nomial logistic regression; by comparing predicted and actual outcomes and by consi-dering Pearson residuals. Unfortunately, ordinal logistic regression, unlike multinomial, does not output the classification table but this can be constructed by checking Pre-dicted category in Outcome. Predicted category is then saved as a variable on the data file which can then be cross-tabulated with the observed or actual category as given by the response variable. This procedure was followed and the results are given in Table 8.2.

Comparing Table 8.2 with Table 8.1, it can be seen that the model predicts more to agree (71%) than actually agree (43%). The model is also much more successful in predicting those who agree. Following the methodology set out in section 6.3, this model reduced prediction errors by 5%.

Pearson residuals can be obtained by checking Cell information in Output (just as in the multinomial). When a continuous explanatory variable, which can take many values, is included in the model the number of cells can be extremely large. This was the case here and so full details are not presented. Nevertheless, the Pearson residuals were examined in detail and they did not give rise to undue concern.

8.4 Fitting the ordinal logistic regression model in Stata

There are two advantages in fitting the ordinal logistic model in Stata; first, odds ratio can be requested and second, any complex design features of the study can be taken into account when estimating the coefficients of the model and their standard errors. However, on the debit side, Stata does not have readily available the test for parallel lines, although a user-written command, omodel, can be obtained by searching Stata's web resources.

SPSS and Stata differ in the way they handle categorical explanatory variables. While SPSS makes the last level of a categorical variable the reference category, Stata makes the first level of a categorical variable (which Stata calls indicator variables) the

Table 8.2 Observed and predicted response category

Observed response category	Predicted response category			
	Definitely disagree	*Tend to disagree*	*Agree*	*Percentage correct*
Definitely disagree	650	397	1360	16.5
Tend to disagree	561	391	2134	12.7
Agree	422	363	3296	80.8
Overall percentage	17.1	12.0	70.9	

reference category (which Stata calls the base category). In order to fit the same model in Stata as in SPSS, dummy variables were created (through the generate command – see section 3.5) for each of the categorical variables. The dummy variables included in the Stata model were the same as those included in the previous SPSS model. (This also meant that the prefix xi: was not required as dummy variables were entered directly and the model command did not need to be instructed to create them.)

The model fitted was exactly the same as the one fitted above by SPSS. The output is shown below:

```
. ologit  infpolr  timeneig educat1 educat2 educat3 locnews1 partciv1

Iteration 0:   log likelihood = -10297.071
Iteration 1:   log likelihood =  -9961.328
Iteration 2:   log likelihood =  -9960.3467
Iteration 3:   log likelihood =  -9960.3465

Ordered logit estimates                     Number of obs   =      9574
                                            LR chi2(6)      =    673.45
                                            Prob > chi2     =    0.0000
Log likelihood = -9960.3465                 Pseudo R2       =    0.0327

-------------------------------------------------------------------------
     infpolr |     Coef.   Std. Err.      z    P>|z|    [95% Conf. Interval]
-------------+-----------------------------------------------------------
    timeneig |   .0079503    .001164     6.83   0.000    .0056689    .0102316
     educat1 |  -.9694336   .0551689   -17.57   0.000   -1.077563   -.8613046
     educat2 |  -.6630881   .0658584   -10.07   0.000   -.7921682    -.534008
     educat3 |  -.4474954   .0497462    -9.00   0.000   -.5449962   -.3499945
    locnews1 |  -.2680136    .044843    -5.98   0.000   -.3559043   -.1801229
    partciv1 |  -.3777386   .0404464    -9.34   0.000   -.4570121   -.2984651
-------------+-----------------------------------------------------------
       _cut1 |  -.9981859   .0574452         (Ancillary parameters)
       _cut2 |   .4707492    .056661
-------------------------------------------------------------------------
```

Figure 8.7 Stata output, ordinal regression.

The first line of the output is the Stata command. Reassuringly, the results from Stata are the same as the results from SPSS. The chi-squared attributable to the model is the same, 673.45, the coefficients are also the same, but Stata calls the thresholds of SPSS, cut points. As mentioned before, Stata gives z (or t) tests rather than the Wald tests favoured by SPSS. But as also mentioned, when there is one degree of freedom (as is the case with each coefficient of the model), z^2 is equal to the Wald statistic. This can be easily verified by comparing the two sets of coefficients. For example the z value for the variable time in the neighbourhood (*timeneig*) given by Stata is 6.83 and $6.83^2 = 46.6$, which apart from rounding is the value of the Wald statistic given in SPSS.

To obtain odds ratios, or was added to the command which was then executed. All other information remained the same, so only the model is shown below.

```
-------------------------------------------------------------------------
     infpolr | Odds Ratio  Std. Err.      z    P>|z|    [95% Conf. Interval]
-------------+-----------------------------------------------------------
    timeneig |   1.007982   .0011733     6.83   0.000    1.005685    1.010284
     educat1 |   .3792978   .0209254   -17.57   0.000    .3404243    .4226104
     educat2 |   .5152577    .033934   -10.07   0.000    .4528618    .5862506
     educat3 |   .6392272   .0317992    -9.00   0.000     .579844    .7046919
    locnews1 |   .7648974   .0343003    -5.98   0.000    .7005397    .8351676
    partciv1 |   .6854096   .0277224    -9.34   0.000    .6331727    .7419562
-------------------------------------------------------------------------
```

Figure 8.8 Stata output, ordinal regression with odds ratios.

Note that the cut points are not given. This is because the cut points are only needed for predictions, which are undertaken on the log scale.

The odds can be readily interpreted. The results indicate that for every additional year living in the neighbourhood, the odds of tending to disagree with the statement 'it was possible to influence political decisions in their local area' increased by 1.008. Those with educational qualifications, a degree (*educat1*), A levels (*educat2*) and GCSEs (*educat3*) compared with those with no educational qualifications (*educat4* – the response category) were less likely to disagree that it is possible to influence local political decisions. Thus it appears that more highly educated respondents are more likely to agree with the proposition.

Reading the local newspaper and participating in civic activities also led respondents to feel that they could influence local political decisions. In the case of reading the local newspaper, the odds reduced by .76 of disagreeing. Alternatively this can be expressed as reading the local newspaper increased the odds by 1.3 (1/.765) of agreeing that it was possible to influence local political decisions.

Further reading

A detailed and more theoretical discussion of ordinal logistic regression can be found in Agresti (1996) and Long (1997). Long (op. cit.) in particular provides further guidance on presenting and interpreting results emanating from the models. Long and Freese (2006) covers much of the material in Long (op. cit.) but also explains how to fit models in Stata.

9 Multilevel modelling

9.1 Introduction

Up to now all the models we have been looking at have had one unit or level of analysis, usually the individual. However, it is often the case in the real world that our research interest involves relating data from more than one unit of analysis or *across different levels*. The best known example of this is from education (and it is no coincidence that educational researchers have been at the forefront of multilevel modelling).

Suppose we are interested in educational attainment, for instance a pupil's score on a particular test at age 16, and we wish to identify the factors that may influence that outcome. We will want to see how a pupil's performance is related to individual characteristics such as IQ (or some other measure of ability prior to age 16 – such as performance at age 11 when they first entered the school), gender and socio-economic status.

But we will also be interested in school effects. Are there features of a school that also affect educational attainment at age 16? Do pupils in state schools do better than pupils in private schools? Is performance higher in girls' schools, boys' schools or mixed schools? Is performance affected by class size (as measured by the pupil/teacher ratio)? Are there other features of the school such as ethos, teaching styles (however measured) that contribute to performance?

Here we have two units of analysis or data at *two levels*: at level one (the lowest level) pupils and at level two (the higher level) schools. This example has only two levels, but in theory there could be any number of levels. (For example, to extend our example, at a higher level to schools are Local Education Authorities.) Hence, we can have *multilevel* data. (The data can also be said to be hierarchical, but I prefer the modern terminology, describing the data structure as multilevel data.)

Another feature of our example is that the data can be said to be *nested*. By this is meant that pupils only attend one school (or they are only at one school at age 16 when the study is conducted). And at the next level, schools only fall within one geographical region. Part of this data structure can be graphically displayed as in Figure 9.1. (In the real world there will be more than one Local Education Authority, more than two schools and more than two pupils.)

There are many examples of nested multilevel data structures in social research. So far we have considered just one, pupils within schools, but other examples include persons within households, workers within industries. A multilevel data structure also arises in many social surveys. In section 2.3 it was stated that many (if not most) large-scale surveys are multistage clustered designs. The British Election Survey, described in section 2.3 and analysed in section 6.6, has a four-level structure; at the highest level

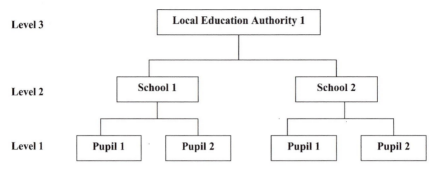

Figure 9.1 Three-level nested data structure.

(level 4) is postal sector, next delivery points (level 3), then households (level 2) and finally, the lowest (level 1) individuals. Multilevel models can also be applied to synthesising results from a collection of independent studies – a statistical technique known as *meta analysis* (Lipsey and Wilson, 2001). A further example of nested hierarchical data occurs in longitudinal research when a cohort of subjects is followed up and interviewed or tested or measured at different time points. If the questions, tests or measurements are the same on each occasion the resulting data structure is known as *repeated measures data*. This last example also illustrates that individuals need not be at the lowest level, level 1. In this example individuals are at level 2, the level 1 data is the repeated measures.

So far we have only presented nested multilevel data, but in many research settings the situation may be more complex. Extending the pupil/school example, if we are also interested in assessing the contribution of the neighbourhood or community that pupils live in we do not have a nested structure as a school's catchment area extends over more than one neighbourhood and pupils from any one neighbourhood can attend different schools. Data structures that are not nested are said to be *cross-classified*. Another example of cross-classified data is patients, doctors and hospitals. Patients are registered with one General Practitioner but GPs can refer their patients on to a number of different hospitals. Thus patients are nested within GPs but the data is cross-classified between GPs and hospitals. This latter example could also lead to yet another data structure where individuals fall within more than one higher level unit. A GP could refer a patient to one hospital to be treated for one illness but to another hospital for a different illness. Such a situation gives rise to a *multiple membership* data structure. Analysing cross-classified and multiple membership data is a little more complex and not considered further here, although they can be accommodated readily by MLwiN – the computer package introduced later in this chapter.

9.2 Methods of analysis and their deficiencies

Let us return to the nested two-level model and consider the situation where the response variable is continuous. In this case we would naturally think of proceeding by fitting a multiple regression model. But what is the sample and what is the unit of analysis? In the pupil/school example the response variable, y, is educational attainment (measured on a continuous scale) which relates to all pupils and is hence a level 1 variable. However, in exploring factors that affect educational attainment of individual pupils, we want to assess the importance of individual factors (gender, socio-economic status etc.) but also characteristics of schools (type, size etc.). In fact the research interest may be to assess the contribution of schools after controlling for individual characteristics. Furthermore, we may also be interested in assessing the importance of particular individual characteristics (level 1) in particular types of schools (level 2), that is, in analysing cross-level interactions.

In the past, researchers have proceeded in various ways but none of them is entirely satisfactory. Kreft and de Leeuw (1998) illustrate the dilemma with an example which considered the relationship between income and educational attainment. The focus of the research was to assess whether, and to what extent, educational attainment determined income. For their study a sample of workers were selected from 12 different industries generating a two-level multilevel dataset with workers at level 1 and industries at level 2. Multiple regression models were fitted with income as the response variable, y, and educational attainment as the explanatory variable, x.

For the first regression the data was pooled across all industries and the sample comprised all the individual workers. That is the regression was fitted to the level 1 data. (Kreft and de Leeuw do not state how many workers were included in the study – but this is of no consequence for the purpose here.) A positive relationship was found in this regression – namely that the higher the educational level achieved, the higher the personal income.

The second regression analysed the data at the industry level (level 2). In this analysis there were 12 units, one for each industry. In order to undertake this analysis an income and educational attainment variable had to be created for each industry. This was achieved by calculating the average income and the average educational attainment for employees within each industry. Fitting a regression to the industry level data resulted in a negative relationship: the higher the average educational attainment of an industry, the lower the average income of employees in that industry. Academia illustrates the issue. At the industry level academics have generally attained a high level of education but on average are not so highly paid (a finding I can verify from personal experience!).

This example shows that data analysed at different levels can produce different, even contradictory, results. 'The logical conclusion is that the variable "education" measures different things, depending on the unit of analysis' (Kreft and de Leeuw, op. cit., p. 3).

Using aggregate measures (as in the industry level analysis) can lead to what is known as the *ecological fallacy*; namely that inferences at the aggregate level do not necessarily hold at the individual level. To give another example, areas that experience high crime may have a high proportion of ethnic minorities but this does not mean that people from ethnic minority backgrounds commit more crime.

When analysing multilevel nested data, problems can arise because (as in this example), workers (at level 1) within an industry (level 2) might be more similar to each other than they are to workers in other industries. (Workers in academia again illustrate this phenomenon.) This is a common finding. Returning to schools and pupils, suppose two schools are selected, an independent school in an affluent part of the country and a comprehensive school in a deprived inner city area, and a random sample of pupils are selected from within each school. The pupils in the school in the affluent area will be very similar to each other in terms of individual characteristics and the pupils in the comprehensive school in the deprived inner city area will also be very similar to each other. The two groups, however, will be very different from each other. The same issue arises in survey research when a multistage, clustered design is adopted; respondents sampled from the same cluster (usually a small geographic area) will be similar to each other on various characteristics.

The extent to which individuals within groups are similar is known as intra-class correlation (denoted by ρ – the Greek letter rho). The intra-class correlation is a measure of group homogeneity and indicates the extent to which individuals share common experiences due to closeness in space or time.

The two regressions undertaken by Kreft and de Leeuw, one with level 1 data (workers) and the other with level 2 data (industries) are, as they point out, inadequate as each ignores the other and the presence of intra-class correlation leads to erroneous inferences. Of course, if the intra-class correlation is zero, nesting (or clustering) has no bearing and the data can be analysed at level 1 without leading to erroneous inferences.

Essentially, to overcome the problems with multilevel data we need to analyse the data at all levels simultaneously taking account of the variation between units at level 1, taking account of the variation between units at level 2 and so on. Multilevel modelling provides a method for analysing data from, and across, different levels. If the purpose is to take into consideration the variation at both levels it implies that we need to have a sufficiently large number of units of analysis at each level in order to obtain accurate measures of the variation at each level. Meeting this requirement has implications for research designs and datasets. Traditionally in social research relatively few level 2 units (schools, hospitals, prisons etc.) have been examined but a large number of subjects within those institutions (pupils, patients, prisoners). Multilevel modelling demands that imbalance be redressed. Experience shows that in most applications it is the lack of a sufficiently large number of level 2 units that inhibits the analysis not the number of level 1 subjects. What is a sufficient sample size for level 2 units is not easily answered and depends on the research problem. However, many would suggest that at least 50 level 2 units are needed.

Throughout this book we will always adopt the more modern and common terminology, multilevel models. However, this form of analysis is also known as hierarchical modelling (in recognition of the fact that the data structure is hierarchical) and sometimes as context modelling. The latter terminology stems from the fact that we often want to analyse relationships between individuals within the context of their wider social settings (pupils within schools, for example).

Before describing multilevel models, note that we could analyse our two-level data at the individual level and enter the higher level units as dummy variables. For example, in the case of workers within industries, we could undertake a regression analysis at level 1 (workers) but enter the 12 industries as up to 11 dummy variables. Similarly, in the schools example we could enter all but one of the schools in our study as dummy variables. However, there are two limitations to this approach. First, a large number of level 2 units (for example, 100 schools) leads to the inclusion of many dummy variables. This is very inefficient. A second limitation of this approach is that while it might indicate the existence of a level 2 (school) effect, it does not say what that effect is attributable to. In reality, identifying the nature of the level 2 effect may be of most interest to us. In the case of schools, we do not simply want to know whether there is a school effect on pupils' performance, but whether the school effect is due to the type of school, the size of the school etc. The advantage of multilevel modelling is that it enables researchers to explore what individual characteristics affect educational performance, what features of schools contribute to performance and to identify whether and if so which interactions between individual characteristics and features of schools contribute to a pupil's performance. Multilevel models also enable us to generalise beyond the schools in our sample.

9.3 Multilevel models

In order to undertake analysis across both levels simultaneously the general linear model needs to be extended accordingly and this requires introducing some additional notation. It is the convention in multilevel modelling to denote the units at level 1 by the suffix i and the units at level 2 by j (and level 3, k, and so on). Thus in the pupil/schools example we have i pupils within j schools.

Hox (2002) recommends developing multilevel models in five progressive steps, starting with the simplest model and systematically moving towards a more complex model if the simpler model is not found to be adequate. Hox's prudent strategy is followed here as it also affords a convenient procedure for explaining multilevel models. However, we do not adopt the notation favoured by Hox (and many other texts) but instead broadly follow the notation of MLwiN as this is the computer software used to fit multilevel models here – and output from MLwiN is presented later.

Step 1: No explanatory variables: the variance components model

The simplest linear model is one that does not include any explanatory variables:

$$y_i = b_0 + e_i \tag{9.1}$$

Here there is just a constant, b_0, and an error term, e_i. This model would not normally be fitted when analysing data at one level but it makes sense when analysing multilevel data for reasons that will become apparent shortly. Equation (9.1) is simply Equation (1.1), the general linear model, with all x variables deleted.

This model, however, does not recognise that the data are drawn from two levels, schools and pupils. To include schools at level 2 we add the suffix j.

$$y_{ij} = b_{0j} + e_{ij} \tag{9.2}$$

The model in Equation (9.2) indicates that the data being analysed relates to the ith pupil within the jth school. Note that the response variable is at level 1. Note also that the suffix j has been added to the constant b_0 which means that each school has a different constant. (Recall from Chapter 4 that the constant in regression is also referred to as the intercept and as the term intercept is used in multilevel modelling it will be adopted from this point onwards.) We could fit schools to this model as a set of dummy variables but the essence of multilevel models is to consider the schools in the dataset as a random sample of all schools. Thus we can postulate that there is a mean school intercept with individual school intercepts varying around that mean. Thus:

$$b_{0j} = b_0 + u_{0j} \tag{9.3}$$

where b_0 is the mean intercept and u_{0j} is the variation of actual school intercepts around that mean intercept. The subscript 0 is included to indicate that this variation is associated with b_0. If we substitute Equation (9.3) in Equation (9.2), the equation becomes:

$$y_{ij} = b_0 + u_{0j} + e_{ij} \qquad (9.4)$$

This equation now includes a fixed constant (mean) intercept for schools, b_0 and has decomposed the variation into two sources, the variation at level 2 (between schools) u_{0j} and the variation at level 1 (between pupils) e_{ij}. Separating the variation in this way has led this model to be known as the *variance components model*.

The importance of the variance components model is twofold. First, it reveals how much of the variation is at level 2 and how much at level 1. In fact, in the multilevel context, the intra-class correlation, ρ, is:

$$\rho = \frac{u_{0j}}{(u_{0j} + e_{ij})} \qquad (9.5)$$

If u_{0j} is zero, or very small and not statistically significant, it can be inferred that there is no level 2 effect and we could simply fit models to the level 1 data disregarding level 2. Thus initially fitting the model without explanatory variables provides important information on whether or not we need continue with a multilevel model.

Note that decomposing the variance in this way is only possible when the response variable is continuous and a multilevel multiple regression model is being fitted.

Second, this model also provides key information by which subsequent models can be judged. Assuming that u_{0j} is not zero and that we need to fit multilevel models, this initial model gives us values of u_{0j}, e_{ij} and -2loglikelihood. Thus from this initial starting point we can assess how far more complex models provide a better fit to the data by gauging how much alternative models reduce u_{0j}, e_{ij} and -2loglikelihood.

Step 2: Adding level 1 explanatory variables: random intercepts model

The next logical and simplistic step is to add explanatory level 1 variables. Including just one explanatory variable, the model becomes:

$$y_{ij} = b_0 + b_1 x_{1ij} + u_{0j} + e_{ij} \qquad (9.6)$$

In our example of schools and pupils, the level 1 variables might be gender, prior educational attainment, IQ, family income. (As in previous models categorical variables would be entered as dummy variables.) Note that the convention adopted throughout has been followed here, of numbering the explanatory variables in sequence starting with 1. The explanatory variable, x_1, has been given the subscripts *ij* to indicate that it is a level 1 variable that varies across individuals and schools. More importantly note that the coefficient of x_{1ij} is b_1 which is a constant and does not change from school to school. What this implies is that the relationship between x (say IQ) and the outcome y (educational attainment at age 16) is the same regardless of which school the pupil attends. This model can be represented diagrammatically.

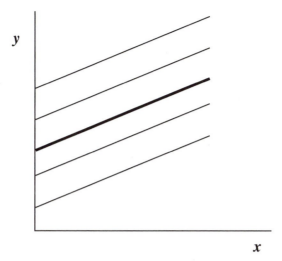

Figure 9.2 Random intercepts model.

It can be seen from Figure 9.2 that the intercepts for individual schools vary around the mean intercept (represented by the thick line). However, the b_1s are constant. The slopes are the same (hence the lines are parallel) indicating that the relationship between x and y is fixed and the same within each school. Put another way, how an individual's characteristic x affects an individual's outcome y is not related or affected by the school they attend. The effect a school has on outcome is the same for each of its pupils but that effect (the intercept) differs between schools. Because *only* the intercepts vary this model is known as the *random intercepts model*. Strictly the first model (with no explanatory variables) is also a random intercepts model but the term is usually reserved for this model. (More confusingly, perhaps, this model is sometimes referred to as the variance components model.)

The random intercepts model can be extended by adding other individual explanatory variables (xs). Alternative models can be assessed (as before) by comparing the differences in –2loglikelihood between models (which is a chi-squared test) and by testing whether a coefficient of an explanatory variable is significantly different from zero (indicating whether the corresponding x variable is contributing to an explanation of y). However, in the multilevel context we can also examine whether the variances e_{ij} and u_{0j} have changed and are significant, indicating whether there is still unexplained variance to be accounted for at either level. By fitting individual explanatory variables we would expect a reduction in e_{ij} – the variation between individuals. However, we might also find some reduction in u_{0j} (the school level variation) because the difference in schools (as represented by their intercepts) might also be attributable to the individual level variables in the schools such as the type of pupils in the schools, that is, school intake.

At this step interaction terms between individual level variables might also be added to the model and tested.

Of course, the choice of level 1 variables should be guided by theory or prior knowledge. As in all statistical modelling the development of the model should not be a solely mechanical process.

Step 3: Adding level 2 explanatory variables to the random intercepts model

Having explored the level 1 explanatory variables, and finding that the model is not adequate as there is still variance at level 2 to be explained (u_{0j} is still high and significant) the next natural step is to identify what characteristics of schools (level 2 explanatory variables, such as type, class size, etc.) explains the variation between schools. Most texts (including Hox, op. cit.) denote level 2 explanatory variables by z rather than x, a convention followed here. This is the only departure from the MLwiN manual which continues to represent level 2 variables by x – the distinction is drawn by the suffixes, ij for level 1 variables and j for level 2 variables. (When it comes to output from the MLwiN package, variable names are used and not x or z.) The model now becomes:

$$y_{ij} = b_0 + b_1 x_{1ij} + b_2 z_{2j} + u_{0j} + e_{ij} \qquad (9.7)$$

The practice of numbering the explanatory variables sequentially is continued, regardless of whether they are level 1 or level 2 variables. Of course, before getting to this step we may have included more xs and possibly interactions between some of the xs, but here just one x is included to indicate that the xs have been considered and at least one has been found to be important.

Note that the zs only have suffix j because they are level 2 variables that only vary between schools and not between individuals within each school. At this step we can include different zs to explore whether it is the type of school or the size of the school, or both, that is important. Interaction terms between any of the zs can be added if that is thought to be appropriate.

As before, the contribution of the level 2 variables z can be assessed by testing the change in –2loglikelihood and by testing the significance of their coefficients b. If any of the level 2 variables are important in explaining y, their inclusion will reduce the variation between schools, that is, u_{0j}. However, the zs will not affect the level 1 variation, e_{ij}.

Step 4: Random slopes model or random coefficients model

In the random intercepts model considered so far it has been assumed that the coefficients of the xs are constant across schools. However, it may be the case that the coefficients vary from school to school because the schools may also influence the effect of x on y. For example, if x is IQ we may find that more academically able pupils do even better in some schools than equally able pupils in other schools. Let us return to the model at the beginning of step 3 and add the suffix j to b_1.

$$y_{ij} = b_0 + b_{1j} x_{1ij} + b_2 z_{2j} + u_{0j} + e_{ij} \qquad (9.8)$$

This signifies that the coefficient, or slope, of x_{1ij} is different for each school. Again if we assume a random sample we can postulate that there is a mean slope b_1 and that the slopes for each school vary around the mean slope. We can represent this model diagrammatically. The average slope in Figure 9.3 is indicated by the thick line and the school slopes vary around this mean slope.

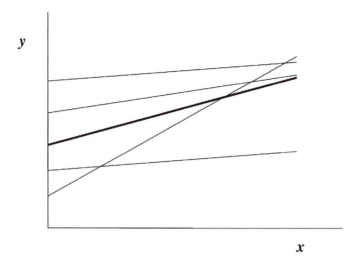

Figure 9.3 Random slopes or random coefficients model.

In terms of our model (as in the case for the intercepts) we can represent b_{1j} as a constant b_1 and a variation around it, or:

$$b_{1j} = b_1 + u_{1j} \qquad (9.9)$$

The suffix 1 has been included to indicate that u_{1j} is the variation associated with b_1.

Adding this to the model we get:

$$y_{ij} = b_0 + b_1 x_{1ij} + u_{0j} + u_{1j} + e_{ij} \qquad (9.10)$$

The fixed part of the model is $b_0 + b_1 x_{1ij}$ and we now have three random terms, u_{0j} (for the variation in the intercepts), u_{1j} (for the variation in the slopes) and e_{ij} (the variation between pupils at level 1).

Because the slopes (or coefficients) are considered to vary this model is known as the *random slopes model* or the *random coefficients model*.

With random slopes models it is also informative to consider the covariance (or correlation) between the intercepts and the slopes, that is, $\text{cov}(u_{0j}, u_{1j})$. A positive covariance indicates that schools that have higher intercepts tend to have steeper slopes and a negative covariance indicates that schools with higher intercepts tend to have less steep slopes.

Note that in this model the intercepts, as before, have also been postulated to vary as well as the slopes. It is possible to consider a random slopes model in which only the slopes vary but not the intercepts. However, given our approach to incrementally increasing the complexity of our model, it is more common to add random slopes to random intercepts than to consider random slopes in isolation.

We can compare this model with other models by comparing the change in –2loglikelihood. But we can also assess whether including random slopes is necessary by considering the significance of u_{1j}.

Note that only the slopes of the level 1 variables, x, are considered to vary, not the slopes of the level 2 variables, z.

Step 5: Including cross-level interactions

The final step is to include interactions between level 1 and level 2 explanatory variables, that is, interactions between an x and a z variable – known as *cross-level interactions*. This model can become very complex and is often difficult to interpret. It also has implications for the way variables are measured, and interpretation is often aided by standardising the variables.

9.4 Statistical software

SPSS can fit a limited range of multilevel models, but only those where the response variable is continuous, that is, a multilevel multiple regression model. Stata has a user-written routine, called gllamm, which can be downloaded from the Stata website. However, my preference is to use MLwiN, software specifically developed to fit multilevel models.

MLwiN was developed in part through sponsorship from the ESRC and is freely available to UK-based academics. There is a charge for other users. The software is well supported by the Centre for Multilevel Modelling, www.cmm.bristol.ac.uk. The website contains details about obtaining the software, training courses and even has video/PowerPoint presentations that can be viewed online. From the website a link takes the user to the TRAMSS (Teaching Resources and Materials for Social Scientists) website where one can download MLwiN and the manual. (Alternatively the researcher could go straight to the TRAMMS website, http://tramss.data-archive.ac.uk.) From the TRAMMS website it is possible for anyone (not just UK-based academics) to download a version of the software, a tutorial dataset and the manual. But the version obtainable from TRAMMS can only be used with the tutorial dataset, it is not possible to analyse one's own data with this version. Nevertheless, it is a very good starting point for learning the software.

As with all new software a little initial investment of time is required to become familiar with it. But the investment is worthwhile. MLwiN fits a wide range of multilevel models, including those where the response variable is continuous or categorical (binary, multinomial, or ordinal). It fits models to nested, repeated measures, cross-classified and multiple membership data structures.

There are a variety of ways of getting data into MLwiN. As with other software, data can be keyed directly and saved but this is not practical with very large files. Data can be 'cut and pasted' into the data editor, although I have found that it is often best to do this in stages, cutting and pasting a subset of the columns (variables) at a time. MLwiN can also read ASCII files. The latest version of MLwiN (version 2.10) can read SPSS files directly. A Stata user-written routine, Stata2mlwin (available from the Stata website), will output a Stata file as an MLwiN file which can then be read by MLwiN.

Once the data is in, it is possible within MLwiN to edit data and obtain basic descriptive statistics. The tutorial at the TRAMMS website describes many of these features so they are not presented in any detail here.

9.5 Fitting models in MLwiN to employment data

Fitting models is straightforward and elegant in MLwiN. The researcher is given a basic model which is then developed by defining the variables and their levels. Variables can be added or deleted in order to specify alternative models. This will be demonstrated in the example that follows but two issues need to be addressed beforehand.

MLwiN requires the data to be sorted in accordance with its nested multilevel structure, that is, first by the highest level, then its next highest level and so on. (The requirements for non-nested, cross-classified data are not considered here.) So with data at two levels, the data needs to be sorted by the level 2 identifier – the level 1 data does not need to be sorted. Anticipating the necessity to structure data, MLwiN has facilities to sort data in the appropriate order.

Second, to fit a multilevel model, MLwiN needs to consider all the terms on the right-hand side of the equations (Equation (9.6), Equation (9.7) and Equation (9.10)) as variables. The trick here is to create a variable x_0 which takes the value 1 for all level 1 subjects (pupils). Although conceived as a variable it is in effect a constant (and is called *cons* in the MLwiN tutorial). Because it takes the value of 1 for every subject, the variable x_0 can be multiplied to any component of the model without changing the value of that component. Full details showing how x_0 is utilised by MLwiN are given in the manual but the point to note here is that an MLwiN data file will need to include a variable with a value of 1 for all subjects that can be declared as x_0. (In anticipation of the requirement, MLwiN has a facility to easily create such a 'variable'.)

The example chosen for the MLwiN tutorial at the TRAMSS website has a continuous response variable and the tutee fits multilevel multiple regression models. However, equally common in social research are situations where the response variable is categorical, often binary, necessitating a multilevel logistic regression. In order to illustrate MLwiN (and to complement the regression model in the tutorial), a multilevel logistic regression model is fitted in the example that follows.

The question to be investigated in this example is to what extent the area in which a person lives affects his or her prospects of employment, after taking account of individual characteristics that affect a person's employability. The dataset combined individual data from the 2003/04 Labour Force Survey and area level data from the 2004 English Indices of Multiple Deprivation. (A more detailed description of the various Indices of Deprivation can be found in section 10.2.) Individuals aged 60 or over had been omitted as many are retired and not seeking employment. The original file included about 160,000 individuals between the ages of 16 and 59 residing in approximately 8000 English local area wards. A ward is the spatial unit used to elect local government councillors. They vary in size but the average number of people in a ward is 5500. Due to the LFS sampling design, the number of individuals in a ward varied between wards; some wards had only one individual sampled whereas others had several hundred.

The original data file is extremely large and a subset was selected for the example here. A sampling strategy was adopted to reduce the number of individuals but to include a large number of wards while avoiding wards with very few individuals. Initially all wards were selected that had between 40 and 45 (inclusive) individuals. This resulted in a subset of 262 wards which met this criterion. Subsequently, individuals aged 16 but less than 25 were omitted in order to exclude the majority who were in education or training. This procedure resulted in a sample of 9,106 individuals, which, together with the 262 wards, was felt to be a good representative sample and adequate for demonstrating multilevel modelling.

The variable of interest, the response variable y, was whether or not a person was employed. Being employed was coded 0 and not employed was coded 1. (Any mature student aged 25 or over in the dataset was coded 0 as they were considered to be economically active.)

For each individual, information was available on their age, gender, and ethnicity, together with other characteristics which might affect their employability such as educational qualifications, socio-economic status, their household composition (in particular whether they were lone parents) and whether they experienced any disability. At the area level, the index of multiple deprivation and its component domains of deprivation were available for each ward together with the proportion of the ward who were aged over 50 and the proportion of the ward who were non-white.

Thus the data is at two levels, level 1 being individuals and level 2 wards.

Step 1: Variance components model

To begin fitting a model in MLwiN the user clicks on the toolbar, Model → Equations which brings up the following screen.

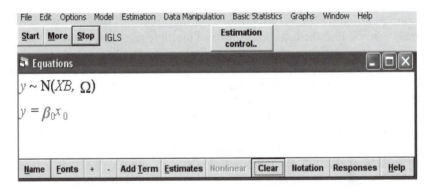

Figure 9.4 Initial MLwiN model screen.

The first line is somewhat different to what we have seen so far and may seem off-putting at first sight, but it defines the model to be fitted by using the components and terminology of the generalised linear model. At this point the reader may wish to consult Appendix 1 for a brief explanation of the generalised linear model in order to understand the representation of the models in MLwiN. The first line specifies the distributional assumptions and the default is N designating a normal distribution which leads to fitting a multiple regression model (suitable when y is a continuous variable). XB is matrix algebra notation stating that there are to be one or more explanatory variables included in the model, each with an associated coefficient, b (the fixed component of the model – see section 1.3 and Appendix 1). Ω (omega) denotes a number of random components to the model.

However, in this example our response variable is binary and we wish to fit a logistic regression. By clicking on N, options for alternative models are presented and Binomial was checked (binomial being the distribution for our binary data). The logit link function was selected to specify fitting a logistic regression (see Appendix 1).

The second line presents the basic variance components model; the only variables included are y and x_0, both of which are shown in red to indicate that they have to be defined. By clicking on y the researcher is invited to specify the response variable, the number of levels and the variables indicating each level. Here y was defined to be the variable *employb*, 2 levels were specified, level 2 being the variable *stwardco*, (standard ward code) and level 1 being the variable *level1* (a unique identifier for each individual). Following these actions the Equations screen changed to:

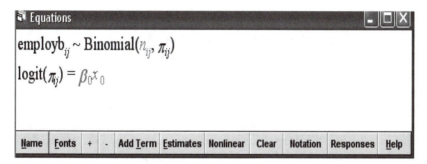

Figure 9.5 MLwiN screen of logistic model.

Binomial is now shown in Figure 9.5 indicating a logistic regression model, but n_{ij} has still to be specified. n_{ij} is the denominator and, in this case, is 1 for each individual – for each '1' individual he/she is either employed (0) or not employed (1). A column of 1s is required and is easily created by clicking Data Manipulation on the toolbar then Generate vector. This 'variable' (which is similar in conception to x_0 – also a column of 1s, but created for a different purpose) has been named *denom*. We also need to specify x_0 and this is done by clicking on it and selecting *cons* (a column of 1s created previously), and checking the '*j*' box to indicate level 2.

Having specified the variables, the researcher clicks Estimates on the bottom toolbar. The parameters to be estimated are shown in blue. By clicking Start on the top toolbar the parameters turn green. Click Estimates again and the estimated values are shown in green as in the Figure 9.6 overleaf.

It can be seen that the variance at level 2, $[u_{0j}]$ is .312, and its standard error (s.e. – given in the brackets) is .042. For models with categorical response variables a value of –2loglikelihood is not given (unlike models with continuous response variables). However, an alternative Wald test can be requested – see manual for details. The Wald test applied here gave a value of 55.2, which, as a chi-squared test with one degree of freedom, is very highly significant (p < .001); the conclusion being that there are significant differences between wards. (Note that a variance cannot be less than 0, i.e. negative, so the test of significance is a one-tailed test assessing whether the variance is greater than 0. See section 3.4 for a discussion of significance tests and a distinction between one and two-tailed tests.)

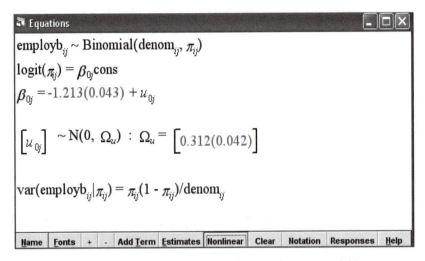

Figure 9.6 MLwiN output, logistic model without explanatory variables.

Note, however, that there is no estimate for the level 1 variance, e_{ij}. This is because a logistic regression model is being fitted and the variance depends on the mean which changes according to the values of the explanatory variables. Because no estimate of e_{ij} is available, the proportion of variance at each level cannot be definitively estimated. Various alternatives have been proposed to provide some indication of the proportion of variance at each level and hence an approximation to the intra-class correlation. The simplest is to assume a threshold (or maximum) value for e_{ij} of 3.29. (See the MLwiN manual for the rationale for this threshold value and for alternative approaches.)

Adopting the threshold value, the intra-class correlation is:

$$\rho = \frac{.312}{(3.29 + .312)} = .087$$

Thus, 8.7% of the variance is at level 2 and 91.3% of the variance is at the individual level, level 1. This is not an uncommon finding as it is often the case that most of the variance is at the individual level. Of importance is that the level 2 variance is significant, vindicating the need for multilevel modelling.

Step 2: Adding level 1 explanatory variables

By clicking on the Add Term button, explanatory variables can be readily included in the model (and deleted by clicking on the variable and clicking delete term). All the level 1 variables were considered and six were found to be related to whether a person was not employed. The six variables were: being a female, of low education, being non-white, disabled, a lone parent and age over 50. An interaction between low education (*lowed*) and *non-white* was also found to be important. The model is displayed in Figure 9.7 below:

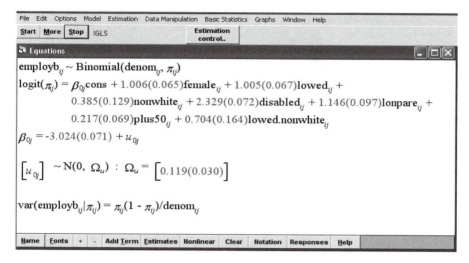

Figure 9.7 MLwiN output, logistic model with level 1 explanatory variables.

Because a logistic regression is fitted, the coefficients (the *b*s) are on the log scale. The odds need to be calculated separately as MLwiN does not do this for you. The odds are given for the final model but until then, log odds are presented. (However, recall from section 3.2 that positive coefficients on the log scale are equivalent to odds greater than 1 and negative coefficients are equivalent to odds less than 1.) All the coefficients in the model are positive and all the variables are coded 0 and 1, 1 being female, low education, non-white, disabled, lone parent and over 50. As not being employed is coded 1, having any of the characteristics of the explanatory variables increases the odds of not being employed. The interaction term is also positive, indicating that being both of low education and non-white further increases the odds of not being employed.

(On a technical note, which need not overly concern us here, and following the recommendation of the manual, estimates of the coefficients were derived using the 2nd order PQL estimation procedure.)

It can be seen that including explanatory variables in this model has considerably reduced the level 2 variance, u_{0j}, which has gone down from .312 to .119. Given that only level 1 (individual level) variables have been fitted, this reduction indicates that much of the difference between wards is attributable to the employability of their residents. However, notwithstanding the reduction, the level 2 variance is still significant, suggesting that level 2 explanatory variables need to be considered.

Step 3: Adding level 2 explanatory variables

The separate indices of deprivation (or domains – see section 10.2) are highly inter-correlated and only the index of multiple deprivation (*zimdscors*) was included in the model. It can be seen from Figure 9.8 below that it was positively and significantly related to not being employed. This variable was standardised so the interpretation of the coefficient is such that a change of one standard deviation in *zimdscors* increases the log odds of not being employed by .224.

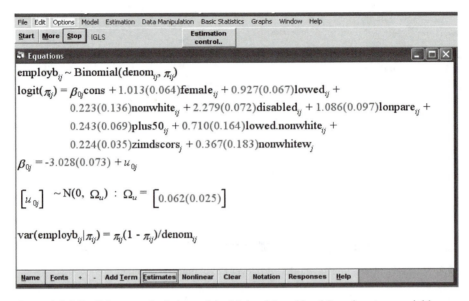

Figure 9.8 MLwiN output, logistic model with level 1 and level 2 explanatory variables.

Of the other two level 2 variables available, the ethnic composition of the ward (the proportion who were non-white), was significantly related to not being employed, but the proportion over 50 was not. The model thus indicates that over and above individual characteristics, those living in socially deprived areas and areas in which a higher proportion of the residents are non-white are more likely not to be employed.

Importantly, the level 2 variance, u_{0j}, has reduced further, from .119 to .062 but is still significant.

Step 4: Random slopes or coefficients

The next step was to allow the coefficients of the explanatory variables to vary. However, none of the random slopes were found to be significant and the model was not improved by this step.

Step 5: Adding cross-level interactions

The final step was to consider any cross-level interactions, that is, interactions between level 1 and level 2 variables. One such interaction was found to be significant, an interaction between an individual being of low education and living in a social deprived area. The final model is shown in Figure 9.10.

The Wald test for this model was 5.4, which as chi-square with 1 df is still significant, but now only at the 5% level not the 1% level. The above model was accepted as the final model and is set out in Table 9.1 where the odds, as well as the log odds are presented.

From the last column of the table it can be seen that all odds are greater than one, which means that having any of the characteristics increases the odds of not being employed. Having a disability has the greatest effect on not being employed, increasing the odds by nearly 10 compared with those with no disability. Being female or having low education or being a lone parent more than double the odds of not being

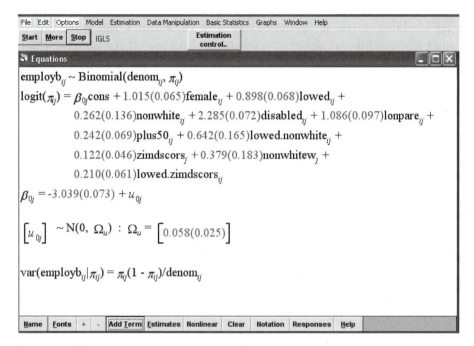

Figure 9.10 MLwiN output, logistic model adding cross-level interaction terms.

Table 9.1 Final model with the odds of being non-employed

Explanatory variable	b	Exp(b) odds
Level 1 explanatory variables		
Female	1.015	2.76
Low education (*lowed*)	.898	2.45
Non-white (*nonwhite*)	.262	1.30
Disabled (*disabled*)	2.285	9.83
Lone parent (*lonepare*)	1.086	2.96
Over 50 (*plus50*)	.242	1.27
Level 1 interactions		
Lowed*nonwhite	.642	1.90
Level 2 explanatory variables		
Standardised index of multiple deprivation (*zimdscors*)	.122	1.13
Proportion non-white in ward (*nonwhitew*)	.379	1.46
Cross-level interactions		
Lowed*zimdscors	.210	1.23

employed. Having low education *and* being non-white further increases the odds of not being employed. Living in deprived areas or in areas with a high proportion of non-whites adversely affects employment, and more so if a person in a deprived area is also of low education.

Further reading

An accessible introduction to multilevel modelling is provided by Plewis (1998).

A good clear, and more detailed, text on multilevel modelling is Hox (2002). Hox explains the methodology and covers a wide range of applications but does not demonstrate how to fit multilevel models using any particular computer software. This is intentional as his aim is to explain general principles and not be tied to one specific computer software.

Further instruction on using MLwiN can be found at the Centre for Multilevel Modelling website www.cmm.bristol.ac.uk and the TRAMSS website http://tramss.data-archive.ac.uk. Only version 1 of MLwiN (and the manual pertaining to this earlier version) is at the TRAMSS website, but version 1 is sufficient to explain the methodology and most of the features of the software. Downloading the software and working through the tutorial, or attending an MLwiN course, are the best ways of becoming familiar with the software.

10 Latent variables and factor analysis

10.1 Introduction

Many concepts or constructs exist in social science, which cannot be measured directly. Consider, for example, alienation, anomie, social deprivation, intelligence, quality of life, fear of crime, business confidence, cost of living: in every case we understand what the term conveys but no natural measurement scale exists. Such variables are called *latent variables*. The list of latent variables in social science seems limitless, so much so that social science could be defined as the study of latent variables. In order to undertake research and analysis on these concepts a measurement scale has to be constructed from *manifest variables*, that is, from variables that provide some indication of the underlying latent variable but which can themselves be measured. In the case of intelligence, individuals can be given tests to gauge their ability at certain tasks or knowledge of particular subjects. In the case of social deprivation, data on the manifestations or indicators of social deprivation (poor housing, high unemployment, etc.) can be pooled to form an index.

In each case we theorise that there is a single individual concept, or a small number of concepts, or latent variables, which lead to many different manifestations. An intelligent person is likely to do well on a battery of different tests. Social deprivation manifests itself in many different but related ways. What the social scientist is attempting to do is distil the underlying social concept(s) from its manifestations. How many dimensions a particular concept has, and how they should be represented, is often at issue. Intelligence, for example, is thought not to be a simple homogeneous concept but multidimensional – proposed dimensions include verbal, numerical and spatial intelligence.

Priority for creating latent variables

On occasions the prime interest may be to produce an agreed measure which will enable changes to be tracked over time. The retail price index is an example here and provides a guide to how the cost of living or inflation is changing from one period to another. In some situations the purpose may be to provide a measure of discrimination between areas. Such a measure is the multiple index of deprivation which ranks local areas of the country from the least to the most deprived. The index thereby informs government decisions on the allocation of resources between areas or identifies areas to be the target of specific interventions.

On other occasions our interest may be more theoretical in exploring the dimensions of a particular concept. The exploration of the theoretical underpinnings of intelligence and fear of crime are examples here.

At other times our interest may be more pragmatic. In a research project involving a survey, a great many questions might be asked tapping respondents' beliefs or attitudes on a particular subject. What is desired is a summary measure which can be incorporated in subsequent analyses. Examples here include the two variables 'left–right scale' and 'libertarian–authoritarian scale'. Both have been derived from responses to a number of specific questions in the British Social Attitudes Survey, although the scales have been used in other surveys, notably the British Election Survey (which was the subject of analysis in section 6.6). Including the responses to all the questions (the manifest variables) would over-complicate a model, resulting in a large number of explanatory variables, and would lead to multicollinearity as the manifest variables are usually highly inter-correlated with each other (see section 3.6).

Of course, the various priorities described above are not mutually exclusive. Often we wish to construct latent variables for several reasons.

10.2 How are latent variables constructed?

Many believe that latent variables are only constructed by factor analysis, and for them latent variables and factor analysis become synonymous. That is not so; while factor analysis has no other purpose than to construct latent variables, there are other and often more appropriate methods for constructing latent variables than factor analysis.

Proxy variables

One could simply choose one of the manifest variables, which is felt to be most representative, to act as a surrogate or proxy for the underlying latent concept. An example here is the number of previous offences committed by an offender, which has been found to be an adequate indicator of previous criminal history in much criminological research.

Obviously 'putting all one's eggs in one basket' has potential problems, especially if the concept has more than one dimension.

Indices

Rather than use one variable we could construct an index from several variables. The simplest method would be to select a range of what were thought to be appropriate manifest variables, add them up and produce a score or an average value. The left–right scale and the libertarian–authoritarian scale are constructed in this way. In the case of the left–right scale, respondents are asked five questions about whether the government should redistribute wealth and whether ordinary people get their fair share of the nation's wealth, whether big business or management benefit at the expense of workers and whether there is one law for the rich and one for the poor. Each question has a five-point scale ranging from 'agree strongly' to 'disagree strongly' and each respondent's answers to the five questions are added and divided by five. Similarly the libertarian–authoritarian scale is constructed from six questions framed to elicit respondents' views on the law, sentencing, discipline, respect and censorship. The same five-point scale forms the responses to the questions which are added together and divided by six.

With the left–right scale and the libertarian–authoritarian scale all individual questions are treated equally. However, each component of an index could be weighted differently, but then a supplementary issue arises: what weight should be given to each variable?

The Retail Price Index (RPI) is calculated by taking a sample of goods and services, which the typical household buys, and items are weighted according to the amount spent on them. Items that are the most important in the spending patterns of the typical household are given a higher weight in the RPI. So, for example food is given a weight of 13% in the overall index, whereas clothes contribute 5.6% of the RPI, motoring 12.8%, alcohol 8.0% and so on.

The three examples given so far can be summed (with or without weights) and averaged because the elements, or variables, are measured on the same metric scale – a five-point attitudinal scale in the case of the left–right and libertarian–authoritarian scales and pounds and pence in the case of the RPI. But another issue arises if manifest variables are themselves measured on different metric scales. Here the way forward is often to standardise the variables in some way, often by transforming them to normal (z) scores.

Factor analysis

Notwithstanding the remarks made earlier, factor analysis is a popular method for identifying and constructing latent variables and is considered in detail below.

As stated above, the Index of Multiple Deprivation is a very important measure as it influences many government decisions, but it is also interesting from a methodological perspective as its construction draws on all the issues raised above. The Index of Multiple Deprivation is a composite of seven latent variable indices, called domains (1 Income, 2 Employment, 3 Health and Disability, 4 Barriers to Housing, 5 Education, Skills and Training, 6 Crime and 7 Living Environment). Each domain is constructed from a selection of manifest variables (for example, the proportion of people claiming benefits, burglary rates etc.). Some domains are simply a summation of their constituent variables (such as Income and Employment) whereas others are constructed using factor analysis (such as Health and Disability and Education, Skills and Training). Each domain is standardised and then weighted prior to being amalgamated to form the Index of Multiple Deprivation. Income and Employment both contribute 22.5% towards the Index of Multiple Deprivation. Health and Education each contribute 13.5% whereas Housing, Crime and the Living Environment each have a weight of 9.3%. (Further details can be found at the government website, www.communities.gov.uk)

10.3 Factor analysis

Factor analysis assumes a linear relation exists between the factors and the manifest variables and postulates a linear model of the form:

$$F_1 = b_{11}x_1 + b_{12}x_2 + b_{13}x_3 + \ldots + b_{1n}x_n \tag{10.1}$$

$$F_2 = b_{21}x_1 + b_{22}x_2 + b_{23}x_3 + \ldots + b_{2n}x_n \tag{10.2}$$

.

.

$$F_n = b_{n1}x_1 + b_{n2}x_2 + b_{n3}x_3 + \ldots + b_{nn}x_n \tag{10.n}$$

Potentially we can have as many factors as there are manifest variables, although our assumption is that only a small number of factors are in any way meaningful or important.

The equations are in the same form as the linear models that we have met in previous chapters. The only difference is that y (the dependent or response variable) is the unmeasured factor F.

Note that there is no constant b_0. This is because the xs have been standardised to avoid the problems that would arise if the xs were measured on different scales. (It is possible to undertake factor analysis on unstandardised variables – and SPSS makes provision for this – but it is the convention to work with standardised variables, which are created automatically by SPSS.)

In factor analysis terminology, the coefficients, b, in the above equations are called factor loadings (although SPSS does not use this term). Because the manifest variables are standardised, the factor loadings can be interpreted as the correlation between the factor and the manifest variable. Like all correlation coefficients their value ranges from -1 to $+1$, with 0 indicating no correlation (or no relationship) between the two. There is no definition of what constitutes a high or low factor loading, but a convention often adopted is that loadings greater than $+0.3$ (or less than -0.3) are considered high whereas loadings in the range -0.3 to $+0.3$ are viewed as low.

For every subject or case in our survey or database we have actual values on each manifest variable (the xs) but we do not have measures of the Fs (the dependent variables) so we cannot fit a regression or similar model, as we would have done previously. However, by applying a few rules that impose certain restrictions, we can transform the relationships between the variables to provide an initial solution. The initial solution is often referred to as the *method of extraction*, as it is the means of getting a set of factors from the data. The transformation (and hence the method of extraction) that is invariably applied is known as Principal Components Analysis (PCA).

Principal components analysis (PCA)

PCA is simply a transformation of the data and thus estimates as many components as there are manifest variables. However, to obtain a PCA solution certain restrictions must be imposed.

First, the sum of squared factor loadings is constrained to be 1. That is, for the first equation

$$(b_{11}^2 + b_{12}^2 + b_{13}^2 + \ldots + b_{1n}^2) = 1$$

Second, unlike the manifest variables, which are invariably highly correlated, the components (factors) are set to be uncorrelated (the correlation coefficient between the components is 0). Uncorrelated components (factors) are also referred to in factor analysis terminology as being orthogonal (this is because they can be presented graphically as being at right angles to each other).

Third, the first component is set to account for the maximum amount of the variance possible. The second component accounts for the largest amount of the variance possible remaining after the first component has been fitted, the third component accounts for the largest amount of variance left after the first and second component has been fitted, and so on.

The attraction of PCA is thus apparent. Having started with a large number of highly inter-correlated variables, PCA transforms the data to a set of uncorrelated components that are arranged in descending order of importance. This means that if the first few components between them explain a large amount of the variation, we can, without much loss of information, replace our more extensive set of manifest variables with a few components. But what is meant by a 'large amount of the variation' and 'a few components'? Before we consider these issues, a further word on the distinction between PCA and factor analysis is required.

PCA is simply a transformation of the data just in the same way that miles can be transformed into kilometres or Fahrenheit into Centigrade. Given a set of data and a set of variables, there can only be one unique PCA solution. PCA is not based on any assumptions about the causative relationship between components and manifest variables or on the interpretation of the components. It is not proposing that the components are themselves latent variables. PCA is neutral on all these issues, it merely rearranges the data subject to the three constraints listed above. However, as PCA is now a standard procedure for undertaking the first step in factor analysis it is common to see the terms used interchangeably or to see the expression 'principal component factor analysis'.

Eigenvalue

The variance of a factor (or component) is known as its eigenvalue, and thus can be used to assess the importance of any factor (or component). If (as is invariably the case) the manifest variables are standardised, the variance of each equals 1 (because that is what standardisation does, it transforms a variable such that its mean = 0 and variance = 1). If we have n manifest variables in our analysis, in standardised form the sum of their variances will be n (as each contributes 1). PCA transforms the data such that the total variance of the components, n, will be redistributed unevenly between the components. The first will have the greatest eigenvalue, the second the next highest, continuing to the nth which will have the lowest eigenvalue. If a factor has an eigenvalue greater than 1 it can be said to have accounted for more of the variance than an individual variable and can thus be thought of as providing a better summary of the data than an individual variable. One rule of thumb is thus to retain in the final factor solution all factors with eigenvalues greater than 1.

If the eigenvalue is divided by n, the total variance (but also the number of manifest variables), the result is the proportion of variance explained by that factor.

Communalities

It was stated above that the factor loading (the b) is the correlation between the manifest variable and the factor. The square of the correlation is the proportion of variance in the manifest variable that can be explained by the factor. If we square and sum all the factor loadings for a manifest variable across the factor equations we have a total known as the communality as it indicates how much of the variance in the manifest variable is accounted for by the combination of the factors. In our initial PCA solution, where we have as many components as manifest variables and all manifest variables appear in every factor equation, the sum of the squares of the factor loadings for any variable will be 1. However, if we drop components from our solution, and retain only those with eigenvalues greater than 1, our communalities will be less than 1 and provide an indication of how much each manifest variable contributes to our reduced solution.

10.4 Example: Fear of crime

Before describing other aspects of factor analysis it is best to consolidate what has been described already by way of an example.

The concept of fear of crime has received much attention in criminology and a range of questions addressing this underlying latent variable are routinely included in the British Crime Survey. That data is analysed here in order to illustrate factor analysis and to demonstrate how to undertake and interpret factor analysis in SPSS.

Respondents to the British Crime Survey 2000 were asked the following nine questions:

Qu1 How safe do you feel in your home alone at night?

Qu2 How safe do you feel while walking alone after dark?

Qu3 How worried are you about having your home broken into and having something stolen?

Qu4 How worried are you about being mugged and robbed?

Qu5 How worried are you about having your car stolen?

Qu6 How worried are you about having things stolen from your car?

Qu7 How worried are you about being raped?

Qu8 How worried are you about being physically attacked by strangers?

Qu9 How worried are you about being physically attacked because of your skin colour, ethnic origin or religion?

Respondents were asked to rate their feelings on a four-point scale. For the first two questions, the options were:

very safe, fairly safe, a bit unsafe, very unsafe

For questions 3 to 9, the options were:

very worried, fairly worried, not very worried, not at all worried

Note that if respondents were fearful of crime their responses would be to the right-hand end of the scale on the first two questions, but towards the left-hand end of the scale on the remaining seven questions. Before embarking on factor analysis we could recode the first two manifest variables so that the scales of all nine 'run' in the same direction. We have chosen not to do that here as the original scales serve as a reminder that when interpreting results (of any analysis) we must have in mind the underlying metric.

Note that responses to all the questions are not continuous variables but ordered variables measured on a Likert scale. In the past (and in many cases in the present) researchers have analysed this kind of attitudinal data as if it were a representation of an underlying interval scale and thus an approximation of a continuous variable. Previously, researchers had little option but to proceed as if the data were continuous, but now other latent variable models are available for categorical data. These models are briefly reviewed at the end of this chapter, but as the purpose here is to illustrate factor analysis as available in SPSS and Stata, we will assume that the variables are continuous variables.

Responses to all the questions are highly correlated as revealed in the correlation matrix presented in Table 10.1.

All the correlation coefficients in Table 10.1 are significant and in the same direction (once we recall that the scale for the first two questions runs in the opposite direction from the other seven). Thus respondents who felt worried or unsafe expressed their anxieties similarly when answering all nine questions.

Let us consider two related issues. First, what are the dimensions of fear of crime? Is there a single underlying construct or is fear of crime more complex and multi-dimensional? We may be interested in this issue in order to reflect on the theory of fear of crime. Second, can we reduce this set of nine highly inter-related manifest variables to a smaller number of uncorrelated summary indices? Our interest here may be more pragmatic. A simple measure of fear may be required as an explanatory variable to be incorporated into models examining other aspects of crime.

It should be noted that one option in answering the nine questions was 'not applicable' and nearly 5000 respondents who did not own a car did not answer questions 5 and 6 ascertaining their concerns about car crime. In addition, some other respondents were coded not applicable on question 7 (worry about rape) and question 9 (worry about being attacked because of their skin colour, ethnic origin or religion). Not applicable was declared a missing value and along with a small number who refused to answer any one of the nine questions were omitted from the analysis. This reduced

Table 10.1 Correlation coefficients between the responses to the nine fear-of-crime questions

	Qu1	Qu2	Qu3	Qu4	Qu5	Qu6	Qu7	Qu8	Qu9
Qu1	1								
Qu2	.44	1							
Qu3	−.26	−.33	1						
Qu4	−.42	−.32	.56	1					
Qu5	−.23	−.20	.48	.44	1				
Qu6	−.17	−.17	.42	.37	.72	1			
Qu7	−.35	−.28	.42	.61	.31	.25	1		
Qu8	−.39	−.32	.50	.71	.40	.35	.72	1	
Qu9	−.20	−.19	.35	.46	.29	.26	.50	.54	1

Note: All correlation coefficients are significant at the 1% level.

the sample from 19,411 to 12,159. The principal purpose here is to explain factor analysis and the analysis was carried out on the reduced sample. However, had our purpose been to explore more thoroughly the substantive issue of fear and worry, consideration would need to be given to the implications of dropping nearly 40% of the sample. People who do not own a car may well be a distinctive group with other characteristics (possibly age, or income) that might or might not predispose them to fear or worry. One approach would be to run alternative analyses including and excluding responses to car crime, rape and personal discriminatory attack and compare the results obtained.

To begin in SPSS we follow: Analyze → Data reduction → Factor, which brings up the dialogue box at Figure 10.1.

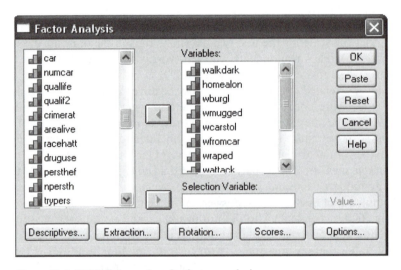

Figure 10.1 SPSS dialogue box for factor analysis.

The nine variables have been entered. Considering in turn each of the buttons at the bottom of the screen:

Descriptives: offers options to produce descriptive statistics and correlations between the manifest variables. Here we opt only to output the default 'initial solution'.

Extraction: offers alternative methods, 'Principal components' is the default (and is most commonly used – although the principal factor method is the default in Stata). A choice is offered between correlation matrix (the default) or covariance matrix. In effect, choosing the correlation matrix means that the solution will be based on standardised manifest variables whereas the covariance matrix means the solution will be based on unstandardised manifest variables. The correlation matrix is chosen here. In this box a choice is offered between extracting a specified number of factors or all factors with an eigenvalue above a certain value. The default is to extract factors with an eigenvalue above 1. Two graphic outputs are offered: 'unrotated factor solution' and 'scree plot'. A scree plot has been chosen and it will be discussed later.

Rotation: varimax has been chosen. Rotation will be discussed later.

Scores: enables factor scores to be calculated and stored on the dataset. We have chosen to save scores.

Options: provides alternative ways of handling missing data. Here we have accepted the default, 'listwise', of omitting cases where data is missing on any of the nine variables.

It can also be seen in the dialogue box that it is possible to undertake the analysis on a subset of the data (for example. men only or children etc.) by entering a Selection Variable. The analysis here is on the entire sample (except those cases where data is missing).

The output from this analysis is presented below. It is actually easier to explain the output in a different order to that produced by SPSS.

Total Variance Explained

Component	Initial Eigenvalues			Extraction Sums of Squared Loadings		
	Total	% of Variance	Cumulative %	Total	% of Variance	Cumulative %
1	4.204	46.711	46.711	4.204	46.711	46.711
2	1.266	14.067	60.778	1.266	14.067	60.778
3	1.010	11.228	72.006	1.010	11.228	72.006
4	.610	6.781	78.787			
5	.592	6.577	85.364			
6	.470	5.224	90.588			
7	.334	3.716	94.304			
8	.277	3.078	97.382			
9	.236	2.618	100.000			

Extraction Method: Principal Component Analysis.

Figure 10.2 SPSS output, PCA eigenvalues.

Because nine manifest variables were entered, nine principal components have been produced. However, only the first three have eigenvalues greater than 1, and as this was the criteria specified, only the first three components are developed further. Dividing the eigenvalue by the number of manifest variables gives the proportion of variance explained by the component (for example, for the first component, 4.204/9 = .46711). It can be seen that the first three components account for 46.7%, 14.1%, 11.2%, or together 72.0% of the variance. Put another way, we can say that 72% of the information contained in the nine original inter-related manifest variables can be summarised in the three uncorrelated components.

The scree plot, shown in Figure 10.3, graphically presents the eigenvalues for the components. (It takes its name from the image of loose scree falling down the side of a mountain.) The scree plot helps decide how many components (factors) should be selected. One criterion is to stop selecting factors at a break point or 'elbow'. The scree plot in this analysis suggests elbows occur after one and, to a lesser extent, three components (factors).

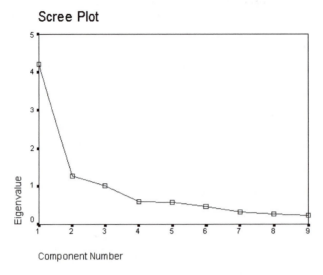

Figure 10.3 SPSS output, scree plot.

Having extracted three components the loadings for each are presented in the Component Matrix box below.

Component Matrix[a]

	Component		
	1	2	3
Feel safe in home alone at night	-.491	.293	.646
Feel safe while walking alone after dark	-.558	.372	.488
Worried about having home broken into and something stolen	.707	.179	-.055
Worried about being mugged and robbed	.828	-.100	.132
Worried about having the car stolen	.659	.613	-.117
Worried about having things stolen from the car	.589	.682	-.122
Worried about being raped	.759	-.310	.271
Worried about being physically attacked by strangers	.841	-.202	.229
Worried about being physically attacked because of skin colour, ethnic origin or religion	.634	-.148	.424

Extraction Method: Principal Component Analysis.

a. 3 components extracted.

Figure 10.4 SPSS output, component matrix.

The loadings are the *b*s of the equations (Equation (10.1), Equation (10.2) etc.) so for the first component (factor) the equation is:

$F_1 = -.491$(feel safe in home) $- .558$(feel safe walking) $+ .707$(worried home broken into) $+ .828$(worried mugged) $+ .659$(worried car stolen) $+ .589$ (worried items stolen from car) $+ .759$(worried being raped) $+ .841$(worried about attack) $+ .634$(worried racial attack)

Similarly, the equation for the second component (factor) F_2 is:

$F_2 = .293$(feel safe in home) $+ .372$(feel safe walking) $+ .179$(worried home broken into) *etc.*

Note that because the manifest variables have been standardised, the *b*s are correlation coefficients and have values between -1 and $+1$.

Note also that a respondent's score on Factor 1 can be calculated by substituting in the above equation their responses on each of the manifest variables – just as predicted scores can be calculated in regression models. When specifying the model in SPSS we opted to have factor scores calculated. Three factor scores were computed and these were added to the database as new variables *fac1_1*, *fac2_1*, and *fac3_1* (which of course can be renamed). All of the three variables can be considered as continuous variables and included as response or explanatory variables in subsequent analyses if required.

The next box presents communalities.

	Initial	Extraction
Feel safe in home alone at night	1.000	.744
Feel safe while walking alone after dark	1.000	.687
Worried about having home broken into and something stolen	1.000	.535
Worried about being mugged and robbed	1.000	.713
Worried about having the car stolen	1.000	.825
Worried about having things stolen from the car	1.000	.827
Worried about being raped	1.000	.746
Worried about being physically attacked by strangers	1.000	.800
Worried about being physically attacked because of skin colour, ethnic origin or religion	1.000	.604

Extraction Method: Principal Component Analysis.

Figure 10.5 SPSS output, communalities.

A communality is the sum of the squares of the loadings for a particular variable across each component. It can be seen that for the initial solution the communality is always 1.0. That is because the initial solution includes all nine components and the sum of squared loadings for any variable across nine components is constrained to be 1.0 (one of the three constraints of PCA mentioned at the outset). Informing us that the initial communalities are 1.0 is not very helpful, but perhaps serves as a reminder of the condition imposed and a check that the program worked successfully. The next column, headed Extraction is more important. It shows the contribution of the extracted components (in this case the first three) in explaining the variation in the manifest variable. The communality for a manifest variable is the sum of squared loadings on the three extracted components. Referring back to Figure 10.4 above, the communality for the first variable is:

$$\text{Communality (feel safe in home alone at night)} = -.491^2 + .293^2 + .646^2$$

$$= .241 + .086 + .417$$

$$= .744$$

which is the value given in Figure 10.5.

It can be seen from Figure 10.5 that all nine manifest variables are related to the combined components, the lowest value being .535 (Qu3: worried about having one's home broken into), the highest being .827 (Qu6: worried about having something stolen from one's car). Had any of the communalities been small this would have suggested dropping that variable(s) from the factor analysis.

10.5 Interpreting the factors and rotation

So far we have merely transformed the responses to the nine questions on fear of crime into a set of components. No attempt has been made to interpret them as latent variables. However, while PCA is invariably adopted to provide an initial solution for factor analysis, in many cases it is also taken to be the final solution and the components are interpreted as factors. For illustration, we attempt to do that here.

We might conclude from the analysis that fear of crime has three dimensions, as represented by the three important components. Looking at the factor loadings in the component matrix it appears that all the questions asking whether respondents are worried about crime are highly positively correlated with factor 1. The first two manifest variables (asking respondents whether they feel safe) are highly negatively correlated with factor 1, although, as pointed out above, the negative sign merely reflects the question wording. Of more importance is the fact that all correlations are quite high. We might conclude, therefore, that there is a general latent variable reflecting people's general level of fear of crime. This finding of a first general factor is not surprising (and not uncommon with attitudinal data) given the significant correlation between all the questions as indicated in Table 10.1.

Looking at the second factor (component), the high loadings are on the questions examining worry about car crime. Respondents are not worried about personal crimes (rape, mugging and physical attacks), all of which are negatively correlated. To a lesser extent respondents are worried about burglary and feel unsafe in their homes. More interestingly (and perhaps an anomaly given their lack of fear of personal crimes) respondents feel unsafe while walking alone after dark.

Loadings on the third factor (component) appear to be the mirror image of component 2. This component seems to indicate a fear of personal crimes but not of property crime.

Thus we might conclude that people have a general fear of crime. However, in addition, some may be more fearful of property, mainly car crime. These might be men and women in particular households or neighbourhoods, who use their cars extensively in the course of their work or in the course of their leisure activities. For others, women perhaps who live in particular neighbourhoods and do not have the same access to a car but rely more on public transport or walking, have additional fears of being physically attacked or sexually assaulted. Further exploration of the data or additional research might test these assumptions and hypotheses.

Alternatively, it could plausibly be argued that because the eigenvalues of the third factor in particular, but also the second, are not much greater than 1, fear of crime is a one-dimensional concept, best represented by the first factor.

Rotation

Having produced an initial solution from PCA and having extracted the components that meet the criteria (in our case those with eigenvalues greater than 1), factor analysis can go on to explore the data to see if further clarification and simplification can be obtained. It is common to find that most variables load highly on the first component, and that was indeed the case here. But factors would be more clearly interpretable if each variable tended to load highly on one factor but low on all other factors. In factor analysis, this further exploration is known as rotation. (The term stems from the graphical representation of factor analysis where the axes of the factors are rotated to form a new relationship to the manifest variables.)

The mathematics need not concern us but the principles do need to be understood. Recall that in order to obtain our initial solution from PCA three constraints were imposed. We shall retain the first, namely that the sum of squared factor loadings is 1. But if we relax one or both of the other two we can obtain other factor solutions.

Orthogonal rotation

Orthogonal rotation is obtained when the third constraint is relaxed, namely that the first component accounts for the maximum amount of the variance but that the second constraint remains intact, namely that the factors are uncorrelated. Of the three orthogonal rotation options in SPSS (varimax, quartimax and equamax) varimax is the most favoured and commonly used method and was selected for this analysis (it is the only orthogonal rotation option within Stata). The output produced is presented in Figure 10.6 overleaf.

Having extracted three components it is these that are rotated. Note that the three rotated factors account for the same proportion as before, 72.0%. However, it can be seen that the first rotated factor explains only 31.1% compared with the first component in the initial solution, which accounted for 46.7%. In the rotated solution the three factors are less divergent in the proportion of variance each explains, or looked at another way, their eigenvalues are closer in value.

Rotation Sums of Squared Loadings		
Total	% of Variance	Cumulative %
2.802	31.136	31.136
2.075	23.054	54.190
1.603	17.816	72.006

Figure 10.6 SPSS output, verimax rotation eigenvalues.

The component matrix showing the loadings from the varimax (orthogonal rotation) is shown in Figure 10.7.

Rotated Component Matrix[a]

	Component		
	1	2	3
Feel safe in home alone at night	-.098	-.128	.847
Feel safe while walking alone after dark	-.265	-.071	.782
Worried about having home broken into and something stolen	.431	.531	-.259
Worried about being mugged and robbed	.725	.330	-.279
Worried about having the car stolen	.208	.878	-.101
Worried about having things stolen from the car	.129	.899	-.047
Worried about being raped	.827	.094	-.230
Worried about being physically attacked by strangers	.826	.235	-.251
Worried about being physically attacked because of skin colour, ethnic origin or religion	.765	.137	.015

Extraction Method: Principal Component Analysis.
Rotation Method: Varimax with Kaiser Normalization.
a. Rotation converged in 5 iterations.

Figure 10.7 SPSS output, rotated component matrix.

The rotation has tended to load the manifest variables more clearly on one factor rather than another but I am not convinced it has simplified the interpretation. It now appears that we have lost the general factor, fear of crime. The loadings suggest that the first factor emphasises fear of violence, the second property crime, in particular car crime. To this extent they are now similar to the original second and third components. However, the third factor now seems to draw a distinction between feelings and worries, being heavily loaded on the first two variables but not the others.

Oblique rotation

Oblique rotation goes one step further by relaxing the second constraint – namely that the factors should remain uncorrelated. The advice generally given is that one should not pursue oblique rotation unless there is good evidence to suggest that the factors are (cor)related. Two options are available in SPSS, direct oblimin and promax. Direct oblimin is generally recommended as this places a constraint on the extent to which factors can be correlated (determined by the value of delta). Direct oblimin is the only oblique rotation method available in Stata. An oblique factor solution was not pursued here.

10.6 Exploratory and confirmatory factor analysis

Factor analysis has come in for a good deal of adverse criticism, perhaps more than any other statistical technique. Its critics claim that it is atheoretical and enables the researcher to try any number of solutions and select the one he or she finds most appealing. All factor analysis solutions are based on the correlation matrix, which may capitalise on chance variation in the data. Arbitrary rules are applied to determine the number of factors to be extracted and there are no formal significance tests to apply. The approach is thus heuristic and inductive, it is claimed.

These criticisms are well founded but similar criticism could be levelled against the application of other techniques. All analyses should be guided by theory or informed knowledge. No technique should be slavishly followed.

Nevertheless, these criticisms have had an effect. Nowadays a distinction is drawn between *exploratory factor analysis* and *confirmatory factor analysis*. What has been described so far is exploratory factor analysis. Confirmatory factor analysis places great emphasis on theoretically informed deductive analysis where the researcher specifies his or her hypothesis and tests that the analysis confirms or refutes that hypothesis. So, for example, the researcher would specify *a priori* the number of factors. Maximum likelihood estimation procedures have been developed, which permit tests of alternative models. Furthermore, standard errors of factors loadings can be estimated, which under standard assumptions can be used to test for significance. Unfortunately SPSS and Stata do not include the option to undertake confirmatory factor analysis or conduct formal tests. Specialist software is required, such as EQS, Lisrel or MPlus. This software also fits structural equation models, which are described in section 11.4.

10.7 Other latent variable models

Factor analysis is the oldest and best known method for creating latent variables. But the assumptions underlying factor analysis are that the latent variables and the manifest variables are continuous and normally distributed. However, analogous methods have been developed for situations where the latent variables and/or the manifest variables are categorical. They are set out in Table 10.2.

Table 10.2 Classification of latent variable methods

Latent variables	Manifest variables Continuous	Categorical
Continuous	Factor analysis	Latent trait analysis
Categorical	Latent profile analysis	Latent class analysis

It can be seen that latent trait analysis is appropriate where the latent variable is continuous but the manifest variables are categorical. (Latent trait analysis is also known as item response theory, IRT.) Conversely, latent profile analysis is appropriate when the latent variable is categorical but the manifest variables are continuous. Finally, latent class analysis is appropriate when both latent and manifest variables are categorical.

Neither SPSS nor Stata fit latent variable models other than factor analysis. If the researcher wishes to fit any of the other three models, the specialist software mentioned above (EQS, Lisrel or MPlus) is required.

Further reading

An accessible and easy to read book on latent variable models, including all those identified in Table 10.2, is Bartholomew *et al.* (2002).

11 Causal modelling: Simultaneous equation models

11.1 Introduction

This chapter describes models that are often referred to as 'causal models', although this term is somewhat misleading as many of the models already presented can be considered as providing evidence of 'causality' if theory dictates that the variables are not merely associated but are causally connected. Furthermore, models for longitudinal data analysis described in the next two chapters are also regarded as providing greater insights and understanding of underlying causal mechanisms and processes. Perhaps the models described in this chapter have attracted the term causal models because the researcher often sets out the relationships and causal connections diagrammatically. Another distinguishing feature of models described in this chapter is that the causal mechanisms considered often lead to a model entailing more than one equation which need to be considered jointly; hence the other term used to describe such models, simultaneous equation models.

Before describing the models, let us define causality. Causality evokes a notion of a sequence, or chain, of events occurring in some temporal order. Moser and Kalton (1993) state that for causality to exist three conditions must be satisfied:

1   There must be an association between the contributory variables.
2   The connection must show that the cause occurs before the effect.
3   The connection between the variables must not disappear when the influences of other variables are taken into account.

The first does not require any further comment. With regard to the second, the connection may be so closely related in time such that changes in cause and effect appear to occur instantaneously or simultaneously. Or, alternatively, limitations in the measuring instruments may lead to the appearance of cause and effect to change at the same time. The relationship between the variables must not be spurious and must persist once control variables are taken into account, by being included in the model for example. This is the essence of the third condition.

Simultaneous equation models can be divided into two groups: recursive and non-recursive. Each will be considered in turn.

11.2 Recursive models: Path analysis, determinants of pay

Path analysis is the oldest causal modelling approach and became popular in sociology in the 1960s. A salient feature, and some would say its strength, lies in the formulation of diagrams to represent underlying complex relationships. Representation in the form of a path diagram is very effective in helping to clarify theoretical assumptions and the sequence of causal events.

To illustrate path analysis we return to the topic analysed in Chapter 4, the determinants of pay. In Chapter 4 a small sample was selected in order to illustrate multiple regression but here we analyse the full dataset and reflect on the temporal sequencing of the determinants of pay.

Theory would lead us to postulate that pay is determined by a variety of factors, such as occupation, the length of time in the current job, whether the job is part-time or full-time, age, sex and ethnicity. However, a person's occupation will in part be determined by the type and level of education received prior to employment. But educational attainment might itself be determined by a person's sex, ethnicity and the historical time period the person was in education (the proportion of people entering higher education has consistently increased over time, for example). Other determinants include a person's intellectual ability (as measured by IQ) and his or her parents' socio-economic status (or class). Unfortunately, information was not available on IQ and class which had to be excluded from this illustrative example.

The set of relationships is represented in Figure 11.1 with the arrows indicating the direction of the causality. The model depicted in Figure 11.1 is known technically as a *recursive model*, which means that the causation is in one direction only, in this case from left to right, reflecting the temporal order of events (for example, education occurs in time before occupation). Although we have chosen to present the model graphically in order to highlight the complexity of the inter-relationships, it could equally have been presented as three separate equations, with three dependent (response) variables: educational qualifications, occupation and hourly pay. Thus path analysis can also be described as a recursive simultaneous equation model.

Having formulated the theoretical model, the next stage is to test the model (and thereby the theoretical assumptions underlying it) on empirical data.

The data

The data used in this analysis is drawn from the 2002 Labour Force Survey (LFS) – a subset of which was analysed in Chapter 4. Persons aged 16 and over are included in the LFS but only those aged 30 to 54 have been selected for the analysis here. Restricting the analysis to those over 30 ensures that they have completed full-time education and are becoming established in their employment careers. (The few over 30 in full-time education were omitted.) A cut-off of under 55 was chosen to exclude many who might be 'running down' their careers or retiring early. Also omitted were those not in work because they were unemployed, in government-sponsored training schemes or not working because of health problems. Hourly pay was chosen and not gross pay to avoid further complications over the number of hours worked. However, to be included, a person's hourly pay needed to be £2 or more. After imposing these criteria for selection, the sample available for analysis comprised 17,242 people.

A total of nine variables are identified in Figure 11.1. Sex has been coded 0 male 1 female. Five birth cohorts, each spanning five years, have been created with cohort 1 being the oldest (50 < 55 age group) and cohort 5 being the youngest group (30 < 35). Ethnic group was dichotomised and coded 0 white 1 all other ethnic groups. Educational qualifications is an ordered six-point scale ranging from 'degree or

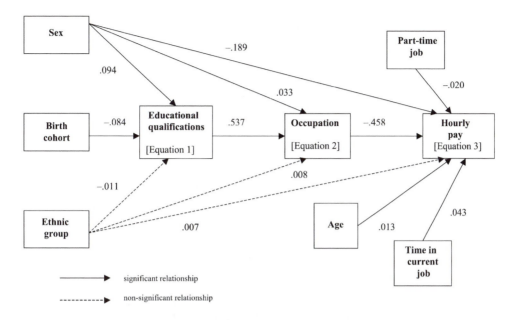

Figure 11.1 Path diagram indicating the determinants of hourly pay.

equivalent' (code 1) to 'no qualifications' (code 6). Similarly, occupation is a nine-point scale ranging from 'managers and senior officials' (code 1) to 'elementary occupations' (code 9). Both have been treated as continuous variables in this analysis. Age is simply the person's age in years. (Obviously age is defined by birth cohort but they have been kept separate to emphasise the different theoretical concepts in the model.) Time in current job is the number of years the person has been in the same job. Part-time is a binary variable, 0 no (full-time) and 1 yes (part-time). Hourly pay is measured to the nearest pence.

Estimating the model

As already stated, the path model depicted in Figure 11.1 is a recursive model and the implication of a recursive model for statistical estimation is that each equation can be estimated separately and independently. When the response variable is continuous, as in this case, ordinary least squares regression procedures, discussed in Chapter 4, can be adopted. Recall, however, that evidence of heteroscedasticity was found in the previous analysis of the LFS data (see section 4.8) and the advice in such circumstances is to calculate robust standard errors. As robust standard errors are readily available in Stata, Stata was preferred to SPSS for this analysis.

There are three equations represented in Figure 11.1.

The first (Eq 1) regresses educational qualifications (the response variable) on sex, birth cohort and ethnic group. (It can be seen in Figure 11.1 that three arrows from the three boxes representing these explanatory variables lead to the box for educational qualifications.) Results of the multiple regression analysis are given in Figure 11.2. The b in the regression command requests beta coefficients, and r robust standard errors.

```
.  reg hiquald  sex bcohort ethnicr,  b r

Regression with robust standard errors              Number of obs =    17242
                                                    F( 3, 17238) =    91.21
                                                    Prob > F      =   0.0000
                                                    R-squared     =   0.0163
                                                    Root MSE      =   1.5039


             |                 Robust
     hiquald |    Coef.     Std. Err.      t     P>|t|                    Beta
-------------+----------------------------------------------------------------
         sex |  .2839897    .0228855    12.41    0.000              .0935682
     bcohort | -.0928282    .0085136   -10.90    0.000             -.0837384
     ethnicr | -.0961995    .0701402    -1.37    0.170             -.0112083
       _cons |  3.346417    .0319767   104.65    0.000                     .
```

Figure 11.2 Stata output for the first equation, educational qualifications.

The results show that sex and birth cohort were significantly related to educational qualifications but that ethnicity was not. The positive coefficient of sex indicates that males, on average, had higher qualifications than females (females were coded 1 and a high score on highest qualification means lower qualifications). As expected given the growth in education over time, the older generation had, on average, lower qualifications than the youngest birth cohort. Although both variables were highly significant (as much due to the large sample size) together they did not explain much of the variance in educational qualifications, R^2 was only .016 (1.6%). Obviously there is much still to explain in terms of the qualifications people obtain. IQ and the socio-economic status of parents would have contributed but are not recorded in the LFS.

The second (Eq 2) regresses occupation on three variables: educational qualifications, sex, and ethnic group. The results are given in Figure 11.3.

```
-----------------------------------------------------------------------------

.  reg occupation sex ethnicr hiquald,  b r

Regression with robust standard errors              Number of obs =    17242
                                                    F( 3, 17238) = 2885.43
                                                    Prob > F      =   0.0000
                                                    R-squared     =   0.2928
                                                    Root MSE      =   2.1951


             |                 Robust
  occupation |    Coef.     Std. Err.      t     P>|t|                    Beta
-------------+----------------------------------------------------------------
         sex |  .1744231    .0340701     5.12    0.000              .0333849
     ethnicr |  .1191777    .0899876     1.32    0.185              .0080664
     hiquald |  .9243222    .0102199    90.44    0.000              .5369622
       _cons |  1.258688    .0343255    36.67    0.000                     .
```

Figure 11.3 Stata output for the second equation, occupation.

It can be seen that sex was significantly related to occupation, in that females had, on average, lower status occupations than males. Ethnicity was not significantly related to occupation, but as expected, qualifications were highly relevant in determining occupation. Sex and, more importantly, highest qualification together explained nearly 30% of the variance in occupation ($R^2 = .293$).

The third (Eq 3) regresses hourly pay on six variables: sex, ethnic group, occupation, part-time job, age, time in current job, sex and ethnic group. The results are shown in Figure 11.4.

```
.  reg  hourpay sex ethnicr occupation ptime age yrscurj, b r

Regression with robust standard errors              Number of obs =    17242
                                                    F(  6, 17235) = 1112.59
                                                    Prob > F      =  0.0000
                                                    R-squared     =  0.2790
                                                    Root MSE      =   6.216

-------------------------------------------------------------------------------
             |               Robust
     hourpay |     Coef.   Std. Err.      t    P>|t|                      Beta
-------------+-----------------------------------------------------------------
         sex | -2.765335   .1147257   -24.10   0.000                 -.1887527
     ethnicr |  .2958281   .2411407     1.23   0.220                  .0071405
  occupation | -1.285325   .0199121   -64.55   0.000                 -.458366
       ptime |  -.334562   .1183261    -2.83   0.005                  -.01966
         age |  .0134416   .0066319     2.03   0.043                  .0128094
      yrscurj |  .0381474   .0063231     6.03   0.000                  .0425781
       _cons |  16.89159   .2813775    60.03   0.000                         .
-------------------------------------------------------------------------------
```

Figure 11.4 Stata output for the third equation, hourly pay.

As in the previous two equations, no support was found for a difference between ethnic groups. All the other five variables were significant. Hourly pay increased with the length of time the respondent had spent in his or her current job. Part-time workers and females received lower hourly pay. Higher status jobs received greater remuneration (the negative coefficient reflects the coding of occupation – lower status jobs having the higher code). The variables together explained 28% of the variance in hourly pay ($R^2 = .279$).

Reflecting on the theoretical model as set out in Figure 11.1, support was found for all the causal connections apart from the influence of ethnicity in any component of the model. At this point we could redraw the diagram omitting the box ethnic group and all the paths leading from it. We could also re-estimate the three equations omitting ethnicity and obtain coefficients for the other variables when ethnicity was not included. However, on doing this, the coefficients for the other variables were found to be little different from those presented above.

It is common practice to write the coefficients on the paths, and these are referred to as path coefficients (although they are simply the regression coefficients). Invariably, the path coefficients reported are the standardised regression coefficients, beta (see Chapter 4) rather than the unstandardised coefficients. The logic here is that the standardised coefficients, by being on a common scale, are directly comparable, showing the relative strength of the causal relationship. For this reason, and following custom, the standardised coefficients are shown in Figure 11.1. Some researchers might reflect the relative strength of a causal path by varying the width of the arrows.

Another practice often followed is to give each path a label. First the variables are numbered and the paths between them are given the corresponding suffixes. For example, if sex was variable 1, birth cohort 2, ethnic group 3 and educational qualifications 4, the path from sex to educational qualifications would be p_{41}, indicating the path to educational qualifications from sex. Yet one more convention, but less often followed, is to write above each dependent variable (connected by a line) an indication of the unexplained variance. This then provides a measure of what is *not* explained by the causal variables. De Vaus (1996) contains an example of a path diagram incorporating all these conventions. However, like all diagrammatic representations there is a trade-off between the visual impact of simplicity and recording all the details of the analysis. I prefer the diagram to readily clarify the conceptual connections underlying the theory. The details can be presented elsewhere.

Total, direct and indirect effects

A considerable advantage of path models is that they clearly show the total effect of one variable on another, even when the effect is mediated through other variables. The total effect of any variable is made up of a direct effect and any indirect effects. Consider the effect of sex on hourly pay. The model as shown in Figure 11.1 reveals that sex influences hourly pay directly but sex also has two indirect effects, one through its effect on occupation (which in turn affects hourly pay) and a second through its effect on educational qualifications (which in turn affects occupation which in turn affects hourly pay). We can calculate the indirect effects by simply multiplying the path coefficients connecting the causal variable to the outcome.

So for the total effect of sex on hourly pay we have:

Direct effect

Sex → hourly pay = −.189

Indirect effects

Sex → occupation → hourly pay (.033 × −.458) = −.015

Sex → educational qualifications → occupation → hourly pay
(.094 × .537 × −.458) = −.023

Total indirect effects = −.015 + −.023 = −.038

Total effect

Direct effect + total indirect effects (−.189 + −.038) = −.227

Of course some variables may only have a direct effect. According to the theory as exemplified by the model, part-time job only has a direct effect on hourly pay. Furthermore, while sex may have indirect effects on hourly pay, sex only has a direct effect on educational qualifications (in our model).

11.3 Non-recursive models: Deterrent effect of solving crime

The previous section considered the situation where causality flowed in one direction only. Unidirectional causality, it was pointed out, greatly simplifies the analysis as it leads to a recursive model where each equation can be estimated separately by ordinary least squares. However, the situation is complicated if theory leads us to postulate that causality is not just in one direction but is in more than one direction simultaneously. It is not uncommon for educationalists to postulate that higher educational attainment enhances self-esteem but that in turn self-esteem results in greater educational attainment. This example implies a contemporaneous feedback in causality which for some theoreticians raises irreconcilable philosophical issues. For them causality cannot 'travel' in two directions simultaneously. In their second condition, quoted at the beginning of this paper, Moser and Kalton (op. cit.) state that the cause must occur before the effect. In practice, however, there may well be a temporal order with causality proceeding in one direction. For example, in the education example:

> Self-esteem in year 1 → educational attainment in year 2 → self-
> esteem in year 3 → educational attainment in year 4 (and so on)

A longitudinal research design, which measures variables at different points in time, is better placed to disentangle the nature of the causality but this is not always possible in much cross-sectional research. In a pure cross-sectional study (where all variables are measured at the same point in time and no historical or retrospective data are collected) we are effectively observing the outcome of the interplay of the various underlying mechanisms at that point in time. A parallel situation occurs in economics when what we observe is what economists call an 'equilibrium mechanism'. Classic examples in economics include the price of a good or commodity or wage rates in a particular industry. When we come to model the determinants of the price of a good, two mechanisms are operating simultaneously, demand for that good and supply of that good. The same two mechanisms, demand and supply, also jointly determine wage rates in a particular industry. In each case, what we observe is the price or wage rates when demand and supply are in equilibrium.

It is not the purpose here to resolve the philosophical debate surrounding causality (if indeed it can be resolved) but it is important to be aware of the debate and to be clear about the rationale when specifying models. The purpose here is to explain the statistical complexities that arise when estimating non-recursive models.

We are now entering the world of econometrics as economists have been at the forefront in developing and applying these methods. In order to illustrate the approach, a simple model is considered which has been developed and applied by economists to estimate the deterrent effects of the criminal justice system. The specific issue to be addressed is whether success in apprehending offenders deters them and potential offenders from committing further crime. If this hypothesis is true, the detection rate (in the UK, the clear-up rate) would be expected to be inversely correlated with the crime rate, such that lower crime rates would be found in areas where a higher proportion of crimes were solved.

To test this hypothesis, data was assembled for 42 police forces in England and Wales. The City of London Police force was omitted as it is found to be an outlier on crime rates – or indeed any 'per capita' measure. (The City of London is primarily a business district with relatively few residents, thus any rate variable, such as the crime rate, where resident population is the denominator, produces an exceptionally high value which is out of line with all other forces.) Crime data for each force relates to the financial year 2003–04.

The crime rate is the number of crimes recorded by the police per 100,000 of the population. The clear-up rate is the percentage of recorded crime that is 'detected' and/or 'solved' by the police. The correlation between the two variables was found to be −.52, which is highly significant, $p < .01$. This result thus provides prima facie evidence confirming the deterrence hypothesis.

Although encouraging, the analysis is deficient as it has not controlled for other factors which affect the crime rate or the clear-up rate. Furthermore, it has not taken into consideration the possible reciprocal relationship between the crime rate and the clear-up rate. Our interest was deterrence – whether offenders are likely to be deterred if they are more likely to be caught. But the level of crime may well affect the clear-up rate. For example, if faced with a large volume of crime, the police may not be able to give each investigation sufficient attention and the clear-up rate may be adversely affected as a consequence. This hypothesis would also suggest a negative correlation between the crime rate and the clear-up rate – which we have observed. Looked at another way, given the empirical result we may ask how much of the inverse correlation is in support of one relationship and how much in support of the other.

Thus we have a simultaneous equation model with two equations:

Crime rate = clear-up rate + (other variables that influence the crime rate)

Clear-up rate = crime rate + (other variables that influence the clear-up rate)

These equations are sometimes referred to as structural equations as they define the structure of the model. However, this should not be confused with structural equation modelling, which is discussed later in this chapter.

In this model, the crime rate and the clear-up rate variables are said to be endogenous variables, that is, their values are determined *within* the model. There will always be one equation for each endogenous variable. The 'other' variables within the brackets, which are yet to be specified, are said to be exogenous variables as their values are predetermined *outside* the model.

We could extend this model further. In what still remains as the most thorough exposition of this method in this area of application, Carr-Hill and Stern (1979) also considered police resources, which may affect both the crime rate and the clear-up rate, and in turn, be affected by them if police resources are adjusted to take account of levels of crime and police performance in solving crime. This led Carr-Hill and Stern to a third equation. They also considered other deterrent effects, in particular the likelihood of an offender being sent to prison. But to illustrate the methodological issues associated with developing and estimating non-recursive models it is sufficient to restrict the model to two equations.

Specification and identification

So far the 'other' variables in each of the equations above have not been specified. Obviously theory and previous research will dictate what other variables should be included, but if the same set of variables is included in each equation there will be no way of distinguishing one equation from the other. This is known as the identification problem. Thus, in order to uniquely identify an equation it must include at least one variable which is significantly related to the dependent variable of that equation, but which is not included in any of the other equations. (The variable needs to be significantly related, because if not it is equivalent to that variable not being in the equation.)

From criminological research it is known that levels of crime are related to the proportion of young males in the population (much crime is committed by young males so areas with a high proportion of young males are likely to experience more crime), social deprivation (deprived areas experience more crime) and density of population (crime is higher in urban areas).

The proportion of young males was simply taken to be the percentage of males between the ages of 15 and 24 of the resident population in each police force area.

Alternative measures of social deprivation were available for each police force area, including the percentage of households headed by a single parent and the proportion of working age people claiming benefits, and the proportion of overcrowded households. All were found to be related to the crime rate, but as expected they were found to be highly correlated with each other. As is customary with variables where the rates are small, the variables were transformed by taking the natural logarithm of the rate. From an initial regression analysis with the crime rate regressed against all the possible social deprivation measures, the log of the percentage of households headed by a single parent was the most significant and once included other variables were found not to be significant. Thus log single parents was chosen as a summary, or proxy, measure to encapsulate social deprivation.

Sparsity of the population was taken as a measure of urbanisation. As the measure varies considerably between forces a log transformation was used in place of the absolute value. Thus the first equation was specified as:

$$\text{Crime rate} = b_{10} + b_{11} \text{ (clear-up rate)} \qquad [\textit{cluprate}]$$
$$+ b_{12} \text{ (proportion males 15–24)} \qquad [\textit{yongmale}]$$
$$+ b_{13} \text{ (log single parents)} \qquad [\textit{lnsigpar}]$$
$$+ b_{14} \text{ (log sparsity)} \qquad [\textit{log\_spar}]$$

(variable names are in square brackets).

An extra subscript has been added to denote the equation. The first subscript denotes the equation, the second denotes the variable to which the coefficient relates.

Having specified the first equation, we turn to the second. Some crimes are more easily detected than others, often because the offence only comes to light once the offender is apprehended. Offences of possession (of knives, drugs etc.) and 'going equipped to steal' would be offences of this kind, which are often termed 'self-detecting crimes'. Many shoplifting offences would also fall into this category. Violence offences have high clear-up rates, especially where the perpetrator is intimately related to, or is an acquaintance of, the victim who can give his or her identity to the police. Thus one large determinant of a police force's clear-up rate is the proportion of crime that is self or readily detected. The degree of urbanisation may also be a factor as it is easier for an offender to preserve anonymity in urban areas than in rural areas. Carr-Hill and Stern (op. cit.) also felt the size of the area would affect the police 'production' of clear-ups through economies or diseconomies of scale. The size of the resident population was taken by them as a proxy for the size of the area and that approach is continued here. Population is measured in units of 100,000. Thus the second equation was specified as:

Clear-up rate = b_{20} + b_{21} (crime rate)   [*crimrate*]

                 + b_{22} (percentage of crime readily detected)   [*crimmix*]

                 + b_{23} (log sparsity)   [*log_spar*]

                 + b_{24} (population)   [*populat*]

(variable names are in square brackets).

Comparing the two equations, it can be seen that the model is identified, in fact it is over-identified in that there is more than one variable unique to each equation: single parents and the proportion of males in the first equation and the proportion of crime that is readily detected and population in the second equation.

The two-equation model can be represented diagrammatically as shown in Figure 11.2.

It can be seen from the diagram that crime rate and clear-up rate are interrelated as indicated by the arrows going back and forth between them. The diagram also reveals that log sparsity of population is an explanatory variable for both the crime rate and the clear-up rate. The other variables are unique to one equation and the model is therefore identified.

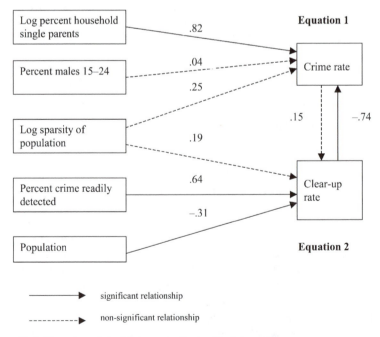

Figure 11.5 Causal model of deterrent effects of solving crime.

Estimating the model

Having specified the model, the next step is to estimate the parameters (the coefficients *b*) of the two-equation model. Here we confront another problem. Because of the contemporaneous feedback or the reciprocal causation between the crime rate and the clear-up rate, acknowledged within the model, the method of ordinary least squares will produce biased estimates of the coefficients (the technical reason being that the explanatory endogenous variable is correlated with the error term – violating one of the assumptions of OLS).

Fortunately estimation procedures have been developed which overcome this problem. One set of techniques estimates all the coefficients simultaneously; they include three-stage least squares (3SLS) and full information maximum likelihood (FIML). The advantage of these methods is that by estimating all the equations simultaneously they are able to take account of *which* variables are in *which* equation. However, a disadvantage of these methods is that the estimates of the coefficients are adversely affected if the wrong variables are in the wrong equations. Three-stage least squares procedures are readily available in Stata but not SPSS. A second method estimates each equation separately but in so doing takes account of the variables in the other equation or equations (but not which equation they are in). The method is known as two-stage least squares (2SLS) and is available in both SPSS and Stata. Two-stage least squares is often found to be as good as the simultaneous estimation procedures, especially with small models and not surprisingly those with two equations (because if the exogenous variable is not in one equation it must be in the other). Two-stage least squares estimation procedures are adopted here to estimate the coefficients of our two-equation model.

As the name implies, there are two stages to the estimation procedure. Take the first equation which has the crime rate as the dependent variable and the clear-up rate as an endogenous variable on the right-hand side as an explanatory variable. The first stage regresses in turn all the endogenous variables appearing on the right-hand side of the equation (in this case there is only one – the clear-up rate) on *all* the exogenous variables in the entire model (that is, in both equations: proportion males 15–24, log single parents, log sparsity, percentage of crime readily detected and population). From this regression, a predicted value of the clear-up rate is estimated from the exogenous variables. The second stage then regresses the crime rate (the dependent variable) on the predicted value of the clear-up rate (derived at stage 1) and the other exogenous variables in the first equation (proportion males 15–24, log single parents, log sparsity). The strength of 2SLS is that having been estimated by the exogenous variables, the predicted value of the clear-up rate (unlike its actual value) can be expected to be uncorrelated with the error term in the first equation, thus overcoming the problem with OLS. It can be shown that the two-stage approach results in more consistent and less biased estimates.

The above two-stage method is repeated in a similar way to obtain estimates of the coefficients in the second equation.

Fitting the model

Simultaneous equation models can be fitted in SPSS by two-stage least squares. The steps are Analyze → Regression → 2-Stage Least Squares. This brings up a dialogue box which asks for Dependent, Explanatory and Instrumental.

For the first equation, Dependent is the crime rate, Explanatory are the variables on the right-hand side: clear-up rate, proportion males 15–24, log single parents, log sparsity. Instrumental are all the exogenous variables in the entire model, which are required at the first stage (proportion males 15–24, log single parents, log sparsity, percentage of crime readily detected and population). SPSS knows that it has to treat clear-up rate as an endogenous variable because it is included as an explanatory variable but it is not included in the list of instrumental variables. Having deduced this fact, SPSS uses the instrumental variables to produce a predicted value of the clear-up rate, before embarking on the second stage.

Fitting the first equation by two-stage least squares in Stata requires the ivreg command (iv standing for instrumental variables). The first variable is the dependent variable and the exogenous variables follow (young males, log single parents, log sparsity). Any endogenous variables in the equation are then placed in brackets followed by = and the other exogenous variables that appear in the other equations – but it is not necessary to repeat the exogenous variables that appear in the equation being estimated. The command for the equation appears as the first line in the output below. The Stata command is a little more complex and errors can be more easily avoided by using the drop-down menus: Statistics → Linear regression and related? Multiple equation models → Instrumental variables & two-stage least squares. This brings up a dialogue box which requests Dependent variable, Independent variables, Endogenous variables and Instrument variables (the last being all other exogenous variables in the entire model).

Reassuringly, SPSS and Stata produced the same results. The output from Stata showing the two-stage least squares estimates of the coefficients of the first equation is shown below.

```
. ivreg crimrate yongmale lnsigpar log_spar ( cluprate = crimmix populat ), bet
> a

Instrumental variables (2SLS) regression

      Source |       SS       df       MS              Number of obs =      42
-------------+------------------------------          F(  4,     37) =   23.43
       Model |  17066.1979      4  4266.54947          Prob > F      =  0.0000
    Residual |  6631.13544     37  179.219877          R-squared     =  0.7202
-------------+------------------------------          Adj R-squared =  0.6899
       Total |  23697.3333     41  577.98374          Root MSE      =  13.387


     crimrate |      Coef.   Std. Err.       t    P>|t|                    Beta
-------------+----------------------------------------------------------------
     cluprate |  -2.857596    .675168    -4.23   0.000               -.7402286
     yongmale |   2.160371   6.273109     0.34   0.733                .0438518
      lnsigpar |   104.3118   21.45801     4.86   0.000                 .819317
     log_spar |   6.371823   4.291213     1.48   0.146                .2504965
        _cons |   471.2878   105.7145     4.46   0.000                       .
-----------------------------------------------------------------------------
Instrumented: cluprate
Instruments:  yongmale lnsigpar log_spar crimmix populat
-----------------------------------------------------------------------------
```

Figure 11.6 Stata output, crime rate regression model.

The model was highly significant, the proportion of variance explained, R^2, was found to be 72%. From the output, it can be seen that the coefficients of the three exogenous explanatory variables are in the hypothesised, positive, direction, namely that more young people, more deprived areas (as indicated by more single parents) and greater urbanisation are associated with more crime. However, the percentage of the population that are young males and the degree of urbanisation were not significantly related to the level of crime in a police force area once the log percentage of single parent households was taken into account. More important, in view of the initial research hypothesis, the clear-up rate remained a significant determinant of the crime rate after controlling for socio-demographic conditions. The beta coefficients are shown in Figure 11.5.

Two-stage least squares estimates of the coefficients of the second equation were found to be:

```
. ivreg cluprate crimmix log_spar populat ( crimrate = yongmale lnsigpar ), be
> ta

Instrumental variables (2SLS) regression

      Source |       SS       df       MS              Number of obs =      42
-------------+------------------------------          F( 4,    37) =    10.74
       Model |  821.111267     4   205.277817          Prob > F      =  0.0000
    Residual |  769.007781    37   20.7839941          R-squared     =  0.5164
-------------+------------------------------          Adj R-squared =  0.4641
       Total |  1590.11905    41   38.7833914          Root MSE      =  4.5589


    cluprate |      Coef.   Std. Err.      t    P>|t|                     Beta
-------------+----------------------------------------------------------------
    crimrate |   .0387994   .0622989     0.62   0.537                 .1497821
     crimmix |   2.838926   .5933898     4.78   0.000                 .6475864
    log_spar |   1.228379   1.488115     0.83   0.414                 .1864255
     populat |  -.1719802    .093084    -1.85   0.073                -.3069296
       _cons |    12.6075   7.084444     1.78   0.083                        .

Instrumented:  crimrate
Instruments:   crimmix log_spar populat yongmale lnsigpar
```

Figure 11.7 Stata output, clear-up rate regression model.

The most important factor in determining the clear-up rate is the percentage of crimes that can be described as readily detectable. In addition, there appears to be some evidence ($p = .073$) of diseconomies of scale in that the larger the population in the police force area the lower the clear-up rate but sparsity (or density) of the population was not significant. When the three variables were taken into account, the crime rate was not found to be a determinant of the clear-up rate. The proportion of variance explained, R^2, for the second equation was found to be 54%. The beta coefficients are shown in Figure 11.5.

To sum up, we started with an inverse correlation between the crime rate and the clear-up rate, which could be interpreted in one of two ways. Having disentangled the two through the specification of the model, it appears that the clear-up rate is a determinant of the crime rate but that the crime rate is not a determinant of the clear-up rate. The analysis provides support for the deterrence hypothesis in that success in solving crime does reduce levels of crime.

Diagnostics: Analysis of residuals

All the models considered in this chapter are multiple regression models. Thus the diagnostic and residual analyses outlined in section 4.8 are appropriate here and should be carried out to assess the adequacy of the models. Having been explained in section 4.8, further discussion is not necessary at this stage.

11.4 Structural equation modelling (SEM)

A technique becoming increasingly popular within social research is structural equation modelling (SEM), or covariance structure modelling as it was previously called. Essentially, SEM extends the recursive and non-recursive models above to include latent variables, which has led SEM to be referred to as 'path analysis with latent variables'. A more accurate description is that SEM combines confirmatory factor analysis with econometric models.

In section 10.6 a distinction was drawn between exploratory factor analysis and confirmatory factor analysis. In exploratory factor analysis the researcher explores how many factors there are and how they relate to the manifest variables. By contrast, in confirmatory factor analysis, the social researcher sets out *a priori* his or her theory and assumptions as to which manifest variables relate to which latent variables. However, the researcher may not merely theorise as to how the manifest variables relate to the latent variables but may postulate relationships between the latent variables themselves, or postulate how they are 'structurally related'. The first step in structural equation modelling is thus confirmatory factor analysis and the second step is to specify the structural relationship between the latent variables. This general theory which includes association and causation between and amongst manifest and latent variables is usually set out in the form of a diagram similar to Figures 11.1 and 11.5, and explains why SEM is often given the short-hand description confirmatory factor analysis and path models. In SEM the diagrams are adapted somewhat in order to incorporate manifest and latent variables. The convention is to represent manifest variables by square boxes (as in Figures 11.1 and 11.5) but to represent latent variables by ovals or circles. Straight lines indicate causal connections but curved lines indicate associations between latent variables. Fitting the structural equation model to the data tests the underlying theory and assumptions. Maximum likelihood statistics are estimated, leading to significance tests which enable the researcher to assess the adequacy of the model and its constituent parts.

Structural equation modelling is not described in any further detail here as many good introductory texts are readily available and because specialist software is required to perform the analysis. Suggested texts are referenced at the end of this chapter. The main SEM programs are Amos, Lisrel, EQS and MPlus. Amos has the advantage of being simple to use (models can be specified by clicking and dragging icons) and it is also available from SPSS. Lisrel and EQS are more sophisticated and well known, especially Lisrel, while the more recent MPlus is gaining rapidly in popularity.

Although details of SEM are not given here, some general observations are in order especially as some of the criticisms (or health warnings) of SEM are not always recorded in texts describing the method.

Advocates point out that SEM represents a considerable advance by enabling researchers to incorporate latent variables in the model, and they stress (as mentioned in the previous chapter) that many variables in social research are latent variables. Confirmatory factor analysis brings factor analysis into the statistical tradition of hypothesis testing. SEM thus enables social scientists to explore and test ever more complex theories about the nature of social phenomena.

Critics warn that in order to estimate structural equation models, many assumptions need to be made and many restrictions imposed. Essentially the same data is being used to estimate factor loadings and regression coefficients. It was pointed out in the previous chapter that restrictions have to be imposed in order to perform factor analysis and further assumptions are required to undertake regression. Without the imposition of restrictions, models are not identifiable. In reality, alternative SEM models may fit the data equally well. But in answer to these criticisms, in all forms of statistical modelling (as we have seen), it is possible to find equally competing models and the choice between them rests on substantive theory, replication in other research on different datasets or some pragmatic rule such as parsimony. Nevertheless, there is a concern that much application of SEM does not explicitly consider the possibility of alternative, but equally plausible models. A further criticism of structural equation modelling is that as there are so many sources of variation in such complex models, the solution may be highly susceptible to chance variation in one element of the model. This suggests that considerable care is required when applying SEM and has led some to suggest a better approach may be to separate the two stages of confirmatory factor analysis and model fitting.

Another limitation is that the statistical theory underpinning SEM is much better formulated for continuous variables where covariances and correlations can be estimated. The theory (and hence the causal models) is not as well developed for categorical variables. However, this general comment can be made about a lot of modelling techniques, including models for longitudinal data discussed in Chapter 12.

Further reading

Simultaneous equation models are well covered in econometrics texts. A suitable starting point is Wooldridge (2003).

A good introduction to Structural Equation Models is Schumacker and Lomax (2004). In addition to explaining SEM, the text serves as a good introduction to fitting models in Amos, EQS and Lisrel.

12 Longitudinal data analysis

12.1 Introduction

Menard (1991) defined longitudinal research as that in which:

- data are collected for each item or variable from two or more distinct periods;
- the subjects or cases are the same, or at least comparable, from one period to the next;
- the analysis involves some comparison of data between or among periods.

Adopting this broad definition encompasses several different research designs and, accordingly, several different approaches to statistical modelling. Each design and the issues it poses for statistical modelling are considered in turn. However, note that the definition of longitudinal research signifies a time frame over which data is collected and referenced. We can conceptualise events in time in two ways. First we can observe the states subjects are in at particular points in the time period, for example, each year we might record whether a person is married or not, employed or not and so on. Following on from this we can monitor transitions between states, that is, moving from being employed to non-employed, for example. Alternatively, or in addition, we can record durations, that is, how long a person is married, employed and so on. Statistical models for durations are considered in Chapter 13.

Longitudinal research is gaining in popularity because it is acknowledged to be superior to cross-sectional research in understanding social change and the processes and causal mechanisms underlying that change. This popularity is reflected in the recent considerable growth in investment by both the ESRC and government departments in longitudinal research studies, especially panel and cohort studies (defined in section 12.4). Longitudinal data is now more readily available but modelling such data raises certain statistical complexities, principally because observations are correlated thus violating the key assumption of independence.

Before discussing statistical models we briefly review the advantages of longitudinal data (although these often more readily reflect the inadequacies of cross-sectional data). One major advantage is that longitudinal research is better placed than cross-sectional research to establish temporal order of events and causality. Statistical models for longitudinal data can also more adequately address the problems posed by unobserved variables (first described in section 3.10). How they overcome the problem of unobserved variables will be explained when statistical models are presented later in this chapter.

For causality to exist, as pointed out in section 11.1, cause must precede effect in time. Take the simplest of examples of a cross-sectional study which collects information on variables x and y measured at the same point in time. If an association is found between x and y, without additional substantive knowledge, it is not possible to say that x causes y or that y causes x. Being measured at the same point in time, it is not possible to establish which variable preceded the other; often the variables are only observed when they are at some equilibrium (see section 11.3). Furthermore, it is possible that both x and y could be caused by an observed value of a third variable z in a previous time period.

However, when commentators make these claims they invariably have in mind a comparison of a 'pure' cross-sectional study where all variables are measured at a single point in time. But in most cross-sectional studies it is common to collect retrospective data of past events, such as 'age left school', 'highest educational qualification attained', 'age of first conviction' and so on. Furthermore, with many variables the temporal sequence is indisputable: schooling precedes employment, and marriage precedes divorce, for example. And, of course, while some variables may change over time (time-varying covariates) such as employment status or marital status, where information on temporal ordering is required, some variables, such as sex and ethnicity, do not. No information on temporal sequencing is required for the latter, time-invariant, covariates.

Nevertheless, while more might be obtained from cross-sectional data than advocates of longitudinal research concede, it is the case that prospective longitudinal research is vastly superior, especially where the research interest is in analysing people's intentions, motivations, opinions, attitudes or feelings, which may change frequently but which are more difficult to recall and temporally locate retrospectively.

Even when time ordering can be established, there are other severe problems with cross-sectional designs, notably in separating age and cohort effects. An interesting finding from the British Crime Survey (BCS; an annual cross-sectional survey) is that a smaller proportion of older women report having been the victim of domestic violence in the previous year than younger women. For example, in the 1996 BCS, 12.0% of women aged 20 to 24 responded that they had been the victim of an assault or threat by a partner or ex-partner, compared with only 0.9% of women aged 55 to 59 (Mirrlees-Black, 1999). This finding could be interpreted as evidence of an age effect, namely that younger women are more likely to be the victim of domestic violence. This is plausible because younger women are likely to be in a relationship with a younger man than are older women and younger men are more likely to be violent than older men.

But could these findings provide evidence of a cohort effect? If society is becoming more violent then more recent generations, that is, younger women (and their younger partners) are experiencing more violence (and committing more violent offences) than experienced by older generations. Of course, the results do not have to be interpreted as either an age or a cohort effect. It is most likely that both age and cohort effects are generating the results. But they are confounded and it is not possible to separate the age effect from the cohort effect. There is evidence of a cohort effect, because in addition to being asked whether they were the victim of domestic violence last year, respondents were also asked if they had ever in their life been the victim of an assault or threat by a partner or ex-partner. Paradoxically, given that older women had longer to experience an incident of domestic violence, life-time prevalence for 20- to 24-year-old women was higher (at 33.7%) than for 55- to 59-year-old women whose life-time prevalence was only 15.9%. (Male respondents were asked the same questions and although the figures are different the patterns between the age groups on both measures is exactly the same.) One cohort explanation has been offered, namely that recent generations are experiencing more violence. But there are other possible cohort explanations. Younger women now tend to enter a greater number of domestic relationships than women of previous generations, thus younger women are more likely to encounter a domestic relationship that is violent. Domestic violence has received greater public attention in recent years, which may have led younger women to perceive it differently from older women and to discuss it more openly and be more willing to report their experiences of it. Older women may be more reticent to tell others about their experiences or to define their experiences as relevant to the survey. Or if incidents are more likely to occur when women are young (age effect), older women's experiences will have been longer ago so may have faded from memory, or may have been favourably revised over time (Mirrlees-Black, op. cit.).

Longitudinal research designs are better placed to separate age and cohort effects and to clarify temporal order and, furthermore, to establish causality. But longitudinal research is no panacea. While longitudinal research is better placed to address the issue of unobserved variables one can never be sure in non-experimental research that some unknown variable is exerting a causal influence. Furthermore, the timeframe in any longitudinal research is finite, which leaves open the possibility that the cause of the results found in the study might be attributable to a variable exerting its influence before the period of reference of the study.

12.2 Time series analysis

In the social sciences, the term time series data usually refers to a long sequence of aggregate data and most commonly macro-economic data. In macro-economics the researcher is studying long-term trends in the economy and the inter-relationships between economic variables as measured over time. The data may be annual, quarterly or monthly aggregate measures (such as GDP, consumption) or rates (unemployment rates, interest rates) or indices (retail price index, share price index).

How long a series needs to be before it qualifies as a time series dataset and amenable to time series analysis has not been precisely defined. But a sequence of about 50 data points is considered a minimum (that is, 50 years of annual data or 12–13 years of quarterly data).

Time series data is not confined to macro-economics, such data exists in other areas. For example, the annual recorded crime rate is available for England and Wales since 1857 and time series data exists on road accident fatalities and on the popularity of political parties. These series can be used to assess the effects of major legislative changes or major political events. For example, the effect of the introduction of seat belts or crash helmets can be gauged by comparing the numbers of road accident fatalities before and after the legislation was implemented. Similarly, Sanders and Ward (1994) analysed times series data to assess the effect of the Falklands War on the government's popularity.

Often the purpose of time series analysis is to discern trends and uncover any seasonal patterns in the data, with a view to forecasting future values of the series. Forecasts can be obtained by extrapolating the series (once its underlying properties are understood) or by fitting a statistical model, the explanatory variables themselves being time series data. We could thus proceed by fitting the general linear model:

$$y_t = b_0 + b_1 \, x_{1t} + b_2 \, x_{2t} + b_3 \, x_{3t} + b_4 \, x_{4t} + \ldots + e_t \qquad (12.1)$$

This is the same model as defined at the outset, that is, Equation (1.1), the difference being that i in Equation (1.1) (which denoted each individual in the sample) has been replaced by t, which denotes that the variables are measured at different time points. A t has been added to each explanatory variable x to denote that they are also times series variables (which is often the case but need not be).

If y is a continuous variable we would think of fitting an ordinary least squares multiple regression model to the data. There is, however, one serious problem with this approach and that is with time series data the e_t tend not to be independent (an important assumption of regression) but are in fact correlated (this correlation is known as serial correlation). Serial correlation arises because values of a variable (e.g. GDP, crime rates) in one year t are closely related to values of the variables in the previous year, $t - 1$, and the year before, $t - 2$, and so on, especially if there is a distinct trend in the series. Serial correlation leads the standard errors of the coefficients, b, to be underestimated, and the t values and R^2 to be overestimated, which can lead to false inferences that variables and models are significant when they are not.

Time series analysis is a technical and specialist branch of statistics and detailed development of the topic is outside the scope of this book. The point being made here is to warn the reader that analysing time series data raises specific issues which need to be addressed appropriately. One cannot simply fit the models discussed in this book. However, SPSS and Stata do have special routines for fitting time series models. Economists, who amongst social scientists make most use of time series analysis, will have been introduced to the topic when studying econometrics. Further reading is given at the end of this chapter for others who may find themselves encountering time series data for the first time and in need of instruction. But I would also advise researchers to seek the help and assistance of an expert if confronted with analysing time series data.

Leaving aside the technical statistical issues, one practical problem often encountered is the comparability of the data over time. During the course of time, definitions, methods of counting and procedures for collecting the data change, which raises concerns as to whether data at one period can be regarded in the same light as data collected at other points. The recorded crime data for England and Wales illustrates the problem. Over time new offences have been created and the rules governing how incidents should be counted as crimes have changed, not to mention the periodic issuing of policy directives to the police regarding their discretion in recording incidents as crimes. Analysing time series data can lead to pitfalls for the unsuspecting.

12.3 Repeated cross-sectional surveys

Many cross-sectional surveys are repeated at regular interviews, often annually, and on each occasion a fresh sample of subjects is drawn from the relevant population. If randomly selected, the samples, though different, will be comparable. To cite one of a large number of possible examples, the Department of Health commissions each year the *Smoking, Drinking and Drug Use Among Young People* survey. The first survey was carried out in 1982 to provide estimates of the proportion of secondary school pupils aged 11 to 15 who smoked. The survey was repeated every two years until 1998 when it became an annual survey. Questions on alcohol consumption were first included in the 1988 survey and questions on the prevalence of drug use were first introduced in 1998.

Repeated cross-sectional surveys provide information on trends at the aggregate level. So, from the survey described above it is possible to establish that the proportion of secondary school pupils who reported that they had ever smoked fell from 53% in 1982 to 39% in 2006. Similarly, the survey has reported that of the young people who said they had drunk alcohol in the last seven days, the mean consumption has nearly doubled, from 5.3 units in 1990 to 10.4 units in 2006. The data from these surveys could be disaggregated to reveal trends for sub-groups (by gender, ethnicity, age and so on).

Being independent random samples, repeated cross-sectional surveys can be pooled to provide a larger sample, which produces more precise estimates of the coefficients in a statistical model and more powerful significance tests of them. However, as some of the underlying relationships may change over time it is customary to include the time periods as a set of dummy variables (with the first time period as the reference category). In some applications the value and significance of the coefficients on the time period dummy variables may be of prime interest, for example, in order to assess whether a change occurred over time, and at what point in time.

However, because the subjects are different from survey to survey, repeated cross-sectional designs cannot assess change at the individual level; for that we need panel studies.

How does times series data differ from repeated cross-sectional surveys? Conceptually they do not differ much. Aggregate time series data can emanate from repeated cross-sectional surveys. However, it is generally the case that cross-sectional surveys have not been repeated often enough to generate a sufficiently long series of data for time series analysis.

12.4 Panel and cohort studies

The essential characteristic of a panel or cohort research design is that the *same* subjects are followed up over time. Subjects need not be individuals, they could be institutions or organisations (firms, schools, hospitals, police forces, etc.). The distinction between a panel study and a cohort study is not important with regard to statistical modelling but a panel study will typically select a random sample of the population at one point in time (which is then followed up). An example of a panel study is the British Household Panel Study (BHPS) which selected a nationally representative sample of 5000 households in Great Britain in 1999 and interviewed all (approximately 10,000) adults within those households. (Further details of the BHPS can be found at its website www.iser.essex.ac.uk.) A cohort, on the other hand, selects a homogeneous group defined by experiencing the same life event (e.g. starting school) which is then followed up. Often (but not necessarily) the group is defined as those being born within a particular period, giving rise to the term birth cohort for this type of cohort. An example here is the National Child Development Study (NCDS) which at its inception selected all children born in a one-week period of 1958. (Details of the British birth cohorts can be found at the website of the Centre for Longitudinal Studies, www.cls.ioe.ac.uk.)

In a panel or cohort study, data on each subject is collected periodically, either after a certain length of time has elapsed, or at key points in the subjects' lives (starting school etc.) or simply when funding becomes available to finance the work involved. Each time the subjects are contacted is known as a panel wave or sweep. Adult members of the households selected in the BHPS have been contacted each year since 1991 and to date there have been seven sweeps of the NCDS.

At each wave, new variables might be added (or some variables may be dropped from previous waves) but many variables will be the same on each occasion, giving rise to repeated measures of those variables, taken at successive waves. (This explains why analysis of such data is often referred to in the statistical literature as the *analysis of repeated measure*.) By obtaining repeated measures to variables it is possible to examine change over time.

A panel component can be built into repeated cross-sectional surveys. The Labour Force Survey gathers information on employment status for a representative sample of working-age people in this country. The survey is conducted each quarter but the design is such that each individual is interviewed for five successive quarters. Thus at any one quarter, a fifth will be newly selected and receiving their first interview, a fifth their second, a fifth their third, and a fifth their fourth, while a fifth will be interviewed for the fifth and last time. The US National Crime Survey has a similar design with some subjects being retained for a period and then being dropped and replaced by other selected subjects. Because of the continuing and evolving nature of the sample, such studies are often called *revolving panel designs*.

Although having distinct advantages in illuminating causality from the sequencing of events over the life course, longitudinal studies, particularly prospective panel and cohort studies, encounter difficulties. Leaving aside cost, attrition is the biggest problem. Over time panel members drop out; they may have died, moved away and not be traceable or refuse to continue to participate. Not only does the panel/cohort reduce in size but those who remain may be a biased subset of the original panel/cohort. This bias may be especially pronounced when examining certain issues (such as homeless-ness or crime) which may have been the cause of the participants leaving the study in the first place.

One other particular problem is what has become known as panel conditioning Participation in a panel, knowledge of the purpose of the research and the kinds of questions that are asked, may lead to responses at one wave being influenced by responses at a previous wave. The revolving panel design facilitates some longitudinal perspective while minimising attrition and panel conditioning.

12.5 Statistical models for panel data

In situations where there are only two panel waves and the response variable is continu-ous it is straightforward to analyse the data by fitting a statistical model. One such model is the *regressor variable model* of the form:

$$y_{i2} = b_0 + b_1 x_{1i} + b_2 x_{2i} + b_3 x_{3i} + \ldots + b_p y_{i1} + e_i \qquad (12.2)$$

Here the response variable is the value of y at the second time period and the value of y at the first time period is included as an explanatory variable.

An alternative model is the *change score model* of the form:

$$y_{i2} - y_{i1} = b_0 + b_1 x_{1i} + b_2 x_{2i} + b_3 x_{3i} + \ldots + e_i \qquad (12.3)$$

The response variable is simply the change in y between the first and second period, or between the two waves.

In both models the xs are explanatory variables that might be postulated to affect the change in the response. They have not been given a time suffix as they could relate to any time period as theory dictates. An explanatory variable could also be the change in x between the two time periods, that is $(x_{pi2} - x_{pi1})$.

Both models can be readily estimated by fitting ordinary least squares (that is, as multiple regression models – described in Chapter 4).

Which of the two models should one choose? For a long time the conventional wisdom was to favour the first model, the regressor variable model. However, that changed following an influential paper by Allison (1990). Allison demonstrated that many of the theoretical arguments against the change score model (which had led the regressor variable model to be preferred) were false and that in many situations statistical theory favoured the change score model.

There is, however, one principal circumstance where the regressor variable model is more appropriate and that is where the initial value of the response y (y_{i1}) affects the subsequent value of y (y_{i2}). This can occur when an initial state the subject is in is likely to influence the extent of change. Allison gives the example of an employee in a high-prestige job looking for another job. The individual is likely to get another high-prestige job irrespective of his/her characteristics, because of the evaluation that potential employers have formed of him/her from his current job. However, even though the regressor variable model would be more appropriate in such circumstances, Allison's view is that the effect of the initial state is so small relative to the other explanatory variables that the change score model may not be seriously affected. His practical advice is that if the choice of model is not clear cut 'there may be no recourse but to do the analysis both ways and to trust only those conclusions that are consistent across methods' (Allison, op cit.).

Models with t *(more than two) panel waves*

We next consider the case where there are more than two measurement periods, or more than two panel waves. Of course in such a situation it is still possible to consider the change between two periods (perhaps the first and the last) and fit a change score or regressor variable model. But this would ignore much of the information, namely the scores at the other, intervening periods.

Let us consider the situation where we have t measures (t waves where a measure is taken) for each of the sample of n subjects. Several different models could be fitted to this data but before presenting each in turn, consider the different types of explanatory variables.

The first type of explanatory variable are those that can vary over time, that is, those that can change from panel wave to panel wave. Many variables fall within this category, for example, income, employment status (not in work, in work etc.) or marital status (single, married, separated etc.). We continue to denote these variables by x. A second type are explanatory variables that do not vary over time. Obvious examples when our subjects are individuals are sex and ethnicity. But if our subjects are hospitals, schools or police forces, their geographical location would not change over time. In order to distinguish time-constant (or invariant) explanatory variables from time-varying explanatory variables we will denote the time-constant variables by z. A third type of explanatory variable are those that are unobserved or not measured. We denote these by x^u. Remember from section 3.10 that estimates are biased if the unobserved variables are correlated with any of the observed explanatory variables. We assume that the effect of the unobserved variables is the same (constant or fixed) over time. Of course, all three types of variable exist, if only implicitly, in all the other models we have discussed in previous chapters of this book. The reason for distinguishing them now is to show how different longitudinal models handle the different types of explanatory variables and how longitudinal models can nullify the effects of time-invariant unobserved variables.

A model could have any number of xs, zs and x^us (although as we cannot observe the x^us we do not know how many there are, so it is common practice to amalgamate all the effects together as one variable). For simplicity we assume one of each type (so there is no need to number them). The model then becomes:

$$y_{it} = b_0 + b_1\, x_{it} + b_2\, z_i + x_i^u + e_{it} \qquad (12.4)$$

Because z does not vary over time (is constant) we do not need a subscript t to denote its value at a particular point in time. Similarly, as we assume x^u does not change over time, it too does not require a subscript t. Furthermore, as we cannot observe x^u we cannot estimate its effect (that is, its coefficient b) so it is not given a coefficient, b, but just included as an overall, unobserved, effect.

Total model or a model for any wave

The longitudinal nature of the data could simply be ignored and the model Equation (1.1) fitted to all the data as if it were a sample of $n \times t$ individuals. Obviously this is incorrect as it assumes a much larger sample of individuals than actually exists (t times as many) and it ignores the fact that there is likely to be intra-correlation, as scores for an individual across waves are likely to be correlated. However, this model is sometimes fitted to 'get a feel for the data' and a sense of the underlying relationships between variables. A more respectable variant on this is to fit a model to cross-sectional data emanating from one particular wave (and the analysis could be repeated for any or all of the waves separately). At least when analysing one wave the sample size used to estimate the parameters and standard errors is correct.

Between model

A more appropriate approach to understanding the underlying relationships between the variables of interest is to average each variable across the t waves and to fit the model to the average values. By taking averages, information from all the t waves are included and given equal weight. Thus the model becomes:

$$\bar{y}_i = b_0 + b_1\, \bar{x}_i + b_2\, z_i + x_i^u + \bar{e}_i \qquad (12.5)$$

Because z and x^u are constant over time, their values are the same each year and thus the same as their average value.

The model in Equation (12.5) is referred to as the between model. The terminology stems from the fact that it ignores (or averages out) variation within subjects across waves but solely examines the differences between subjects.

Note that this model also helps overcome the problem of measurement error. If any of the variables are measured with error at any wave, averaging the variables across waves reduces the bias resulting from measurement error.

Calculating the arithmetic mean of continuous variables is straightforward. If categorical variables are rearranged as dummy variables, coded 0 and 1, then their averages can also be readily calculated. For example, if not employed is coded 0 and employed 1, a person who was not employed at four waves but employed in the other six waves (in a panel study of 10 waves) would have an average score of .6.

When the response variable is continuous, the between model can be estimated by ordinary least squares, as described in section 4.1.

Within (or fixed effects) model

So far we have not taken into account how subjects change over time or the longitudinal nature of the data. To do this we require a model which examines how the change in one variable affects the change in another. A popular approach is to fit the within model. For the within model we subtract from each value of a variable its average value over the time period or panel waves (which is equivalent to subtracting the variable's between value in Equation (12.5)).

The within model is simply the variables in Equation (12.4) minus the variables in Equation (12.5) and is:

$$(y_{it} - \bar{y}_i) = b_0 + b_1 (x_{it} - \bar{x}_i) + (e_{it} - \bar{e}_i) \tag{12.6}$$

As we are fitting a different model, the coefficient b_1 will change between Equation (12.4), Equation (12.5) and Equation (12.6), but for consistency we have kept the same notation.

It can be seen that the data fitted by the within model is the difference between each observation and the mean value. (In some texts, data transformed in this way is called time-demeaned data). Note that the variable z does not appear in the within model. That is because the value of z was constant over time and thus each measure at each panel wave was the same, and the same as its mean. Thus the difference between any value and its mean value is always zero. The implication of this result is that the within model only estimates how the change in the response variable over time is affected by changes in explanatory variables that can themselves change. It does not assess how the response variable changes in respect of time-constant variables such as sex or ethnicity. In practice this is not often a severe limitation as the interest in the longitudinal analysis is invariably to understand change.

Note also that x^u, the unobserved variable which was assumed to be constant (or fixed) over time does not appear in the within model. The within model has thus eliminated the effect of time-invariant unobserved variables. It is for this reason that longitudinal models are regarded as being more resilient to the problems caused by unobserved variables.

The constant term (or intercept), b_0, has also been eliminated by demeaning the data.

The within model is also commonly known as the *fixed effects model*, because of the way it transforms (demeans) the data to remove the fixed effect of the unobserved variables. My preference is to refer to the model as the within model.

The within model can be estimated by ordinary least squares (see section 4.1).

Random effects model

Let us return to our original model in Equation (12.4), repeated here for ease of reference:

$$y_{it} = b_0 + b_1 x_{it} + b_2 z_i + x_i^u + e_{it} \tag{12.4}$$

When introducing Equation (12.4) it was pointed out that correlation between the unobserved variables and the explanatory variables results in biased estimates of the parameters. The advantage of the within model is that it removes the unobserved effect, x^u, but at the cost of also eliminating the time-constant explanatory variables, z.

Assume, however, that x^u is uncorrelated with each of the other explanatory variables (xs and zs) and in all time periods. This is a strong assumption, but there may be grounds for believing it in some situations. If so, then it is unnecessary and inefficient to eliminate x^u by fitting the within model. Under the assumption that x^u is uncorrelated with the other explanatory variables, Equation (12.4) becomes the random effects model. Because x^u is not correlated with any explanatory variables, x^u has a random effect (hence the name random effects model) and can be viewed as another source of random error. However, as the composite error term ($x^u + e$) can be shown to be correlated across the t periods, generalised least squares is required to estimate the model. But, for reasons not given here, generalised least squares does not demean the data and thus does not result in the time-constant explanatory variables, z, being eliminated from the model. Thus, one of the advantages of the random effects model over the fixed effects model is that it retains time-constant explanatory variables.

So which model should be fitted, fixed effects or random effects? Obviously if there is good evidence to suggest that the unobserved variables are correlated with any of the explanatory variables, a fixed effects model is appropriate. If there is evidence to suggest that they are uncorrelated, a random effects model is appropriate. One could simply fit both and compare results and Hausman has developed a formal test of this comparison. The Hausman test is described in the example below.

12.6 Fitting panel data models in Stata

Of the two, Stata is far superior to SPSS when it comes to fitting statistical models to panel data. Stata has a suite of commands prefixed by xt to analyse 'cross-sectional (the x) times-series' (the t) data. The most useful commands to social researchers are possibly xtreg (appropriate when fitting models to continuous response variables) and xtlogit (appropriate for binary response variables). In each case the type of model is specified by adding be (for the between-effects model), fe (for the fixed-effects model), re (for the random-effects model – fitted by generalised least squares) and mle (which fits the random-effects model by the method of maximum likelihood). An example using xtreg is given in the next section but in order to run xtreg (or other xt commands) Stata requires the data to be in a certain format, which has implications for the names given to variables. Essentially, the data must be sorted by panel wave within subject, but if certain conventions are followed when naming variables, other Stata commands can easily convert the data to the required format. The conventions and procedures are best illustrated by a simple example, comprising two subjects and two panel waves. At each wave the subjects' sex, income and hours worked are recorded. The data file will, most likely, be set out as follows:

id	sex	income1	income2	hours1	hours2
1	male	20000	25000	38	42
2	female	25000	15000	37	25

Alternatively, the variables could have been coded in the following order:

   id   sex   income1   hours1   income2   hours2

It does not matter which of the two orders is adopted. Either way, this data layout is referred to as a state-based data structure in Chapter 13 but Stata simply calls it *wide*. However, xt commands require this data to be in what Stata calls *long* format – which is called a person-time (diary) data structure in section 13.6.

The long data structure is set out as follows:

id	panel	sex	income	hours
1	1	male	20000	38
1	2	male	25000	42
2	1	female	25000	37
2	2	female	15000	25

In this long data structure, panel waves are sorted within subject.

Stata can easily convert the *wide* data format to the *long* data format by the reshape command. In this example the command would be:

   . reshape long income hours, i(id) j(panel)

There are two points to note here. First the command only includes the variables that can change at each panel wave (income and hours). Stata will recognise that sex is constant across panel waves and simply repeats the record for each panel wave. Second, the variables that can change must have the same name but a sequential number at the end. Here we added the panel wave number but we could have recorded the year instead.

If required, Stata can just as easily convert a *long* file to a *wide* file. In this example the command is:

   . reshape wide income hours, i(id) j(panel)

12.7 Example from the British Household Panel Study, time spent on housework

Having spent many years illustrating bivariate regression with an example taken from Healey (1996) which examined the relationship between the amount of time husbands spent doing housework and the size of the household, I was attracted to exploring this issue further in the British Household Panel Study (BHPS). The response variable throughout was the number of hours spent on housework per week (*howlng*).

The BHPS began in 1999 and the panel of 5000 households and 10,000 individuals has been contacted each year since then. The data file available from the UK Data Archive contained information for the first eleven panel waves. However, respondents did not appear to be asked about the time they spent on housework in the first wave. Two further waves (the third and ninth) did not contain information on two important explanatory variables and were also omitted. The data was further refined to include only those respondents who answered all the questions of interest at each of the eight panel waves. This resulted in a sample of 4361 individuals.

Without theorising too much, the number of hours spent on housework might depend on:

- the amount of housework there is to do: the primary measure here was the number of rooms in the accommodation (*hsroom*)
- how much time is available for housework: information was recorded on the number of hours normally worked per week (*jbhrs*) and the number of hours spent travelling to and from work (*jbttwt*)
- the composition of the household: as measured by the number of persons in the household (*hhsize*); whether living with spouse or partner (*spinhh*) and whether there were children in the household under 12 years of age (*hhch12*) – both variables were coded no = 0, yes = 1. Monthly household income was also recorded which was transformed by taking natural logarithms (*lnhhinc*)
- the individual characteristics of the respondent: age; sex (male = 0, female = 1); highest educational qualification obtained (*qfedhi* – below A-level = 0, A-level and above = 1), and the health of the respondent recorded on a six-point scale ranging from 1 = excellent to 6 = very poor (*hlstat*).

It can be seen that all the variables were continuous variables or binary/dummy (0, 1) variables. The exception is health which was measured on a six-point ordinal scale, but was treated as continuous in this analysis.

The data from the Data Archive was in the form of an SPSS file and the convention in the BHPS is to prefix the variable name with a letter to denote the panel wave, starting with 'a' for the first wave. Housework was not recorded at the first wave but at the second and onwards: *bhowlng . . . khowlng*. The first task was to rename these to conform to the convention required by Stata; that variables are numbered sequentially, the number coming at the end of the variable name. This is easily achieved in SPSS by the following command:

```
do repeat
a = bhowlng to khowlng / b = howlng1 to howlng8.
compute b = a.
end repeat.
```

It did not matter that the variables for waves *c* and *i* were omitted.

The next step was to save the SPSS file as a Stata file which is possible from SPSS version 14 onwards. The BHPS file structure is, in Stata terminology, wide, so once the data was read into Stata the next task was to convert the file to a long structure in readiness for analysis.

The between model was fitted first; the command and the output are presented in Figure 12.1.

```
. xtreg howlng hsroom jbhrs jbttwt hhsize spinhh hhch12 lnhhinc age sex qfedhi
> hlstat, be i( pid)

Between regression (regression on group means)   Number of obs      =    34888
Group variable (i): pid                          Number of groups   =     4361

R-sq:  within  = 0.0286                           Obs per group: min =        8
       between = 0.4868                                          avg =      8.0
       overall = 0.3466                                          max =        8

                                                  F(11,4349)         =   375.06
sd(u_i + avg(e_i.))=  6.878409                    Prob > F           =   0.0000

------------------------------------------------------------------------------
    howlng |      Coef.   Std. Err.      t    P>|t|     [95% Conf. Interval]
-----------+------------------------------------------------------------------
    hsroom |  -.0819692   .0983227    -0.83   0.405    -.2747317    .1107934
     jbhrs |  -.1367253   .0104034   -13.14   0.000    -.1571213   -.1163292
    jbttwt |  -.0152582   .0101747    -1.50   0.134    -.0352059    .0046895
    hhsize |   1.724643    .156235    11.04   0.000     1.418343    2.030943
    spinhh |   .9682196   .3274471     2.96   0.003     .3262563    1.610183
    hhch12 |   1.173662   .4232217     2.77   0.006     .3439315    2.003392
   lnhhinc |  -.6461363   .2670326    -2.42   0.016    -1.169656   -.1226164
       age |   .0540269   .0097838     5.52   0.000     .0348457    .0732081
       sex |   10.53152   .2189827    48.09   0.000      10.1022    10.96084
    qfedhi |  -1.395297   .2464643    -5.66   0.000    -1.878492    -.912101
    hlstat |  -.1515004    .165222    -0.92   0.359    -.4754198    .1724189
     _cons |   7.164884   1.907572     3.76   0.000     3.425071     10.9047
------------------------------------------------------------------------------
```

Figure 12.1 Stata output, between model.

The output is very similar to the output of multiple regression, presented in Chapter 4. The model in its entirety is very highly significant, as indicated by the *F* statistic. Three R^2 values are given, one each for within, between and overall. It will be seen that these three R^2 are given for all the models. As the between model is being fitted here the between R^2 is the most relevant and indicates that close to 49% of the variance is explained by the model. (The other two R^2 can be interpreted such that if the estimates of this model are used to predict the within model the R^2 is .0286 and this model fitted to the overall data would result in an R^2 of .3466. But to me these are not particularly meaningful, the R^2 pertaining to the between model is the most important.)

The focus here is not to address the substantive issue of the time spent on housework but to demonstrate fitting models for panel data. However, some findings are highlighted in order to clarify interpretation of the model (although interpretation is no different to that of multiple regression). The size of the accommodation (*hsroom*), the time spent travelling to work (*jbttwt*) and the respondent's health (*hlstat*) are not significantly related to the amount of time spent on housework. The most important explanatory variable is *sex*; the model finds that controlling for other variables in the model, women spend about 10.5 hours more than men undertaking housework. Every additional hour at work (*jbhrs*) results in less time (.137 hours) spent on housework.

The second model fitted is the within (or fixed effects) model. The command and output is shown at Figure 12.2.

The *F* test indicates that the within model is significant but the R^2 value is low, at .04

```
. xtreg  howlng hsroom jbhrs jbttwt hhsize spinhh hhch12 lnhhinc age sex qfedhi
> hlstat, fe i( pid)

Fixed-effects (within) regression          Number of obs     =      34888
Group variable (i): pid                    Number of groups  =       4361

R-sq:  within  = 0.0401                     Obs per group: min =          8
       between = 0.0141                                    avg =        8.0
       overall = 0.0176                                    max =          8

                                            F(10,30517)       =     127.50
corr(u_i, Xb)  = -0.1920                     Prob > F          =     0.0000

------------------------------------------------------------------------------
      howlng |     Coef.    Std. Err.      t     P>|t|    [95% Conf. Interval]
-------------+----------------------------------------------------------------
      hsroom | -.0190549    .0529427    -0.36    0.719   -.1228248    .0847149
       jbhrs | -.0968221    .0045857   -21.11    0.000   -.1058103   -.0878338
      jbttwt | -.0080275    .0037757    -2.13    0.034    -.015428   -.0006271
      hhsize |  .3007035    .0788356     3.81    0.000    .1461825    .4552245
      spinhh |  2.012313    .1909816    10.54    0.000    1.637981    2.386645
      hhch12 |  1.465845    .1788635     8.20    0.000    1.115265    1.816425
     lnhhinc |  .0565982    .0956311     0.59    0.554   -.1308427     .244039
         age | -.1774122    .0136301   -13.02    0.000   -.2041278   -.1506967
         sex | (dropped)
      qfedhi |  -.023058    .2722523    -0.08    0.933   -.5566838    .5105678
      hlstat | -.2621001    .0599835    -4.37    0.000   -.3796702     -.14453
       _cons |  20.70835    .7935181    26.10    0.000    19.15303    22.26368
-------------+----------------------------------------------------------------
     sigma_u |  9.7318999
     sigma_e |  6.5322853
         rho |  .68939761   (fraction of variance due to u_i)
------------------------------------------------------------------------------
F test that all u_i=0:     F(4360, 30517) =     9.00         Prob > F = 0.0000
```

Figure 12.2 Stata output, within (or fixed effects) model.

or 4%. Recall that the within model considers how a change in an explanatory variable affects the change in the response variable, which in this case is the change in the number of hours spent on housework. From the model we see that controlling for changes in other variables an increase in the number of hours worked reduces the average time spent on housework (by .097 hours). A change in the number of persons in the household (*hhsize*) increases the time spent on housework (by .3 hours). Because *sex* does not change over time it has been dropped from the model.

Three variables were not significant, size of the accommodation (*hsroom*), log of monthly income (*lnhhinc*) and educational qualifications (*qfedhi*). This implies that a change in any of these variables did not affect changes in the amount of time spent on housework. But is this conclusion justified? It may be that change in an explanatory variable does have an effect on time spent on housework but this effect is masked because in reality the explanatory variable does not change much over time. In other words, some explanatory variables can in theory vary over time but in practice they do not vary much over time and are virtually time-constant variables (like sex and ethnicity). A good example here is educational qualifications, which may change over time for younger people, but for older people they remain constant. Closer inspection of the data on educational qualifications revealed little difference across the eight panel waves, and, as a result, educational qualifications were found to be highly correlated from one wave to another. Thus a change in educational qualifications may change the time spent on housework (and the between model showed educational qualifications to be important) but as there is little change across panel waves in this dataset, a relationship is not revealed.

It can be seen from this model that nearly 70% of the total variation (rho = .689) is attributable to differences between panel members and a little over 30% attributable to changes over time within individuals.

The third model fitted was the random effects model and the command and results are shown in Figure 12.3.

```
. xtreg  howlng hsroom jbhrs jbttwt hhsize spinhh hhch12 lnhhinc age sex qfedhi
> hlstat, re i( pid)

Random-effects GLS regression                   Number of obs      =      34888
Group variable (i): pid                         Number of groups   =       4361

R-sq:  within  = 0.0340                          Obs per group: min =          8
       between = 0.4721                                         avg =        8.0
       overall = 0.3414                                         max =          8

Random effects u_i ~ Gaussian                    Wald chi2(11)      =    4995.46
corr(u_i, X)        = 0 (assumed)                 Prob > chi2        =     0.0000

------------------------------------------------------------------------------
     howlng |     Coef.    Std. Err.      z     P>|z|    [95% Conf. Interval]
------------+-----------------------------------------------------------------
     hsroom | -.0889705    .0459265    -1.94    0.053   -.1789847    .0010437
      jbhrs | -.1035197    .0041961   -24.67    0.000   -.1117439   -.0952955
     jbttwt | -.0099151    .0035532    -2.79    0.005   -.0168792   -.0029509
     hhsize |  .7105946    .0695836    10.21    0.000    .5742132    .8469759
     spinhh |  1.934129    .1628069    11.88    0.000    1.615033    2.253225
     hhch12 |  1.308154    .1637729     7.99    0.000    .9871652    1.629143
    lnhhinc | -.4147853    .0870589    -4.76    0.000   -.5854175   -.2441531
        age |  .0056979    .0065157     0.87    0.382   -.0070727    .0184685
        sex |  10.79277    .2133251    50.59    0.000    10.37466    11.21088
     qfedhi | -1.547989     .174342    -8.88    0.000   -1.889693   -1.206285
     hlstat | -.285964     .0563472    -5.08    0.000   -.3964026   -.1755255
      _cons |  9.454102    .6855105    13.79    0.000    8.110526    10.79768
------------+-----------------------------------------------------------------
    sigma_u |  6.4790942
    sigma_e |  6.5322853
        rho |  .49591203   (fraction of variance due to u_i)
------------------------------------------------------------------------------
```

Figure 12.3 Stata, output, random effects model.

Because of the theory behind the random effects model and the procedures for estimating it, the *F* test is not appropriate and a Wald chi-squared statistic is given instead. The Wald test shows that the model is highly significant. Note that unlike the fixed effects model, *sex*, a time invariant covariate, is included in the random effects model. Broadly, the coefficients are not too dissimilar to those of the within (fixed effects) model but many of the significance levels have changed. This model suggests that about half of the variance is attributable to variation at the individual level and half attributable to within individuals over time.

However, which model is to be preferred, the within model or the random effects model? To answer this we can use the Hausman test, which compares the coefficients of the two models. The null hypothesis is that they are not different and we can adopt the random effects model because we can conclude that the unobserved variables are not correlated with the explanatory variables. To undertake the Hausman test in Stata the random effects model is run as above (but is not shown again here). The estimates are saved so that they can be compared with the within (fixed effects) estimates. The within model is then fitted. These commands are shown below.

. estimates store random_effects

. xtreg howlng hsroom jbhrs jbttwt hhsize spinhh hhch12 lnhhinc age sex qfedhi
> hlstat, fe i (pid)

The output from the within model is not shown; it is the same as given earlier. Then the Hausman command is entered as below.

```
. hausman . random_effects

                  ---- Coefficients ----
             |       (b)          (B)          (b-B)      sqrt(diag(V_b-V_B))
             |        .        random_eff~s    Difference         S.E.
-------------+-----------------------------------------------------------------
    hsroom   |    -.0190549     -.0889705      .0699156         .0263379
     jbhrs   |    -.0968221     -.1035197      .0066976         .0018498
    jbttwt   |    -.0080275     -.0099151      .0018875         .0012769
    hhsize   |     .3007035      .7105946     -.409891          .0370563
    spinhh   |    2.012313      1.934129       .0781844         .0998392
    hhch12   |    1.465845      1.308154       .1576911         .0719068
   lnhhinc   |     .0565982     -.4147853      .4713835         .0395734
       age   |    -.1774122      .0056979     -.1831101         .0119718
    qfedhi   |    -.023058      -1.547989      1.524931         .209108
    hlstat   |    -.2621001     -.285964       .0238639         .0205672
-------------+-----------------------------------------------------------------
                        b = consistent under Ho and Ha; obtained from xtreg
           B = inconsistent under Ha, efficient under Ho; obtained from xtreg

    Test:  Ho:  difference in coefficients not systematic

             chi2(10) = (b-B)'[(V_b-V_B)^(-1)](b-B)
                      =       360.50
          Prob>chi2 =        0.0000
```

Figure 12.4 Stata output, Hausman test of models.

The test only compares coefficients that appear in both models so sex is omitted in the comparison table above. The Hausman chi-squared test is highly significant, indicating a difference between the models and that it is not safe to accept the stricter assumptions underlying the random effects model. The test gives support to the within (fixed effects) model.

12.8 Relationship between panel models and multilevel models

At this point readers may have noticed a correspondence between the within and random effects models presented above and the multilevel models discussed in Chapter 9, and rightly so as there are similarities. Indeed the random effects model above is a multilevel model. Repeated measurement arising from panel studies is a two-level data structure, but with the individuals at level 2 and the repeated measures, collected at each wave, at level 1.

Longitudinal data can thus be analysed by adopting the methodology of multilevel models. Further details are not given here but the texts referred to in Chapter 9 all contain sections on fitting multilevel models to longitudinal data.

Further reading

Readers wishing to understand more fully the limitations of cross-sectional data for drawing causal inferences and how many of these limitations can be overcome with longitudinal research designs are referred to Davies (1994) and to the Introduction in either Blossfeld and Rohwer (1995) or Blossfeld *et al.* (2007) – the Introduction to both books is virtually identical – or to Blossfeld and Rohwer (1997).

The econometrics literature is a good source of instruction on analysing time series data. Wooldridge (2003) explains fitting regression models to time series data and to panel data.

An informative introduction to modelling time series analysis, including an example comparing results from different models, is Sanders and Ward (1994).

The further reading listed at the end of Chapter 9 explains fitting multilevel models to longitudinal data.

13 Event history models

Life course events occur at specific points in time and in relation to other life events. People experience a period of time (or spell) in one situation (or state) before moving to another state, which they will occupy for a further spell; for example being single and then getting married. The first part of this chapter presents models that have been developed to analyse data on the duration of spells and the interrelationship between spells and other characteristics or influences. Survival models, which are applicable when a spell ends in a single event, are discussed. Discrete time models are appropriate in a much wider range of applications (and subsume survival models) and are presented in the second part of this chapter.

13.1 Time to an event: Survival models

Often in social research we know whether an event occurred and we also know when it occurred. From this information the time interval to an event from some other fixed event can be calculated. Many examples exist, such as the time to getting a job after leaving education or after becoming unemployed, the period of time to committing an offence following release from prison or the length of a marriage before it ends in separation or death. Knowing the time to an event is additional information, providing greater insights than simply knowing whether an event occurred or not.

Time is a continuous variable which suggests that the researcher could simply proceed by fitting multiple regression models (see Chapter 4), length of time to the event, or duration, being the dependent or response variable. However, multiple regression results in biased estimates if the data are censored – as is usually the case. Censoring is discussed in detail below but is, essentially, the inability to observe events before or after a defined cut-off point. To overcome this limitation, special statistical models have been developed, which are generically known as survival models. These models were initially developed for, and have been applied extensively in, medical research and engineering where the dependent variable might typically be the length of survival following some form of medical treatment or the time to failure of a particular piece of equipment. A key concept in survival models is the hazard rate. Furthermore, over time some of the explanatory variables may themselves change in value – these variables are known as time-varying covariates. All of these three concepts are best explained by way of examples, which are now described.

Example 1: Reoffending by parolees

In Tarling (1993), I explored the application of survival models to identify factors associated with reoffending by prisoners released from prison on parole licence. The sample comprised 738 men serving prison sentences of over 18 months and who were released from prison during the 1980s. All 738 offenders were followed up for 30 months following release and, if they were subsequently reconvicted of a further offence, the date of the commission of the offence was recorded. In the 30-month follow-up period, 510 (69%) men were known to have committed a further offence, leaving 228 not having committed an offence within the follow-up period. Length of time to the event (the first offence committed following release; an offender may have committed more than one offence in the follow-up period) was measured in days.

Socio-demographic information was available on each offender, together with details of his criminal career. The principal covariates available for analysis were:

- type of offence committed which led to the index prison sentence
- age at conviction
- age at first conviction
- type of occupation
- employment status at time of original conviction
- marital status
- living arrangements following release form prison
- employment arrangements following release from prison
- reconviction prediction score.

Most of the above variables are self-explanatory except, perhaps, the last. The reconviction prediction score (RPS) is a simple points score, expressed as a percentage, indicating the probability of reconviction within two years following release from prison. It is a weighted sum of many criminal history and background variables (including those above) shown to be related to reconviction.

Example 2: Training for Work

The second example is from an evaluation of Training for Work (TfW) conducted by Payne *et al.* (1999). Training for Work was a government-sponsored programme which aimed to assist long-term unemployed people find jobs through skills training and work experience. A nationally representative sample of 822 people who had been unemployed for more than six months and had participated in TfW, were selected. Each participant was individually matched with a person of the same gender, from the same geographical area, of a similar age and with a similar employment history but who had not participated in TfW. This matched comparison sample comprised 815 people.

Members of the first sample had completed TfW in the autumn of 1995 and both samples were interviewed in spring 1996 and re-interviewed in summer 1997. The time period started when a person became unemployed. The date they obtained a job was recorded (they could have obtained a job while on the training programme or some time afterwards). A total of 696 had not obtained a job by the summer of 1997. The time difference, measured in months, between becoming unemployed and obtaining a job (or the summer of 1997 for those that did not obtain a job before then) was calculated and became the variable *duration*.

The objective of the study was to assess whether or not the Training for Work programme was effective in helping unemployed people get jobs as well as identifying factors that were associated with a return to work.

Although the models are traditionally called survival models – stemming from their first fields of application (where patients survive until they die or components work until they stop functioning), the above two examples illustrate that this nomenclature can be misleading. In the first, prisoners could perhaps be considered to be surviving crime free and failed when they reoffended. However, in the second, unemployed people were without a job and succeeded (not failed) in obtaining one. Perhaps more neutral terms, such as duration models or event occurrence would be more helpful. Nevertheless, when applying and interpreting these models (as with other models) the researcher has to be clear which way the variables are coded and what the outcome is defined to be.

Censoring

In many research studies, subjects can only be followed up for a certain period of time and information is not available beyond that 'cut-off point', which is known in survival models as the censoring point. Consider the first example above. Prisoners were followed up for 30 months, but not beyond that point. It was stated that after 30 months 510 had reoffended, but what of the other 228? All we know is that they did not commit offences within the 30 months when we stopped observing them. Some may have committed offences at a later date, but we have no information on that (although we know from other studies which have followed up prisoners for a longer period that many more will reoffend later). In this study, 30 months is the censoring point.

In the TfW example above, subjects were only followed up until the summer of 1997. Their employment history beyond that censoring point is not known. Some of the 696 still unemployed at summer 1997 will have successfully obtained a job later, but we do not know that.

In a follow-up study, such as the two described above, the data are said to be censored to the right, that is we have information at the beginning of the time period but no information beyond a cut-off point at the end of the study. This is depicted graphically as case A in Figure 13.1. Censoring to the right can also arise within the study period if a different event occurs which prematurely terminates the follow-up period. Such a situation (depicted as case B) would result if a subject died or emigrated during the study period or left or opted out of the study for some other reason.

Right censoring is the most common but data can also be censored to the left, that is, at the beginning of the time period. This often occurs in retrospective studies which rely on administrative records. Those records may only contain information back to a certain point in time (for example, when the subjects started school). Left-censored data is depicted as case C in Figure 13.1. To complete the picture it is possible to have data censored to both the left and the right (case D) or not censored at all (case E).

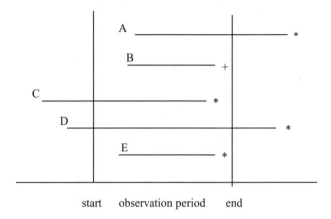

start   observation period   end

* occurrence of the event of interest
+ occurrence of an event not of interest

Figure 13.1 Censored data.

Hazard rate

The hazard rate $h(t)$ (also known as the risk) is defined to be the number that fail at time t expressed as a proportion of those in the sample that have survived up to time t. Note the second half of the definition; it is not the proportion of the whole sample but the proportion of those that have survived up to time t, that is, the whole sample excluding those that have already failed before time t.

The hazard rate for the parole sample is presented in Table 13.1. Although the duration was measured in days, the data have been grouped into six-month periods for illustrative purposes.

The last column of Table 13.1 shows the proportion of the entire sample that reoffended for the first time in each of the five six-month periods. Typically it shows a sharp decline as those who reoffended in one period are not counted if they fail again in a later period. However, discounting those that have failed in previous periods shows those that remain at risk at the start of the subsequent period (column 3). Expressing those reoffending in the period as a proportion of those still at risk produces the hazard rate (column 4). It can be seen that the hazard rate also declines but not at the same rate. In fact it is virtually constant during the first 12 months. A declining hazard is not uncommon, as it is often the case that if a person survives for a period then his or her

Table 13.1 Number and proportion of parolees reoffending and the hazard rate

Time period (months)	Number reoffending	Number at risk	Hazard rate	Proportion of sample reoffending
0 < 6	209	738	.28	.28
6 < 12	137	529	.26	.19
12 < 18	81	392	.21	.11
18 < 24	59	311	.19	.08
24 < 30	24	252	.10	.03

chances of ultimately surviving improve. Or put another way, if a person is to fail they are more likely to do so fairly quickly.

However, depending on the situation, hazard rates can decrease, increase or remain constant throughout the period (or even change direction throughout the period). The direction, or shape, of the hazard rate can influence the choice of survival model adopted. However, Cox proposed a model, Cox's proportional hazards model (or Cox's regression model), which makes no assumptions about the distribution of the hazard. For this reason, and its ability to incorporate covariates, it has been widely adopted, almost to the point of being the standard initial procedure. It is presented in section 13.2 and an example of its application is in section 13.4. (For a discussion of other models, see Tarling, 1993.)

Time-varying covariates

The concept of time-varying covariates was introduced in section 12.5 but is restated and extended here. When researching social processes over time, events can occur or statuses change within the time period under investigation. Of course some variables do not change and are fixed and immutable. Sex and ethnicity are examples of fixed variables.

Some variables become fixed once the study period has been defined. Consider Example 1 – as soon as the prisoners had been selected for the study their number of previous offences became fixed. Had the study been undertaken later, or had they been selected for a subsequent study, their number of previous convictions may well have been different.

Other variables, however, change during the course of the study period, and these are known as time-varying (or time-dependent) covariates. One set of such variables may be thought of as 'clocks', the most obvious here being age – in Example 1 all the prisoners were 30 months older at the end of the follow-up period than they were when released from prison. But other variables are also of this type, for example the length of time a person is unemployed increases up to the point that they get a job. These variables can be important in a study as risk is often related to time. An older person may find it more difficult to get a job, or the longer a person has been unemployed the more difficult it may be to get a job.

During the study period, events may occur which change the status of the research subject. These events and changes of state can affect the outcome under investigation. In the first example, a prisoner might get married or divorced during the follow-up period, changing their status from single to married in the first instance or married to divorced in the second. Either change of status may affect the offender's risk of reoffending. In the second example, a significant event may be the birth of a child. Such an event may influence when either or both parents get a job and the type of employment they seek.

13.2 Cox's proportional hazards model

In the early 1970s, Cox proposed the proportional hazards model which is a simple and elegant model for analysing survival data. The advantage of this model is that it alleviates the problem of knowing the underlying distribution of the hazard rate and is therefore extremely flexible and suitable in a wide range of applications. It takes into account censored data and can accommodate some covariates which vary over time. Furthermore, it is readily available in SPSS and Stata and has been applied universally.

In Cox's model the failure rate or hazard rate, $h(t)$, at time t is related to the covariates as:

$$h(t) = h_0(t)\, e^{b_1 x_1 + b_2 x_2 + b_3 x_3 + \ldots}$$

where:

$h_0(t)$ is the baseline hazard function when the x_p are set equal to 0, that is, the expected risk without the influence of the explanatory variables, x_p

x_p are the explanatory variables

b_p are the coefficients of the xs.

The one assumption underlying the model is that $h(t)$ and $h_0(t)$ are proportional and a method for checking that assumption is given later.

An alternative way of expressing Cox's model is to divide both sides of the equation by $h_0(t)$, resulting in:

$$\frac{h(t)}{h_0(t)} = e^{b_1 x_1 + b_2 x_2 + b_3 x_3 + \ldots}$$

The left-hand side, the response variable, is the relative hazard or the hazard ratio and is the change in risk (hazard) associated with the xs.

The component $e^{b_p x_p}$ is the risk associated with the value of x_p relative to a value of $x_p = 0$. Here the bs are on the log scale as in the logistic, multinomial and ordered regression models presented earlier. As with those models, the b_ps can be readily interpreted. For example, if b_p is positive this indicates that an increase in x_p will increase the hazard rate or risk. In the first example, an increase in risk would decrease the length of time to reoffend.

The model can be developed further by taking the natural logarithm of all the components, resulting in:

$$\log\left[\frac{h(t)}{h_0(t)}\right] = b_1 x_1 + b_2 x_2 + b_3 x_3 + \ldots$$

The bs are now the odds or Exp(B) as discussed in previous models.

The proportional hazards model is for continuous time and, in theory, ties (events occurring at the same time) should not exist. In practice, they often do, as failure times might be grouped as in the second example where time to obtaining a job was measured to the nearest month. Methods for handling tied data are available and should be followed if this is a serious problem. However, the occurrence of ties was not such a problem in the first example as time to reoffend was measured in days.

Cox's regression model was applied to the data in Example 1. The best fitting model is presented in Table 13.2.

It can be seen that all three variables were significant, their t-values well in excess of 1.96 (the 5% level).

Interpreting the coefficients in Table 13.2 is similar to interpreting the coefficients in the other models discussed so far. The Bs indicate the effect of the xs on the log of the hazard. The Exp(B)s indicate the effects of the xs on the hazard. Considering the first explanatory variable, for each additional year of age at conviction the hazard is multiplied by .950 after taking into account other variables in the model. Thus the older an offender is at the time of conviction the less likely that he will reoffend. The effect of the

Table 13.2 Cox's proportional hazards model: time to reoffend by prisoners released on parole licence

Covariates	B	Exp(B)	t value
Age at conviction	−0.051	.950	5.7
Number of previous convictions	0.041	1.042	3.5
Reconviction prediction score	0.022	1.022	6.1

other two explanatory variables is in the opposite direction, in that the greater the number of previous convictions or the larger the value of the reconviction prediction score, the greater the hazard and the more likely it is that the offender will reoffend. For each additional previous conviction, the hazard increases by 4.2% and for each unit increase in the reconviction prediction score, the hazard increases by 2.2%.

13.3 Comparing survival times between two or more groups

When the focus of interest is to examine the impact of a particular treatment or intervention, a suitable starting point is to compare the survival rates for the different groups. The objective of the Training for Work study, it will be recalled, was to assess the effect of this programme in getting people into jobs by comparing the time those participating in TfW (the trainee sample) took to obtain a job with those in the comparison group who did not participate in TfW. The Kaplan–Meier method is invariably adopted when survival rates need to be compared as it estimates the survival rates, displays them graphically and provides significance tests in order that inferences may be drawn about the difference between them. The procedure in SPSS is:

Analyze → Survival → Kaplan–Meier

Which brings up the following dialogue box:

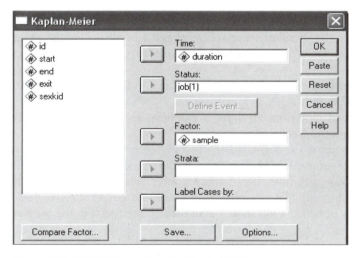

Figure 13.2 SPSS dialogue box for Kaplan–Meier.

The researcher has then to specify the variable containing the Time to the event – in this case the variable *duration*. Status requires the variable that records whether the event occurred. In this study it is *job* and once stated lights up the Define Event bar immediately below. Define Event must be completed by giving the code (or range of codes) that indicates that the event has occurred. Code 1 of *job* indicates in the data file that the person obtained a job. Factor requests the variable that distinguishes between the group(s) that are to be compared. Here *sample* is a binary variable, code 1 for the comparison group and code 2 for the trainee group.

The output is voluminous, giving a detailed table of survival times for the groups (although this can be omitted by 'unchecking' the box Survival table(s) in options). The summary information provided is shown in Table 13.3.

Table 13.3 Mean and median survival times for comparison group and participation group in Training for Work

	Survival time	Standard error	95% confidence interval	
Comparison group				
Mean (limited to 142)	68.3	2.7	63.1	73.6
Median	49.0	3.5	42.1	55.8
Participation group				
Mean (limited to 142)	49.8	2.0	45.8	53.7
Median	30.0	1.3	27.5	32.5

The mean survival time is given for both groups, but note it is not the arithmetic mean but the area under the survival curve (shown below) for the uncensored cases. The detailed calculation of the mean given need not concern us unduly except that we cannot replicate the estimates by calculating the mean in the original dataset. Of more importance is that the means for both groups are calculated in the same way and are comparable. The confidence intervals for the two groups do not overlap, which indicates that the survival rates for the two groups are significantly different – although significance will be tested formally later.

The median for the two groups is also given. The median survival time is the time of the first event at which the cumulative survival reaches 0.5 or 50%. Like the mean, the confidence intervals indicate that the medians for the two groups are significantly different.

(limited to 142) simply states the longest survival time in the data – in this case the censoring point at 142 months.

By choosing Survival plot from Options, a graphical representation is produced, which is shown in Figure 13.3 opposite.

The comparison group is the higher of the two curves and indicates that those in the comparison group survive longer than those in the trainee group. However, it will be recalled that *duration* was time to obtaining a job. Thus surviving longer means taking longer to obtain a job. The trainee group (the lower curve) survived less well, which meant that they obtained a job sooner than their counterparts in the comparison group.

Survival Functions

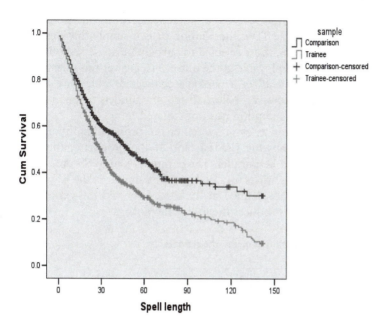

Figure 13.3 SPSS output, Kaplan–Meier survival functions.

Are these survival curves significantly different? Did those participating in TfW obtain jobs more quickly? That question has already been answered by examining the confidence intervals. However, further confirmation can be obtained by requesting significance tests (click on Compare Factor and check the appropriate boxes). Three tests are available (Log Rank, Breslow and Tarone–Ware) and all were requested here (by checking the appropriate boxes). There is little difference between the tests and only in exceptional circumstances would they result in a different inference or conclusion to be drawn.

Test Statistics for Equality of Survival Distributions for trainee

	Statistic	df	Significance
Log Rank	34.06	1	.0000
Breslow	21.21	1	.0000
Tarone-Ware	26.59	1	.0000

Figure 13.4 SPSS output, tests of equality of survival curves.

The results show that all three are highly significant and indicate that trainees obtained a job more quickly than members of the comparison group.

13.4 Fitting Cox's proportional hazards regression model to Training for Work data

The previous Kaplan–Meier analysis revealed a difference between the two groups, but is the difference attributable to the TfW intervention or is it simply that despite being matched on certain characteristics, those selected to participate possessed other characteristics that made them more employable at the outset? To answer this question and to identify those characteristics that affect a person's chances of obtaining a job, Cox regression models were fitted. However, before fitting any models it was necessary to check that the proportionality assumption was not violated.

A simple but useful method for assessing whether the proportionality assumption holds is to examine the log minus log (LML) plot. If the proportionality assumption holds, the two curves should be parallel. The commands in SPSS are Analyze → Survival → Cox Regression which brings up a dialogue box similar to the Kaplan–Meier dialogue box. Time and Status are defined in the same way and the variable *sample* should be entered in Strata. This produces the following plot.

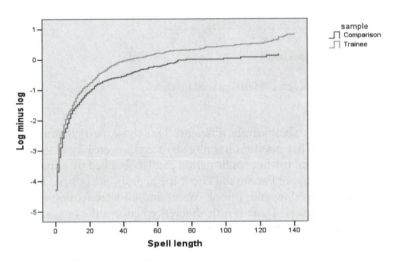

Figure 13.5 SPSS output, LML plot.

It can be seen in the plot above that the curves are broadly parallel in the TfW study so we can have confidence in fitting Cox's proportional hazards models.

To fit models in SPSS, follow the instructions given above but covariates need to be specified and any that are categorical need to be identified as such. In the model fitted here three variables were included, all categorical: *sample* (whether in the comparison group or the trainee group) (note: if continuing from the previous analysis, *sample* will need to be deleted from the Strata box), *health* (with three categories: no problems, has problems, registered disabled) and *driving* (doesn't have a driving licence and does have a driving licence). The variables, the way they were coded and which were entered in the model, are given in Figure 13.6. Following previous conventions, the highest code was taken as the reference category. The model is set out in Figure 13.7.

Categorical Variable Codings[b,c,d]

		Frequency	(1)	(2)
sample[a]	1=Comparison	807	1	
	2=trainee	815	0	
health[a]	1=No problems	1209	1	0
	2=Has problem	332	0	1
	3=Registered disabled	81	0	0
driving[a]	1=No	675	1	
	2=Yes	947	0	

a. Indicator Parameter Coding

b. Category variable: sample

c. Category variable: health (Long-term health and disability)

d. Category variable: driving (Has full driving licience)

Figure 13.6 SPSS output, categorical variable codings.

Variables in the Equation

	B	SE	Wald	df	Sig.	Exp(B)
sample	-.382	.067	32.582	1	.000	.682
health			51.540	2	.000	
health(1)	.650	.175	13.739	1	.000	1.916
health(2)	.048	.192	.062	1	.804	1.049
driving	-.479	.069	47.729	1	.000	.619

Figure 13.7 SPSS output, proportional hazards model.

The model was very highly significant, the reduction in the -2Loglikelihood was 143.7, with 4 degrees of freedom, which compared with the chi-squared distribution is highly significant, $p < .001$.

Considering each variable separately, not participating in TfW meant the 'risk' of getting a job was reduced to .682 compared with those who participated. Or, looked at the other way, participants' chances of getting a job were one and a half times better (1/.682) than non-participants.

Compared with the reference category, registered disabled, those with no health problems are very nearly twice as likely to get a job. However, the chances of those with health problems are little different (and not statistically significantly so) from those who are registered disabled (although the relatively small numbers in these two categories should be noted).

Similarly, not having a driving licence reduced the risk of obtaining a job, or having a licence increased the chances by 1.6 (1/.619) compared with those without a driving licence. This finding reflects the fact that being able to drive opens more opportunities for employment: either in being able to travel to a wider range of jobs or to take up the kind of work that involves driving a vehicle.

Undertaking survival analysis in Stata is straightforward as Stata has a suite of built-in dedicated commands (all prefixed st – for survival-time). A particular advantage of Stata is its flexibility in being able to perform survival analysis working from a variety of data structures. The main data structures are described in section 13.6 and the Stata command stset can declare any of these to be survival-time data, informing Stata of the key variables for subsequent analysis: duration, event, whether censored, as well as noting which are fixed and time-varying covariates.

The Cox regression model is appropriate in situations where the focus of interest is time to a single event; and especially where there are no (or very few) ties, the proportionality assumption is not violated and preferably where there are no time-varying covariates.

13.5 Discrete time models

A relatively recent innovation has been the development of discrete time models which are the subject of the second part of this chapter. Discrete time models provide an alternative to survival models and the Cox regression model can be fitted as a discrete time model. But discrete time models offer additional flexibility for analysing longitudinal data where events occur at different points in time or at different stages of a life course. Discrete time modelling is particularly suited to social data as people are often in a number of discrete states (a job, a particular residence) or events occur at certain points (vote at elections, birth of a child) which do not change frequently. This contrasts with medical or engineering applications where variables change frequently and continuously over time (blood pressure, performance of a component). Before discussing the models it is necessary to clarify what is meant by discrete time and the implications it has for different data structures.

13.6 Data structures

To illustrate data structures, let us consider the following hypothetical example in which four people are studied over a four-year period (years 1 to 4). The first three were unemployed at the start of the study whereas the fourth was employed from the outset. Information was collected on any change in employment status during the four years, together with the length of time each person had been unemployed before the start of the study, each subject's sex, marital status (and any changes in marital status throughout the four years) and if and when any children were born in the study period.

The first subject was a man who had been unemployed for two years before the start of the study, but got a full-time job in year 2. He was married at the start of the study but divorced in year 4. He had no children.

The second subject was a female who was unemployed for one year before the start of the study. She was married throughout the four-year study period and had a child in year 2. She returned to work part-time in year 3.

The third subject was a male who had also been unemployed for one year before the study. He was single at the start of the study but married in year 2. His wife gave birth to a child in year 4. He remained unemployed throughout the four-year study period.

The fourth subject, a male, was in part-time employment at the start of the study but became unemployed in year 3. He had been in continuous employment before the start of the study. He was divorced and did not have any children.

Until recently, and certainly in most historical studies, the structure of the database would be either of two types, state-based or event-based.

State-based data structure records the status of each person in each year. For this hypothetical study the data might be coded as in Table 13.4:

Table 13.4 State-based data structure

Person ID	Sex	Marital status at Yr 1	Marital status at Yr 2	Marital status at Yr 3	Marital status at Yr 4	Job at Yr 1	Job at Yr 2	Job at Yr 3	Job at Yr 4	Child at Yr 1	Child at Yr 2	Child at Yr 3	Child at Yr 4	Time previously unemployed
id	sex	msyr1	msyr2	msyr3	msyr4	jobyr1	jobyr2	jobyr3	jobyr4	childyr1	childyr2	childyr3	childyr4	prunemp
1	M	married	married	married	divorced	no	yes (FT)	yes (FT)	yes (FT)	no	no	no	no	2
2	F	married	married	married	married	no	no	yes (PT)	yes (PT)	no	yes	no	no	1
3	M	single	married	married	married	no	no	no	no	no	no	no	yes	1
4	M	divorced	divorced	divorced	divorced	yes	yes	no	no	no	no	no	no	0

Note: The second row of the heading lists the variable names used in the SPSS syntax.

Table 13.5 Event-based data structure

Person ID	Sex	Time married	Time divorced	Child born	Time previously unemployed	Time start job	Time end job	Type job
Id	sex	marryr	divorcyr	childyr	prunemp	job1st	job1end	job1type
1	M	Yr 1	Yr 4	–	2	Yr 2	Yr 4	FT
2	F	Yr 1	–	Yr 2	1	Yr 3	Yr 4	PT
3	M	Yr 2	–	Yr 4	1	–	–	–
4	M	–	Yr 1	–	0	Yr 1	Yr 2	PT

Note: The second row of the heading lists the variable names used in the SPSS syntax.

This data structure is of a similar form to that often constructed in longitudinal research. The British Household Panel Study data file analysed in the previous chapter is of this type, where the years here would be the panel waves in the BHPS. Stata calls this a wide file.

Event-based data structure records the dates at which events occur. For this hypothetical study the data might be coded as shown in Table 13.5.

Comparing state-based and event-based data structures, it can be that the state-based structure is often larger than its event-based counterpart, especially if data is recorded over a large number of time periods. It is usually the case in event-based structures that no more than three variables are needed to describe the event: its start time, end time and the type of event.

If the data was coded in either of the formats illustrated above, and the purpose of the study was to fit a survival model (as in section 13.4) in order to analyse time to getting a job, two additional variables would need to be derived: (1) time or duration to getting a job from the start of the study, and (2) whether the person got a job or whether their record was censored. In our example, the first two subjects did get a job but the third had not got a job by the end of the study – the censoring point. The fourth person already had a job at the start so would be excluded from any study that examined time to getting a job.

Spell-based (or episode-based) data structure Recent advances in statistical software have increased the popularity of spell-based/episode-based data structures, which record each spell experienced by each subject. For this hypothetical study the data would be as shown in Table 13.6.

Spell data structures require a little more by way of explanation. Another way that we can conceptualise the data is that for each individual we have a sequence of spells (or episodes) of time spent in discrete states, such as being single, married, divorced or unemployed, employed etc. An event occurs causing a person to transfer from one state to another; for example, a person gets a job and transfers from state unemployed to state employed. In constructing the data we have to create a new spell whenever *any* of the non-time variables change value. Take subject 1; he enters the study in a set of states – his first spell. He remains in this set for one year, when the set changes because he gets a job. He thus enters a new, second, spell which lasts unchanged for two years.

Table 13.6 Spell-based (or episode-based) data structure

Person ID	Start year	End year	Sex	Marital status	Children	Time previously unemployed	Employment status	Spell number	Spell length
1	1	1	M	married	0	2	unemp	1	1
1	2	3	M	married	0	2	FT	2	2
1	4	4	M	divorced	0	2	FT	3	1
2	1	1	F	married	0	1	unemp	1	1
2	2	2	F	married	1	1	unemp	2	1
2	3	4	F	married	1	1	PT	3	2
3	1	1	M	single	0	1	unemp	1	1
3	2	3	M	married	0	1	unemp	2	2
3	4	4	M	married	1	1	unemp	3	1
4	1	2	M	divorced	0	0	PT	1	2
4	3	4	M	divorced	0	0	unemp	2	2

Note: Blank rows have been included to indicate more clearly data for the three subjects.

This spell ends when he gets divorced whereupon he starts a different, third, spell which continues to the end of the study period.

Person-time (diary) data structure The essential prerequisite of discrete time models is to rearrange the data into discrete time periods, such as months or years, and then to record for each subject their value on each variable of interest in each of the time periods. In other words, the data is set out like a diary. For the hypothetical study the data structure would be as shown in Table 13.7. Stata calls this data structure a long file.

It can be seen that each person contributes four rows of data to the database, one for each time period, years in this case. Some covariates remain constant throughout the period, in this case sex and time previously unemployed. Others, time-varying covariates, can change during any one of the time periods. A subject can marry or get divorced at any time and their employment status can also change.

Note the variable year started job (*startjob*) which records the year in which each subject first obtained a job. The first person started a job in year 2, the second person in year 3, the third person did not get a job during the study and was given the code 0, whereas the fourth person was employed at the start of the study and was coded 1. The variable, *startjob*, is not essential as a record (the information is embedded in the employment status (*job*) variable). However, it is needed when writing SPSS syntax code to reconfigure the data to fit different models.

One of the great advantages of arranging the data in the person-time format is that it is easy to accommodate time-varying covariates. (Something that is not so easy in survival models.) Another advantage is that models fitted to person-time data do not experience problems with ties, that is, where more than one individual experiences the same event at the same time. The other major advantage is that we can, with this data structure, fit standard models, such as logistic regression.

Table 13.7 Person-time (diary) data structure

Person ID	Year	Sex	Marital status	Employment status (job)	Year started job	Child born	Time previously unemployed
1	1	M	married	unemployed	2	no	2
1	2	M	married	job (FT)	2	no	2
1	3	M	married	job (FT)	2	no	2
1	4	M	divorced	job (FT)	2	no	2
2	1	F	married	unemployed	3	no	1
2	2	F	married	unemployed	3	yes	1
2	3	F	married	job (PT)	3	no	1
2	4	F	married	job (PT)	3	no	1
3	1	M	single	unemployed	0	no	1
3	2	M	married	unemployed	0	no	1
3	3	M	married	unemployed	0	no	1
3	4	M	married	unemployed	0	yes	1
4	1	M	divorced	job (PT)	1	no	0
4	2	M	divorced	job (PT)	1	no	0
4	3	M	divorced	unemployed	1	no	0
4	4	M	divorced	unemployed	1	no	0

Note: Blank rows have been included to indicate more clearly data for the four subjects.

A drawback when undertaking discrete time modelling is that invariably the data has to be rearranged in person-time (diary) format and the person-diary file has to be rearranged further to meet the particular requirement of the type of model to be fitted. Thus to undertake such analyses usually entails some data manipulation and data handling skills on the part of the researcher. Section 13.11 offers guidance on arranging data into the appropriate format.

Fortunately, one former impediment to fitting discrete time models has largely been eradicated. Setting out data in the person-time format greatly expands the size of the database, and it can be seen in our example that four lines of data (one for each subject) in the event-based or state-based file expanded by a factor of four (one for each year) in our person-time file. And had our time period been months and not years (which might have been more appropriate) the size of our database would have expanded by a factor of 12. In the early days of applying discrete time models researchers suffered from a lack of computer power to handle the large databases generated. However, more recent technological advances in computing make these concerns a thing of the past.

We next consider different discrete time models but before doing so, note that by viewing history in the person-time (diary) format we can model the probability of moving from one state to another. The probability of moving to one state from another is the hazard rate (or risk rate) – which was defined in section 13.1. In this context it is also called the transition rate, reflecting the rate at which subjects transfer from one state to another.

13.7 Time to a single event

Modelling time to a single event is the analysis we were carrying out when fitting survival models. Discrete time models provide an equivalent but alternative method to survival analysis. However, before we can fit the discrete time model the data needs to be restructured. Let us assume that our focus of interest is the event of getting a job after a spell of unemployment. If the subject gets a job the event has occurred but if they do not get a job within the study period we regard the data as being censored. Data for all time periods up to and including the event (getting a job) are retained in the restructured dataset. If the person does not get a job all time periods are retained, that is up to the censoring point.

The dataset for the subjects in our hypothetical example would be as shown in Table 13.8.

In this analysis our interest was in the single event getting a job; both a full-time and a part-time job were regarded equally, no distinction was made between them. The first subject contributed two rows (representing the first two years) to the database, that is, up to and including the year he got a job. The second subject contributed three rows, as she got a job in the third year and the third subject four rows as he got a job in year 4. The final subject had a job at the beginning of the study period and was excluded. Looked at another way, for subjects who get a job, time periods are retained when the event is coded 0 and the first row when it is coded 1. If a person does not get a job, all the time periods are retained. In this case, no row contains 1 (because the event has not occurred), and the data for this subject is regarded as censored.

Having constructed the binary (0, 1) variable getting a job it can be designated as the response variable in a logistic regression analysis. Any or all of the variables sex, marital status, birth of a child and time previously unemployed can be entered as independent variables (time previously unemployed as a covariate, the others as categorical, factors or indicator variables). Marital status and birth of a child can vary over time. Interactions between variables can also be created.

Before fitting logistic regression, note the similarity between this analysis and the survival analysis discussed earlier. In the survival analysis we also had a binary variable

Table 13.8 Dataset for the subjects in the hypothetical example

Person ID	Year	Sex	Marital status	Child born	Time previously unemployed	Event (job) 0 No, 1 Yes
1	1	M	married	no	2	0
1	2	M	married	no	2	1
2	1	F	married	no	1	0
2	2	F	married	yes	1	0
2	3	F	married	no	1	1
3	1	M	single	no	1	0
3	2	M	married	no	1	0
3	3	M	married	no	1	0
3	4	M	married	yes	1	0

Note: Subject 4 is not included because he had a job at the start of the study.

which recorded whether or not the event had occurred. However, in the survival analysis the variable *duration* recorded the time to the event (getting a job). In the discrete time approach we also measure duration but it is represented as separate rows (years) leading up to the event. The Cox regression can be shown to be equivalent to the logistic discrete time model when the time intervals in the latter are very small. In practice, however, model estimates often do not change greatly if the size of the discrete time periods is altered, say from one month to three months.

As we are in effect analysing the same problem but in two different ways we would expect to obtain the same results and hence draw the same inference. Reassuringly, we do indeed get the same result. A logistic regression model was fitted to the TfW discrete time dataset and the same three variables were included as in the Cox regression survival model presented in section 13.4: participation on the programme, the subject's health and whether or not the subject held a driving licence. The results of the logistic regression are given below:

Variables in the Equation

		B	S.E.	Wald	df	Sig.	Exp(B)
Step 1[a]	sample(1)	-.384	.068	32.223	1	.000	.681
	health			56.607	2	.000	
	health(1)	.668	.176	14.344	1	.000	1.951
	health(2)	.029	.193	.023	1	.880	1.030
	driving(1)	-.537	.070	59.639	1	.000	.584
	Constant	-4.170	.177	552.967	1	.000	.015

a. Variable(s) entered on step 1: sample, health, driving.

Figure 13.8 SPSS output, proportional hazards model fittted as logistic regression.

Comparing the two models, we see that the variables display the same relationship with the response variable, the coefficients are virtually the same as are the significance levels. What small differences there are, are attributable to the slightly different numerical methods adopted to fit each model and the problems caused by ties in the data.

13.8 Competing risk models

In the previous section, our focus of interest was in a single event, getting a job. However, a spell of unemployment may well end in various (competing) ways: a person may obtain a full-time job or a part-time job, or he/she may leave the labour market (to become a student, housewife, retire and so on). Analysing time to different outcomes is known as competing risk modelling.

Fitting discrete time models to competing risks is a straightforward extension of discrete time models to a single event. We simply model each outcome separately as if it was a single event but regard exits to all other outcomes as censored. (Other approaches could be pursued leading to multinomial models, but here we stay with the simpler and more straightforward approach proposed by Allison, 1984.)

In our example, suppose we were interested in whether people obtained a full-time or

Table 13.9 Dataset for competing risk model, modelling time to full-time job

Person ID	Year	Sex	Marital status	Child born	Time previously unemployed	Event (full-time job) 0 No, 1 Yes
1	1	M	married	no	2	0
1	2	M	married	no	2	1
2	1	F	married	no	1	0
2	2	F	married	yes	1	0
2	3	F	married	no	1	0
3	1	M	single	no	1	0
3	2	M	married	no	1	0
3	3	M	married	no	1	0
3	4	M	married	yes	1	0

a part-time job. It will be recalled that in our example the first subject got a full-time job whereas the second person got a part-time job.

Modelling time to full-time job our database would be as shown in Table 13.9.

It can be seen that this dataset has the same number of rows as the dataset for the single event model. The difference being that the code for a part-time job is 0, indicating that it is to be treated as censored.

We would then fit a logistic regression to this data, the event full-time job being our response variable.

Modelling time to part-time job our database would be similar, except that obtaining a part-time job would be coded 1 while obtaining a full-time job would be coded 0, indicating that it is to be treated as censored.

A logistic regression model can now be fitted to this data, the event part-time job being the response variable.

It may well be, indeed it is very likely, that the best model for full-time job turns out to be different from the model for part-time job. But this simply reflects the different characteristics of people taking up full-time or part-time employment. The age and sex of the respondent and the number and age of their children may have a significant influence on whether a person seeks full-time or part-time employment.

13.9 Repeated events or multiple spells

So far we have only considered time to an event (although that event could lead to different outcomes and competing risk models). In reality, however, people may experience more than one occasion (or spell) in a particular state, for example, a person may be unemployed on more than one occasion during their life or a person may reoffend on more than one occasion during a fixed period following release from prison. Thus events may be repeated or people may experience multiple spells in a state. To incorporate this additional information we can treat each spell as a separate observation. To keep the discussion simple, here we will only consider the case where we have one outcome, getting a job.

Suppose in our hypothetical study we followed up each of the four subjects for ten

Table 13.10 Repeated events or multiple spells, database entry for subject with three spells of unemployment

Person ID	Year	Sex	Marital status	Child born	Time previously unemployed	Event (job) 0 No, 1 Yes
1	1	M	married	no	2	0
1	2	M	married	no	2	1
1	5	M	divorced	no	2	0
1	6	M	divorced	no	2	0
1	7	M	divorced	no	2	1
1	9	M	divorced	no	2	0
1	10	M	divorced	no	2	0

years, not four. Consider the first subject: he was unemployed in the first year but obtained a job in year 2 and was still employed in year 4, the end of the study. Further suppose that he lost his job in year 5 but was re-employed in year 7. He then become unemployed in year 9 and was still unemployed in year 10. This subject has experienced three spells of unemployment and would thus contribute three separate observations. His entry in the database would be as shown in Table 13.10.

Having constructed the database, we would proceed as before by fitting a logistic regression model with the event job as the response variable.

It should be noted that pooling repeated events or multiple spells in the way described above is only theoretically justified if each spell is statistically independent of the other spells. However, we would expect that people who are prone to be unemployed will be frequently unemployed. This finding of itself does not violate the assumption of independence so long as the periods of unemployment are entirely accounted for by the explanatory variables, such as sex, age, number of children etc., but there is always the potential problem of unobserved variables or unobserved heterogeneity (which was discussed in section 3.10). One way to minimise this potential problem is to include as an explanatory variable a subject's relevant previous history, such as, in this example, the number of previous spells of unemployment (or, in the case of reoffending, the number of offences prior to the study period).

13.10 Multiple states

The final class of models considers the situation in which we have multiple spells and multiple outcomes. So, for example, in an employment career a person may obtain a job, leave the labour market, obtain a job and then become unemployed etc. and he/she may experience any number of different states throughout his/her career. If we have three possible states, employed, unemployed, not in the labour market, a person can transfer from the state they are currently in (the origin state) to either of the other two (the destination state). In this example there are six possible transitions:

1   job to unemployment
2   unemployment to job

3   job to not in the labour market
4   not in the labour market to job
5   unemployment to not in the labour market
6   not in the labour market to unemployment

One approach to analysing these transitions is to fit six separate logistic regression models, one for each transition. For the first (job to unemployment) the database would comprise all spells that start in the state job. The end of the spell is defined by a transition to state unemployment, with all other transitions (in this case the other can only be to not in the labour market) treated as censored.

13.11 Guidance on restructuring data to fit survival and discrete time models

Comparing the two, Stata has a much wider range of data manipulation commands than SPSS and is, in general, better suited to handling different datasets especially those which contain more than one record per case.

In determining how to proceed, two issues need to be considered. First, what models are to be fitted and, second, how is the data structured? To take the second point first, in reality, when undertaking statistical modelling, the social researcher will have available existing data for secondary analysis and the data structure will already be determined. It could be in state-, event- or spell-based format. SPSS cannot read spell-based data directly so if the data was in this format the researcher would need to use Stata. Alternatively the researcher could be assembling a new data file and has a choice of which data structure to adopt. In this situation, especially if the aim is to fit more complex models (such as multiple state models), it may be more efficient and advantageous to adopt a spell-based (Stata prefers the term episodes) structure and proceed using the wider range of facilities available in Stata. But adopting a spell-based structure rules out analysis in SPSS. If analysis in SPSS is a possibility, a state-based structure is perhaps the best compromise and this is the structure adopted by many panel studies, including the British Household Panel Study analysed in section 12.7.

Returning to the first consideration, if the intention is to carry out survival analysis, Stata has a suite of built-in 'st' commands and the command stset can read a variety of data structures directly. As stated, it is not possible in SPSS to read spell-based datasets directly and state- and event-based data would usually require certain variables to be derived (for example *duration*) – although this is relatively straightforward.

If the purpose is to fit discrete time models, data manipulation is required in SPSS and Stata. Unfortunately, Stata does not have a suite of built-in commands for discrete time modelling similar to the 'st' commands for survival analysis. However, Stata does have a command, reshape (explained in section 12.6) which converts state-based data structures (which Stata calls wide) to person-time (diary) data (which Stata calls long) and a command stsplit to convert spell-based (episodes) data structures to person-time (diary) data.

To convert the event-based data structures to person-time (diary) data requires rather more Stata commands and code, which is given below for the four-person hypothetical dataset. The variables in this dataset have been coded as follows:

Sex:	1 male, 2 female
Marital status:	1 single, 2 married, 3 divorced
Children	0 no, 1 yes
Employment status	0 unemployed, 1 part-time job, 2 full-time job.

The Stata code is:

```
expand=4;
sort id;
by id: gen year=_n;

by id: list;

gen ms=1;
replace ms=2 if marryr <= year;
replace ms=3 if (divorcyr <= year & divorcyr <.);

gen job = job1type
replace job=0 if  year < job1st;
replace job=0 if  year >job1end;

gen childb=0;
replace childb=1 if childyr==year;

by id: list id year sex ms job job1st childb prunemp;
```

The expand=4 command writes out the line for each person four times as that was the maximum number of years in the data. All fixed explanatory variables are repeated for each year (line). The code shown generates the time-varying covariate states which can change from year to year.

SPSS syntax

State- or event-based data can be converted to person-time (diary) structure in SPSS. The diary data then has to be further adapted in order to fit time to a single event or competing risk models. SPSS syntax to perform these data manipulations for the hypothetical dataset is given below.

Converting the state-based data structure to the person-time (diary) structure

```
get file='path and filename'.

*create a vector with as many elements as number of years (here 4)

vector job=jobyr1 to jobyr4.
compute startjob=0.
```

```
loop #i = 1 to 4.
. do if (job(#i)>0).
. compute startjob=#i.
. break.
. end if.
end loop.
execute.
```

*change variables to cases to make one row for each of the years (here 4)

```
VARSTOCASES /MAKE job FROM jobyr1 to jobyr4
/MAKE ms FROM msyr1 to msyr4
/MAKE child FROM childyr1 to childyr4
/INDEX = year(4)
/KEEP = id sex startjob prunemp
/NULL = KEEP.
```

save outfile= 'path and file name'

execute.

Transforming event-based data structures to person-time diary structure is a little more difficult and is accomplished most easily by first converting event-based data to state-based data then converting state-based to person-time, following the instructions above.

get file='path and file name'.

```
compute jobyr1=0.
compute jobyr2=0.
compute jobyr3=0.
compute jobyr4=0.
```

* create as many jobyr variables as the maximum time period in the dataset (here 4).

* this should be the largest value found in the 'jobstart' and 'jobend' variables

* the vector and loops below range over these variables.

vector job=jobyr1 to jobyr4.

```
loop #i = 1 to 4.
* First job.
. if (#i ge job1st and #i le job1end) job(#i)=job1type.
. if (#i gt job1end) job(#i)=0.

end loop.
```

save outfile= 'path and file name'.

execute.

Note that the above code only converted the job data. Similar code would need to be included to generate the child born and marital status state for each time period.

Having converted the job data into state-based form (with job1type in the state) we can use the SPSS syntax for the state-based data to convert to the person-time diary data structure.

Time to a single event data file

In the model in section 13.7, we were interested in the time to getting a job of any kind, regardless of whether it was a full-time or part-time job. We thus need to recode the data: unemployed = 0 (which it is in any case) and part-time and full-time = 1 (that is recode full-time to equal 1).

Referring back to the database in section 13.7 and the commentary following it, the dataset required retains rows when the event is coded 0 and the first row when it is coded 1. The appropriate rows can be selected from the person-time diary file by the following command:

select if (year < startjob or (year = startjob and year > 1) or startjob = 0)

Competing risk models

Structuring the data for competing risk models is a simple and straightforward extension to single event data structures. All that is required is to recode job. In our example, if we were interested in the event part-time job, unemployed and full-time job are coded 0 and part-time job coded 1. Similarly if the interest was full-time job, unemployed and part-time are coded 0 and full-time job coded 1.

Further reading

Elliott (2002) provides a good introduction to event history modelling as well as an interesting application, including fitting models with SABRE. Allison (1984) is a classic text and discusses the models presented here as well as alternative models, together with details of the statistical theory underpinning the models. The early chapters of Blossfeld and Rohwer (1995) provide an excellent discussion of causality and statistical modelling and the impact of different research designs (an alternative source is Blossfeld and Rohwer, 1997). The chapters also discuss data structures and the various types of censoring.

References

Agresti, A. (1996) *An Introduction to Categorical Data Analysis*. New York: John Wiley.

Agresti, A. and Finlay, B. (1997) *Statistical Methods for the Social Sciences 3rd Edn.* New Jersey: Prentice Hall.

Allison, P. A. (1990) Change scores as dependent variables in regression analysis. *Sociological Methodology*, 20, 93–114.

Allison, P. A. (1999) *Multiple Regression: A Primer*. Thousand Oaks, CA: Pine Forge Press.

Allison, P. D. (1984) *Event History Analysis: Regression for Longitudinal Event Data*. Beverly Hills: Sage.

Allison, P. D. (2002) *Missing Data*. Quantitative Applications in the Social Sciences, No 136. London: Sage.

Bartholomew, D. J., Steele, F., Moustaki, I and Galbraith, J. I. (2002) *The Analysis and Interpretation of Multivariate Data for Social Scientists*. London: Chapman & Hall/CRC.

Blossfeld, H. P. and Rohwer, G. (1995) *Techniques of Event History Modelling: New Approaches to Causal Analysis*. London: Lawrence Erlbaum Associates.

Blossfeld, H. P. and Rohwer, G. (1997) Causal inference, time and observation plans in the social sciences. *Quality and Quantity*, 31, 361–84.

Blossfeld, H. P., Golsch, K. and Rohwer, G. (2007) *Event History Analysis with Stata*. London: Lawrence Erlbaum Associates.

Carr-Hill, R. A. and Stern, N. H. (1979) *Crime, the Police and Criminal Statistics*. London: Academic Press.

Crockett, A. (2006) *Weighting the Social Surveys*. Economic and Social Data Service (ESDS) website (www.esds.ac.uk).

Davies, R. B. (1994) From cross-sectional to longitudinal analysis. In: Dale, A. and Davies, R. B. (eds) *Analyzing Social and Political Change: A casebook of methods*. London: Sage.

De Vaus, D. A. (1996) *Surveys in Social Research 4th Edn.* London: UCL Press.

De Vaus, D. (2001) *Research Design in Survey Research*. London: Sage.

De Vaus, D. (2002) *Analyzing Social Science Data*. London: Sage.

Dobson, A. J. (2002) *An Introduction to Generalized Linear Models 2nd Edn.* London: Chapman & Hall/CRC.

Elliott, J. (2002) The value of event history techniques for understanding social processes: modelling women's employment behaviour after motherhood. *International Journal of Social Research Methodology*, 5, 2, 107–32.

Fielding, J. and Gilbert, N. (2006) *Understanding Social Statistics 2nd Edn.* London: Sage.

Groves, R., Floyd, J., Fowler, M., Couper, J., Lepkowski, E., Singer, E. and Tourangeau, R. (2004) *Survey Methodology*. New Jersey: Wiley.

Healey, J. F. (1996) *Statistics: A tool for social research 4th Edn.* Belmont, CA: Wadsworth.

Hox, J. (2002) *Multilevel Analysis: Techniques and Applications*. London: Lawrence Erlbaum Associates.

Kreft, I. and De Leeuw, J. (1998) *Introducing Multilevel Modeling*. London: Sage.

Lipsey, M. W. and Wilson, D. B. (2001) *Practical Meta-Analysis*. Thousand Oaks, CA: Sage.

Long, J. S. (1997) *Regression Models for Categorical and Limited Dependent Variables*. London: Sage.

Long, J. S. and Freese, J. (2006) *Regression Models for Categorical Dependent Variables Using Stata, 2nd Edn*. College Station, TX: Stata Press.

Menard, S. (1991) *Longitudinal Research*. Quantitative Applications in the Social Sciences, 76. London: Sage.

Mirrlees-Black, C. (1999) *Domestic Violence: Findings from a new British crime survey self-completion questionnaire*. Home Office Research Study No. 191. London: Home Office.

Moser, C. A. and Kalton, G. (1993) *Survey Methods in Social Investigation*. Aldershot: Dartmouth.

Norman, P. and Wathan, J. (updated by Rafferty, A.) (2006) *Using SPSS for Windows*. Economic and Social Data Service (ESDS) website (www.esds.ac.uk).

Payne, J., Payne, C., Lissenburgh, S. and Range, M. (1999) *Work-Based Training and Job Prospects for the Unemployed: An Evaluation of Training for Work*. Research Report RR96. Sudbury, Suffolk: DfEE (now DfES) Publications.

Plewis, I. (1998) *Multilevel Models*. Social Research Update, Issue 23. University of Surrey: Department of Sociology. Available at http//:sru.soc.surrey.ac.uk/

Rafferty, A. (2006) *Introduction to Stata using the UK Labour Force Survey*. Economic and Social Data Service (ESDS) website (www.esds.ac.uk).

Sanders, D. and Ward, H. (1994) Time-series techniques for repeated cross-section data. In: Dale, A. and Davies, R. (eds) *Analyzing Social and Political Change*. London: Sage.

Schumacker, R. E. and Lomax, R. G. (2004) *A Beginner's Guide to Structural Equation Modelling 2nd Edn*. London: Lawrence Erlbaum Associates.

Tarling, R. (1993) *Analysing Offending: Data, Models and Interpretations*. London: HMSO.

Wooldridge, J. (2003) *Introductory Econometrics 2nd Edn*. Belmont, CA: South-Western.

Websites

British Household Panel Study (BHPS)
www.iser.essex.ac.uk
This site provides details of the history and development of the BHPS.

Centre for Longitudinal Studies (CLS)
www.cls.ioe.ac.uk
The CLS is an ESRC Resource Centre, based at the Institute of Education, University of London. CLS houses three of Britain's birth cohort studies: 1958 National Child Development Study, 1970 British Cohort Study and the Millennium Cohort Study.

Centre for Multilevel Modelling
www.cmm.bristol.ac.uk
The Centre is the home of MLwiN where further details of the software, newsletters and training events can be obtained.

The Economic and Social Data Service (ESDS)
www.esds.ac.uk
The ESDS is a UK national data service providing access and support for an extensive range of key economic and social data, both quantitative and qualitative. As well as providing descriptions of major datasets and support on the secondary use of them, the ESDS website contains guides on Stata, SPSS and on weighting data. The site also provides details of training datasets especially created as a resource for students and lecturers.

Missing data
www.missingdata.org.uk
This is an ESRC resource centre developing procedures for handling missing data.

SPSS
www.spss.com
The SPSS website provides details of the software.

Stata
www.stata.com
The Stata website contains details of the software and a bookstore of available Stata texts.

Statistical Modelling for Social Researchers
www.routledge.com/textbooks/9780415448406
This website has been designed to accompany this book. It hosts many of the datasets analysed in the book and suggests further exercises that readers may wish to undertake to enhance their knowledge and skills of statistical modelling.

Training Resources and Materials for Social Scientists (TRAMSS)
http.//trams.data-archive.ac.uk
This site provides details of MLwiN and SABRE. A trial version of MLwiN can be downloaded together with Version 1 of the manual and a tutorial dataset. SABRE is freeware software and can be downloaded.

UK Data Archive
www.data-archive.ac.uk
As the name implies, the Data Archive is the main repository of major UK datasets.

Datasets

Department for Education and Skills, *Training for Work 1995–97* [computer file]. Copyright: Crown copyright.

Heath, A. *et al.*, *British General Election Study, 1997* [computer file]. 2nd edn. Colchester, Essex: UK Data Archive [distributor], 28 May 1999. SN 3887. Copyright Social and Community Planning Research.

Home Office. *Police Force Area Statistics, 2003–04* [computer file]. Copyright: Crown copyright.

Home Office. *Offenders Sentenced for Shop Theft, 2001* [computer file]. Copyright: Crown copyright.

Home Office. Communities Group and BMRB. Social Research, *Home Office Citizenship Survey, 2001* [computer file]. Colchester, Essex: UK Data Archive [distributor], November 2003. SN 4754. Copyright: Crown copyright.

Office for National Statistics and Department for Communities and Local Government, *Labour Force Survey, 2003–04 and Indices of Deprivation, 2004* [computer file]. Copyright: Crown copyright.

University of Essex, Institute for Social and Economic Research, *British Household Panel Survey: Waves 1–15, 1991–2006* [computer file]. 3rd edn. Colchester, Essex: UK Data Archive [distributor], June 2007. SN 5151. Copyright: Institute for Social and Economic Research.

University of Manchester, Cathie Marsh Centre for Census and Survey Research. ESDS Government, *British Crime Survey, 2000: Teaching Dataset* [computer file]. Home Office. Research, Development and Statistics Directorate, National Centre for Social Research [original data producer(s)]. Colchester, Essex: UK Data Archive [distributor], November 2003. SN 4740. Copyright: Crown copyright held jointly with the Economic and Social Data Service.

University of Manchester, Cathie Marsh Centre for Census and Survey Research. ESDS Government, *Labour Force Survey, 2002: Teaching Dataset* [computer file]. Office for National Statistics. Labour Market Statistics Group, Department of Finance and Personnel (Northern Ireland). Central Survey Unit [original data producer(s)]. Colchester, Essex: UK Data Archive [distributor], November 2003. SN 4736. Copyright: Crown copyright held jointly with the Economic and Social Data Service.

Appendix 1: The generalised linear model

A significant development in statistical modelling occurred in the 1970s with the realisation that many of the models discussed in this book were related and could be viewed as different members of the same family: the generalised linear model (GLM). It is not necessary to understand the generalised linear model in order to apply the individual models in research settings or to undertake the analyses outlined in this book in SPSS and Stata. However, the terminology and concepts of the generalised linear model are found in more advanced texts on statistical modelling (for example, Dobson 2002). Furthermore, some computer software, and importantly for us MLwiN (used in Chapter 9 to fit multilevel models), is adopting the terminology and notation of GLM. In anticipation that sooner or later readers will come across the GLM, but more immediately to understand MLwiN, a brief description is given here.

In section 1.3 we set out the general linear model and noted its constituents.

The systematic component comprises the explanatory variables:

$$b_0 + b_1 x_{1i} + b_2 x_{2i} + \ldots + b_p x_{pi}$$

The random component, e, is assumed to have a particular distribution associated with a particular response variable. For example, if the response variable, y, is continuous we assume that the random component is normally distributed, whereas if the response variable is binary we may assume that the distribution of the random component is binomial.

Generalised linear models have a third component:

The link function specifies the relationship between the systematic and random components of the model. More precisely, the link function specifies how the mean of the random component relates to the explanatory variables.

Many models can be defined by the distributions assumed for the random component and their link function. The most common models, which are described in this book, are listed in Table A.1.

Table A.1 Types of model expressed as GLM

Model	Random component	Link
Multiple regression	Normal	Identity
Logistic regression	Binomial	Logit
Multinomial logistic regression	Multinomial	Generalised logit
Loglinear models	Poisson	Log

In multiple regression we assume the random component (error term) is normally distributed and model the mean directly, so the link is 'identical' to the mean. In logistic regression the logit of the mean is modelled, in the multinomial the generalised logit and in loglinear models the log of the mean is modelled.

Appendix 2: Handling tabular data

On occasions, the researcher will receive data in tabular form – much official data is presented in this way, for example, in National Statistics publications. Similarly, tabular data is presented in research papers, reports and textbooks.

To illustrate the procedures for inputting and analysing tabular data, we draw on the data on the sentences awarded to adults convicted of shop theft. A two-way table of sentence by sex was presented in Table 3.1. The data was further analysed in Chapters 6 and 7 where other variables were included in various multinomial logistic regression and loglinear models. The actual data file available for analysis contained data for each offender in the standard format, that is, one row for each offender. However, suppose the data had not been available in that format but had appeared as a table in a published report. In order to make the example meaningful but at the same time manageable we consider a three-way table in which sentence has been cross-classified by sex and the extent to which the offenders had committed previous offences. The data is presented in Table A.2. In any published presentation of this data, totals, subtotals and percentages would be given to highlight the relationships between the three variables, but that is not the purpose here. These three variables were included in the multinomial model fitted in section 6.2.

Table A.2 Number of offenders awarded different sentences, by sex and previous criminal history

	Male	*Female*
No previous convictions		
Custody	44	12
Community penalty	46	24
Fine	82	39
Discharge	70	83
1 to 4 previous convictions		
Custody	63	11
Community penalty	108	69
Fine	148	68
Discharge	101	79
5 or more previous convictions		
Custody	543	67
Community penalty	383	88
Fine	365	44
Discharge	258	65

Cell notation

First we need a systematic way of referring to the cells of the table, and the convention adopted is to define each cell as:

$$C_{ijk...}$$

where: C is the cell
     i refers to the row
     j refers to the column
     k refers to the layer
     . . . and so on, depending on the dimensions of the table.

To some extent it is arbitrary which variable is the row, the column and so on as tables can always be presented and rearranged in a different order.

In Table A.2, the rows are taken to be the types of sentence, such that:

row 1 is custody
row 2 is community penalty
row 3 is fine
row 4 is discharge.

The columns are the sex of the offender, such that:

column 1 is male
column 2 is female.

The layers record the extent of the offender's previous criminal history, such that:

layer 1 is no previous convictions
layer 2 is between 1 and 4 previous convictions
layer 3 is 5 or more previous convictions.

Thus for example:

C_{111} (custody, male, no previous convictions) contains 44 such offenders
C_{122} (custody, female, 1–4 previous convictions) contains 11 offenders
C_{313} (fine, male, 5 or more previous convictions) contains 365 offenders
C_{423} (discharge, female, 5 or more previous convictions) contains 65 offenders.

Inputting tabular data

The data in Table A.2 can be entered into SPSS or Stata by creating a data file with 24 rows, one corresponding to each cell of the table. The file has four variables, *sentence*, *sex*, *precons*, and a fourth variable whose value is the number in the cell, which we will name *count*.

The data file showing just the four exemplary cells given above would be:

Table A.3 Data file for sentencing data in Table A.2

sentence	sex	precons	count
1	1	1	44
–	–	–	–
1	2	2	11
–	–	–	–
3	1	3	365
–	–	–	–
4	2	3	65

The data file as inputted has 24 rows but the original sample comprised 2860 offenders. To convert the table to the original sample we need to weight the combinations of the characteristics by the number in the cell; for example, we need to effectively produce 44 offenders who were classified *sentence 1* (custody), *sex 1* (male) and *precons 1* (no previous convictions).

This is accomplished in SPSS by Data → Weight Cases

Which brings up the following box:

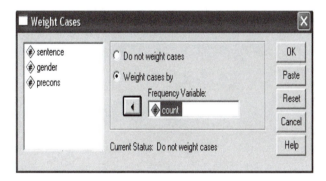

Figure A.1 SPSS dialogue box for weighting cases.

Weight cases by has been checked and *count* entered into Frequency Variable.
In Stata a similar procedure is adopted:

```
.input sentence sex precons count
1 1 1 44
:
1 2 2 11
:
3 1 3 365
:
4 2 3 65
.end
```

The data is then weighted in any commands to analyse the data. For example to produce a two-way table between sentence and sex:

    tab sentence sex [fw=count]

where fw is an abbreviation for frequency weight.

Index